About the Authors

Darren Rowse is the guy behind `ProBlogger.net`, which has become one of the leading places on the Web for information about making money from

The authors Chris Garrett (left) and Darren Rowse (right).

blogs. He is a full-time blogger himself, making a six-figure income from blogging since 2005. In addition to his blogging at ProBlogger, Darren also founded and edits the popular Digital Photography School (`http://digital-photographyschool.com`). Darren lives in Melbourne, Australia with his wife, Vanessa, and sons, Xavier, Henri and Louis. In his spare time, he's a mad photographer and has an interest in emerging forms of church and spirituality.

Chris Garrett is a writer, Internet marketing coach, and, of course, professional blogger. As well as his own blog, chrisg.com, he runs an online training class called the Authority Blogger Course (`http://AuthorityBlogger.com`) and writes for many sites, including CopyBlogger, and occasionally a blog you might have heard of called ProBlogger. He is now back living in Canada with his wife, Clare; his daughter, Amy; his dog, Benji; and his grumpy old cat, Tigger. When he is not at the computer (rare) you can bet he is out taking mediocre pictures with his digital camera.

ProBlogger

ProBlogger

Secrets for Blogging Your Way to a Six-Figure Income

THIRD EDITION

Darren Rowse
and
Chris Garrett

John Wiley & Sons, Inc.

ProBlogger: Secrets for Blogging Your Way to a Six-Figure Income, Third Edition

Published by
John Wiley & Sons, Inc.
10475 Crosspoint Boulevard
Indianapolis, IN 46256
www.wiley.com

Copyright © 2012 by John Wiley & Sons, Inc., Indianapolis, Indiana

Published simultaneously in Canada

ISBN: 978-1-118-19955-8
ISBN: 978-1-118-22825-8 (ebk)
ISBN: 978-1-118-24069-4 (ebk)
ISBN: 978-1-118-26539-0 (ebk)

Manufactured in the United States of America

10 9 8 7 6 5 4 3 2

Dedicated to our families, friends, and the bloggers we have yet to meet.

Credits

Executive Editor
Robert Elliott

Project Editor
Maureen Spears

Technical Editor
Rebecca Leaman

Senior Production Editor
Debra Banninger

Copy Editor
Kim Cofer

Editorial Manager
Mary Beth Wakefield

Freelancer Editorial Manager
Rosemarie Graham

Associate Director of Marketing
David Mayhew

Marketing Manager
Ashley Zurcher

Business Manager
Amy Knies

Production Manager
Tim Tate

Vice President and Executive Group Publisher
Richard Swadley

Vice President and Executive Publisher
Neil Edde

Associate Publisher
Jim Minatel

Project Coordinator, Cover
Katie Crocker

Compositor
Maureen Forys, Happenstance Type-O-Rama

Proofreader
Nancy Carrasco

Indexer
Robert Swanson

Cover Image
© Franck Boston/iStockPhoto

Cover Designer
Ryan Sneed

Acknowledgments

From Darren Rowse — A blogger is only ever as good as those around them. I dedicate this book to those in my life who make me better at what I do and who I am. To my family, especially Vanessa, who encouraged me to pursue this "crazy blogging thing"; and to the readers of ProBlogger, who have taught me so much about blogging.

From Chris Garrett — Thanks to my family for supporting me with love and cake, my smart chrisg.com readers, my lovely customers, and to the great folks at Wiley for helping us get to the end with (most of) our sanity intact.

Contents

Introduction

Becoming a ProBlogger: Darren's Story of Blogging

During the first year of my blogging career, I worked three jobs simultaneously, studied part-time, and blogged on the side.

A common misconception that first-time readers arriving at `ProBlogger` `.net` have is that the six-figure income I've earned from blogging was something that I achieved overnight. It wasn't.

Though blogging has enabled a growing number of people to earn an income, the process is rarely a quick one. For this reason I'd like to share my own story of blogging—from hobbyist to full-time blogger.

So, grab a coffee, make yourself comfortable, and relax—this could take a little while.

Once Upon a Time...

In November 2002, when I first hit "Publish" on my original (and short-lived) blog, I did so believing that this "blogging thing," which I'd only just heard of that day, would be nothing more than a bit of fun.

I started this blog for a number of reasons, but it was largely out of curiosity, the idea of having a new hobby, and the hope that perhaps I might meet some new people with similar interests to mine.

At the time I was working three jobs.

My Three Jobs

My main job at the time was as a minister of a church, three days per week. It was a part-time job (I was not "the" minister, but one of four working in a team), and my responsibility was to work with young people.

I was engaged to be married (to Vanessa, or "V," as I call her) and trying to save for a wedding and pay off a car loan and college fees, so I had also taken on a number of part-time jobs (minister's wages are not fantastic at the best of times, but part-time they are even less spectacular).

My second job was working for an online department store. Although that might sound interesting and useful for what was to come in blogging, it was not. I was the warehouse "dog's-body," and my job consisted largely of sweeping, cleaning, lifting boxes, packing orders, and other menial and boring tasks. Still, it helped pay the rent.

My third job was as a casual laborer. I was on-call with an employment agency and did all kinds of temping work ranging from mind-numbing production-line work on a conveyor belt to helping to assemble circuses (don't ask).

Alongside these jobs I was finishing off my theology degree part-time—a long-term endeavor which took 10 years to complete.

This was my life that fateful day when I first got the taste for blogging.

Hobby Blogger

I'd like to say that at the moment I hit "Publish" on my first blog that the earth shook and a light from heaven came down and I was suddenly transformed into a full-time blogger—but as we all know, it usually doesn't happen that way, and it didn't for me.

In fact, for the first 12 or so months of my blogging very little changed. If anything, I became busier as a result of taking on an extra subject at college and leaving my job as a minister to lead a team starting a new, "emerging church."

Blogging at this time was a hobby and a way to connect with others who were thinking through issues of the "emerging church."

My blog LivingRoom (www.livingroom.org.au/blog) became reasonably popular in emerging-church circles that year, and my site-hosting and ISP costs (I was still on dial-up) began to escalate.

It was after about a year of blogging that I accidentally started Digital Photography Blog; it was originally a photoblog, but no one looked at my images, and the review that I wrote of my camera got a lot of traffic. In an attempt to help cover my hosting costs, I decided to add some AdSense ads and the Amazon Affiliate program to this blog. I just wanted to cover expenses.

I quickly discovered that my hope of covering my costs was realistic, not simply because of AdSense, but also because I put it on an established blog that was getting several thousand readers per day (this is important to keep in mind).

Even with established traffic the earnings in the early days were not high. In my first month (October 2003), I averaged about $1.40 per day, and that was with lots of curiosity clicks from my readers; by November, I'd hit $3 a day.

The money was minimal, but it covered my costs, and I began to wonder if with the extra few dollars a month I might be able to save up for a new computer (up to this point I was blogging on dial-up from a six-year-old PC that worked most days). My other lofty goal was to save for a professional blog design.

December saw daily earnings hit $6 per day, January $9, February $10, and March $15—hardly big dollars, but I began to wonder what would happen if I saw the same sorts of increases in income over a longer period of time. By that I don't mean adding $2 to $3 to the daily average per month, but what would happen if I could sustain 30-, 40-, or even 50-percent growth each month?

I began to think in terms of exponential growth.

Part-Time Blogger

Around this time, I had a little more time on my hands and was in need of another part-time job.

My study was winding down (I finally graduated), and other jobs ended. "V" (my wife by now) began to hint that maybe I should start looking for another part-time job (rightfully so), and we decided that when I finished my degree at the end of June, I'd need to get serious about finding another two days of work per week. All this time I was secretly doing the calculations in my mind to see how much I'd need to earn per day to be able to call blogging my part-time job.

April's earnings came in and averaged around $20 per day, and I realized that I just might have myself a part-time job already. The beauty of blogging income is that it earns you money seven days per week, so I totaled $140 per week.

I began to work harder (largely after hours and late into the night), with the hope of getting earnings up high enough to convince "V" to let me pass on getting a "real" part-time job and to concentrate on blogging.

The work paid off: In May earnings hit $32 per day, and by the end of June, I'd broken $1,000 in a month for the first time and was bringing in $48 per day.

It was crunch-time, and "V" and I had to consider our next move. I could probably keep growing things each month by working after hours on blogging and go find another job—or I could put the two free days that had been taken up by study into blogging and see if I could make a go of it.

I decided to put six more months of effort into blogging to see where it would end up. At the end of the six months, "V" and I would assess the situation again—the threat of getting a "real job" still loomed. I also got my new computer and the professional blog design that I'd been eyeing.

I'll pause here in my story to say that this was a bit of a freaky moment for both "V" and me. Neither of us had started a small business, and though I've always had something of an entrepreneurial spirit, we are both fairly conservative people in many ways. Although the figures indicated that there was potential on many other levels, it just seemed plain weird.

I mean, who makes their income blogging? Needless to say, we didn't tell many people of our decision, and when we did tell a few family and friends, there were plenty of raised eyebrows and lots of comments like, "That's nice, but are you going to get a real job?" and, "How's your little hobby business going?"

I'll stop going into the monthly earnings at this point except to say that investing the two days per week into blogging proved to be one of the best decisions we made. I will stress that this decision came after I'd already been blogging for 19 months and after establishing a number of blogs that were earning reasonable money.

Quitting jobs is not something I recommend people just do off-the-cuff in their early days of blogging. Work up over time, because though it worked out for me, there are plenty of others for whom it has taken a lot longer, and some for whom it just hasn't worked at all.

Throughout the second half of 2004, I continued to put two days per week into blogging while maintaining another three days a week of other work (some church work and some warehousing). It was more than two days per week in practice because I continued to work long hours in the evenings to keep things moving forward, and at times worked literally around the clock (like during the Olympics when I partnered with another blogger to run a blog on the games).

This was a time when I began numerous blogs (I had 20 at one point) and experimented with many different income streams and advertising systems. It was during this time that I also started blogging seriously about blogging and had an active blog-tips section on my LivingRoom blog. This didn't go down too well with some of my readers there, and so I decided to move all of those tips to a new blog called ProBlogger.net. It launched on September 23, 2004.

Full-Time Blogger—Eventually

By mid December of 2004 we had pretty much decided that 2005 would see me go full-time as a blogger. I'd already ditched most of my warehousing work because the earnings from blogging had continued to rise, and my paid church work had ended as we transitioned the church to a voluntary leadership model.

All was going well, with some amazing figures in terms of earnings in November and December, until what felt a little like disaster happened in mid December. Google did one of its notorious updates where some bloggers go way up in search results and others go way down—I was in the latter group and most of my blogs virtually disappeared from Google, taking with them almost three-quarters of my traffic and earnings. Ouch!

Things looked a little uncertain for the first time in more than six months, and I wondered if the next Google update would see things back to where they were or get worse. The Google update in mid December left us at a level where we could still get by, but it was time for a contingency plan. I even went out and got another part-time job for a while.

The next Google update brought things back to a level just under what they were before. The experience did teach me many lessons, including the importance of diversifying your interests, not relying only on search-engine traffic, and expecting the unexpected when working online.

2005 was a massive year. I worked the part-time job that I'd got during the "Google crash" and worked full-time on my blogging (a juggling act, but both were worthwhile). I continued to diversify my efforts, which resulted in new blogs and partnerships, including developing a course called Six Figure Blogging with another blogger, Andy Wibbels. The name for the course came as I realized that I'd in fact grown my blogging to a point where I earned more than $100,000 per year from the medium—a staggering realization.

Since 2005 the business has continued to evolve with a number of developments, including:

- **Starting a blog network—b5media**—With a small group of other bloggers, b5media began as a handful of blogs networked together but grew to be over 300 blogs that employed hundreds of bloggers from around the world. The business took on $2 million of venture-capital investment in 2006 and has continued to grow. I am no longer active with the company but remain a minor shareholder.

- **Launching** TwiTip.com—With the rise in Twitter I saw an opportunity to create a Twitter Tips blog.
- **Moving into e-book publishing**—As I saw the economy begin to decline in 2008, I started making plans for diversifying my income by selling products of my own. In 2009, I launched two e-books from my main two blogs: "31 Days to Build a Better Blog" and "The Essential Portrait Guide." Since this time I have launched a total of 14 e-books from ProBlogger and Digital Photography School. See them at http://www.problogger.net/learn and http://www.digital-photography-school.com/learn. e-book sales are now my number-1 source of income.
- **Starting the ProBlogger community**—As another diversification move, I started ProBlogger.com, a community companion site for ProBlogger.net. This paid membership site has grown to well over 2000 members and is a place where bloggers gather to take the principles taught on the free blog further.
- **Launching** ProBloggerAcademy.com—I launched a series of courses on different aspects of blogging with my co-author, Chris Garrett.
- **Launching** FeelGooder.com—This is a blog with "life tips" aimed at helping people live life to the fullest.

Lessons from My Journey

So why am I telling this story? Is it just a self-gratification thing? I have enjoyed reminiscing, but there's more to it than that. The main reason I wanted to tell the story is because I think it's important to keep emphasizing a number of points:

1. **Blogging for an income takes time.** Although there are stories of people making good money from blogs faster than I have (I've been at it since 2002, remember), there are many others whose growth has been slower. I've had my share of luck, have worked insane hours, and I started out at a time when blogging was a lot less competitive than it is now. All of these things have contributed to my success. It took me more than 1.5 years to be able to call blogging a part-time job, and another year before I went full-time. Building up to going pro as a blogger takes time.

2. **Take it one step at a time.** Unless you have a massive pile of cash somewhere or a sugar daddy (or mommy) to cover your expenses, you need

to approach blogging professionally one step at a time. My approach was to always have a backup plan and to increase the time I dedicated to blogging only gradually as it started to show me earnings that justified it. My wife and I decided what level of income I needed to earn and agreed that as long as blogging was bringing in less than that, I would need other work. We put a time limit on it. If income hadn't reached the level we wanted within that timeframe, I would have been looking for work. Though this might sound a little rigid or a bit of a downer, I didn't want to run off ahead of "V" in my own direction without our decisions being joint ones that we were both comfortable with. "V" has been incredibly supportive in all this and has allowed me to follow my dreams even when they seemed quite bizarre—but there have also been times when she's rightly been the voice of reason and pulled me back to earth.

3. **It takes hard work and discipline.** As I mentioned a number of times in this story, there have been countless nights when I've worked into the wee hours of the morning blogging. Though I have better boundaries these days, it wasn't unusual for me to post 50 times per day over 12 hours in front of the screen. I love blogging, so this isn't a chore all of the time, but I'd be lying if I said there weren't days (and weeks) that I didn't want to slack off and ignore my business. Friends talking about starting a home-based business often say to me that they'd never be able to do it because they'd be too tempted to never work. I always thought I'd be like this too, but I've worked hard at being disciplined and working hard, and I credit a lot of my success to that discipline.

4. **Follow your dreams.** The main point of this story was to communicate the preceding three points and to give a realistic view of the process of becoming a pro blogger. I never want to be accused of giving an unbalanced view of blogging or hyping it up as a get-rich-quick thing.

Having said all this, it would also be irresponsible of me not to say that it is possible to make money blogging—and for some (but not all), it is possible to make very good money doing it.

There is a growing number of bloggers earning a full-time living from blogging (we employ a few at b5media), and even more who supplement their income on a part-time basis while spending other time doing other work, raising a family, or studying.

My hope is that this book will help the number of people making a living from blogging increase even further.

Chris Garrett's Blogging Story

My blogging story is quite different from Darren's and, in fact, Darren plays quite a pivotal role in it.

The early part of my career consisted of various IT and programming roles until I discovered the Internet or, more accurately, the Internet found me! I was working for a college in the U.K. when the management decided we should have Internet infrastructure and a website. The task for setting all this up fell to me.

Although I had experienced the Internet in a limited way, and had been online for a while—first through "bulletin boards" then later using Usenet discussion groups—it was my first experience of the Mosaic web browser that switched me on to the Internet in a real way, and this project meant learning everything, and in detail. I was hooked from that moment.

As well as the college website, I built my own, one after another. I built sites around my favorite Usenet newsgroups, and, of course, I had a personal homepage. Then I started doing sites on the side for local companies. Around this time, the mid-'90s, I started my science-fiction website (it could be this was my first "blog," depending on your definition). It was a reverse-chronologically organized website with regularly updated content and comments (via a "guest book"). Later, in 1999, I started an online diary as I moved away, changed jobs, got married, and started a family.

After that I took various web-marketing and advertising agency roles and looked for ways to increase my connections and job marketability. This, combined with a naturally helpful nature, and also being a complete geek, meant that I was active on discussion lists and forums. Getting known in those geek communities led to writing work, which led to co-authoring a couple of programming books, which led to even more of a geek profile.

Around this time I started trying to supplement my meager salary with building affiliate marketing websites. Though I had some successes hawking magazine subscriptions, lawyer leads, and loans, my heart really wasn't in it. My programming websites still did very well, bringing in leads for my programmer-training sideline and freelance writing.

It was Darren and Google AdSense that switched me on to professional blogging. I fell out with AdSense almost as quickly as I fell in, but thanks to Darren I knew this blogging thing was a perfect fit for me.

Since those early days my blogging has progressed from a hobby side-business to being the source of all my income. We will return to more of my story later in the book, but suffice it to say right now, without blogging I don't know where I would be today. Unlike Darren, the majority of my income comes from selling consultancy, coaching, and running online courses such as my Authority Blogger Course.

1 Blogging for Money

I t is hard to miss the word *blog* today. We hear blogs mentioned in the media, see them all over the World Wide Web, and we even hear them discussed now in business and social situations. In many cases the term *blogger* is used not just to describe a person who writes a blog, but also someone who earns money doing it.

This chapter examines what blogging actually is and what it involves; it then examines the different types of bloggers, and the truth about making money blogging.

Before you get into earning money from a blog, you need to know what exactly a blog is.

What Is a Blog?

So what exactly is a blog? Because you are at the beginning of a blogging book, this is definitely an issue we need to be clear on!

We can answer this question in a number of ways, ranging from the broad to the highly technical. To put it as clearly as possible, *a blog is a particular type of website.* You can see an example in Figure 1-1.

Studies have shown that although awareness of blogs is increasing, many people frequent blogs without realizing it. This is fine; the key thing is that readers get value out of it. Anyone who has been reading blogs for a while, though, will know there is more to blogging than just publishing any old website.

Though blogs started out as informal lists of links and personal journals, they have evolved into a far more varied medium. In addition to diary blogs and link blogs, there are now CEO blogs, educational blogs, marketing blogs—you name it!

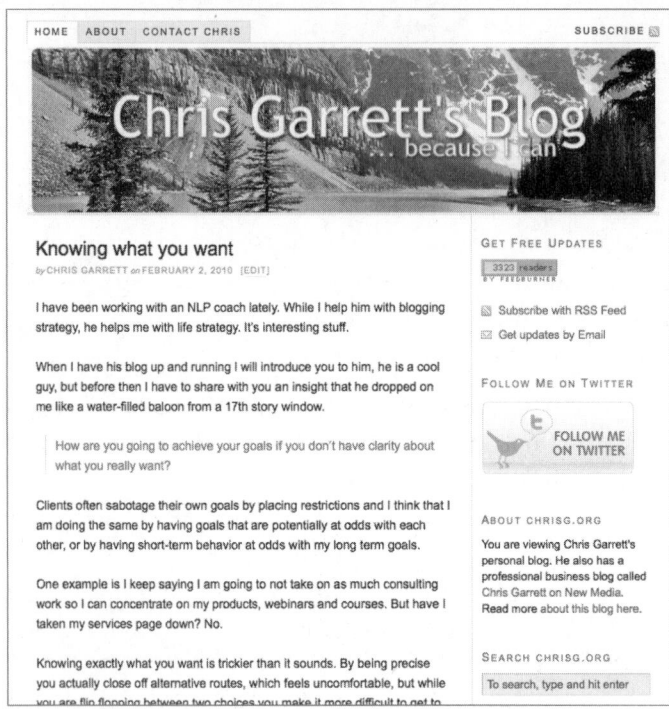

Figure 1-1: Chris's personal blog is a pretty typical blog (http://chrisg.org).

Even blogs on a seemingly similar topic can be approached very differently. Just compare chrisg.com (www.chrisg.com) and ProBlogger (ProBlogger.net), the blogs belonging to the authors of this book. You can see that although blogs have a lot of features in common, they can also be implemented with your own individual style.

What Makes Blogs Different?

If blogs are just websites, what makes them so different?

In my opinion, three main areas differentiate a blog from any other type of site:

- **Content**—Blogs are usually updated more often than traditional websites are, and this keeps visitors coming back more often. The content is also normally arranged in reverse-chronological order with the most recent *post* (article) at the top of the main page and the older entries toward the bottom.

- **Syndication**—Not only can blog followers read a blog in their web browser just like they can any other website, but a blog almost certainly provides the content in the form of a *feed*. In other words, the articles posted to the site are provided in a machine-readable format, allowing people with the appropriate software to read the blog posts as they are published without actually visiting the site.
- **Conversation**—The style of a blog is quite different from other types of websites; there is more of a conversational and community feel. Unlike a purely informational site, or a traditional news site, blogs are written with the bloggers communicating directly to their audience, and replies are expected in the form of comments. In addition to the conversation happening on each blog, conversation also happens between blogs, with one blog post attracting replies and responses on others.

EXERCISE

The best way to really get a feel for what makes blogs so special is to go out and read a few.

Find as many interesting blogs as you can and note the following:

1. What appeals to you?
2. What does not appeal to you?
3. What sort of content do the blogs you looked at provide?
4. How often do they update?
5. What sort of reader reaction do they get?

When you find a couple of blogs that you enjoy reading regularly, you will begin to appreciate the subtle differences in style and approach to other forms of web publishing. You might also appreciate the pleasure that blogs provide over and above their potential to generate financial gain!

The Added Benefits of Blogging

Yes, blogging has many benefits. Although many bloggers get pleasure just from the process of writing, and of course we cannot overlook the bloggers who make money, blogging may help you achieve other goals:

- **Fame**—A successful blog has the potential to get you noticed and help you build a more visible profile in your business market, pastime, or community.

- **Contacts**—Blogs are excellent ways to get to know people and network. Because blogs naturally lead to conversation, a well-read blog will put you in contact with a wide variety of people.
- **Traffic**—Attracting highly targeted visitors alone could be a big draw, especially if you have products or services to sell. Website owners are always looking for new sources of traffic, and blogs are a proven way to generate more visits and increased loyalty.
- **Sales**—In addition to gaining more attention, over time, your articles can help you generate trust and build credibility, which is critical to making sales.

I love blogging. It is great to be able to work from home, on my own schedule, while helping and meeting so many people. I can't imagine a better way to earn a living!

Making Money with Blogs

We've already mentioned a couple of times that blogs can make you money, but so far we have offered no explanation of how that is the case. This section takes a look at how bloggers make money. While you read this, you may want to think about tactics that appeal to you.

An Introduction to Professional Blogging

Over the past few years, blogging has changed a great deal and has evolved in many ways. What was once an activity limited to a very small number of people has now exploded into a mini-industry. As the number of bloggers has exploded, so has the number of tools and services available for bloggers.

Online activities that once involved a good deal of perseverance and a lot of technical proficiency can now be quickly and easily performed by anyone with a few clicks and some typing. Web publishing has arrived for the masses.

With these developments and a growing awareness, some individuals have succeeded in profiting from their blogs. In the beginning it was almost unheard of for someone to earn money from a blog; in fact, for many, profit was seen as counter to blogging culture. This soon changed. As the first pioneers shared their income achievements, the focus on making money from blogging has increased. Now, although financial gain might not be expected, it is certainly much more accepted.

Over recent years the term *professional blogger* arrived to describe anyone who approaches blogging not as simply a hobby, but as a professional money-earning activity.

How Much Could You Earn?

It should be stressed before we go any further that bloggers need to enter into an examination of this topic with realistic expectations. Although millions of bloggers are experimenting with professional blogging, most bloggers are not getting rich and are only supplementing their income by blogging.

Although some bloggers, like Darren and I, do make a full-time living from blogging, and some bloggers make way more than either of us do, many more bloggers use their blogging income to subsidize gadget purchases or to offset some Internet costs.

Just like in most walks of life, those who succeed are the few who put in the effort to make a go of it over the long haul, whereas most others fall by the wayside before they really get going.

Pro Blogging Is Not a Get-Rich-Quick Tactic

It sometimes disappoints people when we tell them to look elsewhere if they want instant riches. Unfortunately for the impatient, it takes time to build a profitable blog. You do not just become a professional blogger overnight any more than you instantly become a professional golfer. If only this were the case! Although blogging involves you making a decision that you are going to earn money from blogging, it is also something you have to work toward over time.

Yes, you *could* make a lot of money from blogging. Read the stories that are going around on blogs of people making decent full-time incomes from blogging and you will get an idea of the sort of earning potential that exists. Take care also to read about and investigate the hard work and time investment required by bloggers who have created a financially viable blog. Remember that for every well-publicized success story you do read about, there are plenty of others around, who have tried and failed, that you do not read about. A lot more people struggle to make more than a few dollars from their blogs than who earn those headline-making five-figures-a-month totals.

Don't get us wrong; we're not saying this to dampen the excitement and dreams of pro bloggers! The whole point of this book is to help you achieve exactly those dreams, but we think it is the responsibility of those of us who are "talking up" blogging to also keep giving reality checks. No magic wands, no hidden tricks, and no secret handshakes can bring you immediate success, but with time, energy, and determination, you can get there.

Direct and Indirect Earning Methods

We go into more detail about exactly how you can earn money from a blog later in this book, but making money from blogging is achieved with two broad categories of tactics: *direct* and *indirect monetization*.

Most blogs and bloggers tend to use one or the other of these methods, but there is nothing to stop bloggers from experimenting with elements of both.

Direct Monetization

Direct methods include strategies that enable bloggers to earn an income directly *from* their blogs. Examples include the following:

- Advertising
- Sponsorships
- Affiliate commissions
- Paid reviews

As you can see in Figure 1-2, Darren creates revenue directly through displaying advertising.

Figure 1-2: Sponsor advertisements on ProBlogger.net.

Indirect Monetization

Indirect methods include those in which bloggers earn an income *because* of their blog. This could be taking your blog-derived authority, credibility, and expertise and using it for any of the following:

- Freelance contracts
- Books and e-books
- Speaking engagements
- Consultancy opportunities
- Service contracts
- Running courses, classes, and workshops
- Membership sites and paid communities

When you visit my blog, you will not see any paid advertisements, but you will see banners and references (Figure 1-3) to my own indirect monetization methods and the occasional recommended resource.

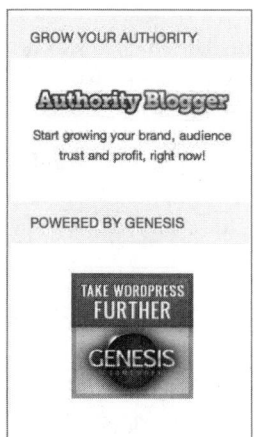

Figure 1-3: Using a blog to sell products and services.

Maintaining a Blog Income Mix

Direct and indirect is not necessarily an either-or choice. In fact, one of the big mistakes we often see is bloggers focusing on only one specific source of revenue, let alone one monetization *type*.

Although there is something to be said for maximizing what you discover works for you, thinking it will give you the best result, this in fact often leads to increased risk. You do want to get good at the income streams you choose to pursue, but you don't want to be over-dependant because things on the Internet can and do change rapidly and in unexpected ways, catching people off-guard.

One of Chris's coaching clients, Shane Ketterman, discovered this in the most painful way possible. He had built up his blog to be very successful, very quickly. Traffic was growing via Google, and because of his fantastic quantity of traffic, he was making a lot of money via Google AdSense, to the point where he gave notice at his employment to go full-time as a blogger. Unfortunately, Shane put off implementing Chris's advice to build his e-mail subscriber base and diversify his income streams.

Then Google changed the way it ranked websites, taking the majority of his traffic away practically overnight, and therefore most of his income vanished with no way to get it back.

Thankfully the story does have a positive ending, as you will see later in this book (in Chapter 6)! Right now, use it as a lesson of what *not* to do, because Shane could have very easily been in the situation of begging for his job back.

What should Shane have done? He should have maintained a mixture of traffic and monetization strategies.

Although Chris mostly focuses on indirect monetization, which is what he is known for, he doesn't focus on one product or service, but has a variety. As well as his most well-known offerings (the Authority Blogger course and his private coaching), he also makes a certain amount of his income from affiliate and joint venture projects (including ProBlogger projects with Darren).

On the other hand, while Darren is famous for direct monetization, in particular AdSense and Chitika, an increasing share of his revenue comes from publishing e-books (see Figure 1-4).

Maintaining a mixture of income streams means you are making as much out of your available opportunities as you can, plus you are offsetting the risk of loss of income as much as possible.

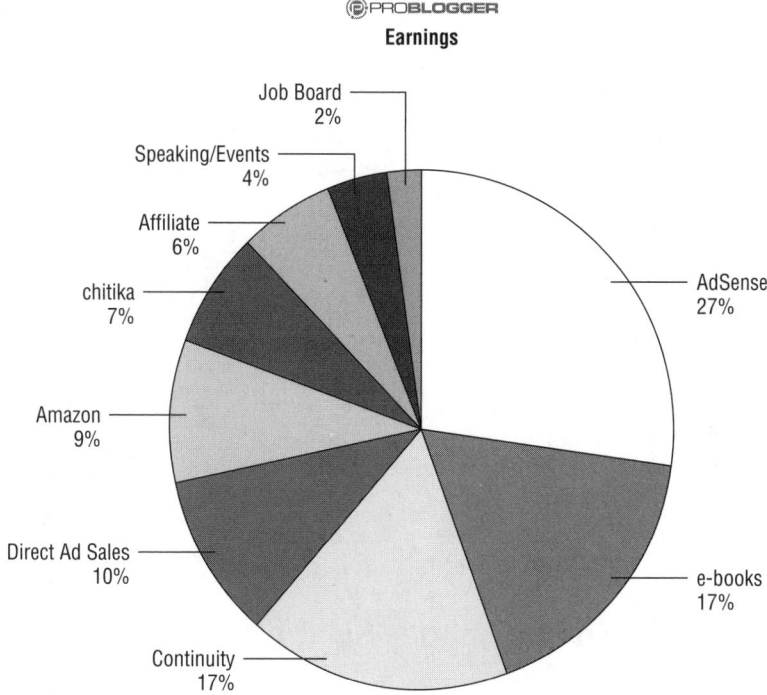

Figure 1-4: Darren's top revenue streams.

Passive and Active Income

A big appeal for making money out of blogs, or in fact web publishing in general, is that many people see it as a passive income or income that is earned even when they are not actively working.

Although some aspects of blogging can be seen as allowing a passive income—for example, advertising can earn you money while you are asleep, you can take days off, and so on—in actual fact you do need to keep working at it to make a steady or increasing income.

Blogs that stay still, do not get cared for, or are obviously built with automated or ripped-off content ultimately decline and disappear. When a blog attracts no visitors, the blogger will not earn income.

Is Pro Blogging Right for You?

Darren and I speak to bloggers every day who have heard the stories of blogs that make big money and who want to try to make an income from blogging. One of the pieces of advice that we offer, knowing full well that it doesn't always get through, is that it is worth taking time out to ask yourself whether making money with a blog is right for you.

Although this might seem to be a silly or even insulting question to some, it is meant to help you examine your intentions. Not every blogger is suited to blogging for money.

Many new bloggers find that the enthusiasm and ideas come easily at first, but after the first flush of energy has passed it becomes harder and harder to write every day, let alone keep up with all the other activities required to maintain a blog. When your income depends on keeping it up, you might find some of the feelings of excitement and enjoyment have turned to resentment and blogging has become a chore.

Which Monetization Method Is Right for You?

It is not always obvious which style of monetization you might want to follow. Each monetization tactic is appropriate to a different style of blog and blogger.

Consider the following approaches to blogging and see if they fit you. We have noted which category they *primarily* fall under.

- **Indirect**—Here are some common reasons for blogging that fall in the indirect monetization category:
  - You blog to help promote your business.
  - You blog because you want to sell your products.
  - You blog because you want to promote your writing.
  - You blog because you want to make yourself known.
- **Direct**—Here are some common reasons for blogging that fall in the direct monetization category:
  - You blog for recreational purposes, about your interests and hobbies.
  - You blog to make money in your spare time.
  - You blog about products and write reviews.

Now, there is nothing wrong with blogging for more than one reason, and a mix of strategies is certainly possible, but bloggers considering adding income streams to their blogs need to be aware of the possibility that the implications of going in that direction might impact their other goals.

Let me share some scenarios of real cases that Darren and I have come across where putting ads on a blog wasn't a good idea. Although they might seem specific, I am sure they represent the story of many bloggers and that you can imagine many more scenarios.

Business Blogs Advertising for Competitors

Many entrepreneurs hate the thought of leaving money on the table, so when they hear about blog advertising they think they have found a way to make money from wasted traffic. In fact, what tends to happen is that the ads that are served up by their blogs are for other competing businesses in their field. Although they could block some of the ads, most often more ads come in to replace them. If you are promoting your own products or services, be extremely careful about displaying banners or any offers other than your own. In many cases the space you give over to advertising could be more profitably used to sell your own offering.

Reader Uproar

One blogger who Darren spoke to told him about the day she added graphical banner ads to her blog that sparked a mutiny among her readers. Previously loyal readers expressed outrage that she'd gone that route. Whereas on some blogs, the readers' sense of ownership is not very high, on other blogs—for one reason or another—readers take great offense when bloggers change the rules midstream, especially when it comes to intrusive or animated banner ads. Depending on the community levels and the way you introduce the ads, you can end up losing readership when you advertise, and you need to consider whether the benefits of the income that ads generate outweigh the disadvantages of losing readers.

Money Obsession

Perhaps one of the saddest examples is of a blogger who had been running a really interesting and reasonably successful blog. Although you wouldn't call him an A-lister, he had a growing and loyal following. Seeing this growth, he got bitten by the "money from blogging" bug so badly that it ended up killing his blog. He deleted from his archive any content that had no income-earning potential and introduced so many ads onto his blog that it was hard to find the actual content. Eventually he ended up writing only on topics that he thought would be earners. By doing so, he lost the vast majority of his readership and ended up with a pretty uninteresting and garish blog.

Distractions and Clutter

A number of bloggers try some advertising and then later pull the ads, largely because the payoff isn't worth giving the space to the ads. Ads contribute an element of clutter to your blog and if the conversion isn't sufficient, using ads can seem quite pointless. Opinions on the usefulness of ads versus the disadvantages of the clutter they create vary from blogger to blogger and sometimes depend on the type of ad chosen and the topic that the blogger is writing about, but it's one of the main reasons we see for bloggers to *remove* advertising.

Loss of Reputation

Reputations are increasingly important and very hard to build. It does not take much to lose any trust you have built up. Some bloggers manage to build their reputation, gather an audience, and then wash what they built down the drain. After advertising, many bloggers look to affiliate commissions and paid reviews for their next source of income. The problems start when they consider only the commission value and start promoting affiliate products of which they have no knowledge. Inevitably, some of those products will be subpar or even actually rip people off. In promoting defective products or writing inaccurate reviews those bloggers betray their audience, something it is very hard to recover from.

How to Make Blog Advertising Work for You

Here are the key tips to keep in mind when you are considering adding advertising to your blog:

- Put your reader and content first.
- Don't let ads dominate.
- Ensure only relevant and appropriate ads are displayed.
- Write reviews only for products that you have used.
- Promote affiliate offers only when you are sure they are a good value. Disclose your affiliate relationship so as not to fall foul of the U.S. Federal Trade Commission and other government regulations.

Stick to these tips and you should be fine in most cases.

Blog Strategies

When they think of earning money from blogging, many people think of only one model:

1. Set up a blog.
2. Make it popular.
3. Earn from advertising.

In fact, there are other models to consider.

Multiple Blogs

First of all, there is no reason why you should have only one blog. Darren and I each have more than one blog. Although your earnings on an individual blog might not set the world alight, if you have multiple blogs and earn a couple of hundred dollars *per blog*, it could make for quite a nice salary.

Freelance Blogging

In addition to owning my own blogs, I make a percentage of my income writing for other people. It is enjoyable, can be lucrative, and is actually great marketing for my own blog and me.

Obviously I think it is a good deal for the blogger, but what about the person hiring the blogger? People hire a freelance blogger to blog for them for several reasons.

- **Ability**—There is the writing itself and then all the other things a blogger needs to do, such as traffic building and promotion, design tweaks, technical stuff like installing plug-ins and programming, and so on.
- **Time**—If you are busy running your business but you know you would benefit from a blog, you might hire someone else to do the actual writing. I know many bloggers who have built up mini-networks of blogs this way without doing much of the actual blogging.
- **Network**—As you will see later in this book, success can be as dependent on other people as on your own efforts. Sometimes people hire other bloggers who they know are well-connected to gain access to people and communities otherwise out of reach for them.

- **Knowledge**—At times you might need a subject-matter expert to write on certain topics. Rather than learning it all yourself, you can outsource those articles.
- **Credibility**—Hiring an already-popular blogger is also an advantage because you can leverage his or her credibility and traffic to boost your own. There's nothing like having a well-known, big-name blogger to drive people to your site.

Building and Flipping

A concept familiar in the real-world real-estate market, building and flipping has transferred over to the virtual world of property development. Essentially, it is possible to grow a blog's value and then sell it. You could build from scratch, or find an under-developed property, buy it, give it a makeover, and then sell it for a profit. See Chapter 6 for more on this approach.

EXERCISE

After reading the preceding sections you will have a good idea of the sorts of revenue options that are out there. Take some time to think about which appeal to you and why. Most monetization techniques take a good amount of testing, but knowing in advance where your motivations lie will give you an idea of which strategies you are going to have the energy to persist with.

Measuring a Blog's Success

If you are building a blog to earn money directly, or if you are hoping to make sales from your blog, then money is your obvious metric to determine how well you are doing. What if direct income or sales leads are not part of your plan? How can you measure the success of your blog then?

Every blogger you speak to seems to have a unique perspective on what determines a successful blog. For some it could be about traffic, others prioritize the number of subscribers, and some bloggers count comments as the best measure. Each metric means different things to different people.

The following sections cover a few measures of success that different bloggers use to evaluate how their blogs are going. Some will be more or less relevant for different blogs and will depend on the goals and objectives of the blogger.

Traffic

The most common ways that bloggers use to evaluate a blog are the different measures of *traffic*. Different bloggers seem to have their own preferences regarding different aspects of traffic, plus each tool you use to measure traffic gives a different result due to the differing methodologies used. It is very rare to find two different tools that agree on any one result, so when measuring traffic it is best to stick to your favorite service and use it to show progress rather than obsessing over the actual numbers. Figure 1-5 shows an example traffic graph for ProBlogger.

Figure 1-5: Alexa graph showing the launch of ProBlogger.

Unique Visitors

The idea behind tracking *unique visitors* is to count the number of people who visit your blog. The problem in determining this accurately is that there is no way to know with any confidence who is visiting unless you get each person to log in every time they read.

To get a rough idea of how many unique people visit a blog, you can use techniques such as counting each unique IP address (a number given to each device connected to the Internet) or recording *cookies* (small text entries saved by your web browser for later retrieval). All methods have proponents and problems. For example, your IP address today might be different tomorrow, or many different computers could be simultaneously surfing under one number due to differences in how networks are organized. Cookies have a lot of fans, but they are less reliable than they once were because so many people delete them manually or automatically via security and privacy software.

A further complication is that, if you have readers who choose to take your content in feed form rather than view your blog in their web browser, your audience is actually larger than this statistic represents.

Advertisers, especially, like to know how many unique visitors your blog attracts in a given month, and if you are going to sell your blog, this metric is extremely important also. See Chapter 6 for more on selling your blog.

Visits

An individual visitor could make several visits to a blog. You can measure visits more reliably than you can unique visitors, but to compare results you have to agree on what constitutes a visit.

Visits are also sometimes termed *visitor sessions*. Depending on who you listen to and which software you use to measure, a session could be calculated in several ways. One popular way to define a session is as an unbroken stream of page views after a certain period of inactivity. If someone visits two pages ten minutes apart, is that two page views in one session or two visits?

Many website owners take note of average session length as a way to determine how long people spend on their site. As websites become less about downloading pages and focus more on interactivity within a page, session length is gaining attraction. The longer visitors spend looking at your content the better, because it means they were more engaged, and according to media types, gaining more affinity with your brand.

Page Views

Page views are the total number of pages read in a web browser. Most bloggers like to know how many page views they attract on a daily and a monthly basis.

In addition to the total page views, you should monitor the ratio of pages viewed per visitor. It is best to have a high number of pages viewed and for the average visitor to read more than one page.

Each article you write will receive its own page views, and by comparing individual page counts you can work out which articles are gaining the most attention, giving you an idea what content your audience finds most interesting.

Hits

Hit counts measure the number of requests sent to the server for a file.

This is a dated and largely unhelpful metric because every request for any file is counted. Although it sounds useful, in actual fact it gives you little actionable information. If you have a page containing four images, one request for that page is counted as five hits. To increase your hits, you can add images to the page!

Because of the misleading nature of the metric, few people use it seriously, and the term *hits* is often incorrectly used in conversation and the media; what they actually mean is that *hits* describes traffic in general, or specifically visits or page views.

Bounce Rate

A metric you will see often is your *bounce rate*, and though it may be useful, it can be extremely misleading and confusing. The easiest way to describe bounce rate is as the percentage of people who view only one page of your site and then go away.

Why is this confusing or misleading? After all, you want people to stick around and view more of your content, right?

The problem is that the way blogs are consumed leads to high bounce rates. Consider the behavior of blog subscribers. They see your headline in their Feedreader software or in their e-mail, they click through, they read, then the majority will move on to other things. Or they might visit your homepage, subscribe, and from that point on read your blog on their iPad!

Giving people related content and categories, encouraging commenting, and so on, can all help reduce the number of people who read one article and then vanish.

So take your bounce rate less seriously when thinking about a blog than other types of websites, but do consider it in your metrics mix.

Subscribers

Bloggers can vary from being indifferent about subscriber counts to being obsessed with them. Why are subscribers so important?

Counting a blog's subscribers gives a good indication of how popular it really is because subscribers are the people who want to read your content long-term and have signed up to receive updates so they never miss one. These are your loyal readers, the people you can hopefully count on to come back again and again.

Whereas the metrics mentioned before are important, and they are traditional measures for any website, subscribers are critical to blogs. A visit could be a person arriving, not finding what he or she needs, and going away never to return. A subscriber has made a small commitment to you and demonstrates you are providing something useful and compelling.

Subscribers are usually split into RSS subscribers and e-mail subscribers, although the lines are blurring.

RSS Subscribers

RSS subscribers are the people who use your feed to read articles. They use a Feedreader (service or software application) to pull down updates to your feed and might never actually visit your blog at all.

The most popular feed-measurement service is FeedBurner (found at FeedBurner.com, which is now owned by Google) and because of this, most bloggers rely on that service to compare progress against each other. Many feed-reader services provide an indication of how many readers are subscribing to a feed, but FeedBurner is the most trusted service because it provides a semi-reliable count across all of them.

Although nearly all bloggers rely on FeedBurner, even the company would admit that counting feed readers is not an exact science. Numbers fluctuate every day, and glitches can make it seem like you have lost or gained readers almost randomly. The best idea is to use the count as a progress guide and not an exact count of individuals.

E-Mail Subscribers

In addition to RSS readers, many bloggers publish their content over e-mail. Services are available that allow you to take your RSS feed and deliver e-mail updates automatically, and specialist e-mail-newsletter-publishing services such as AWeber (www.aweber.com) allow you to create messages or import your content.

An advantage of using e-mail lists over using RSS is that when a visitor subscribes you get his e-mail address. A list of e-mail addresses is a reliable indicator of how many individuals you have subscribed, plus that list is a valuable asset to have.

Comments, Feedback, and Interaction

Much as we all want readers, when a blog is truly engaging, you will attract comments. Comments show that your visitors want to interact with you. They allow you to build a sense of community, further encouraging readers to return time and again. You can see an example comment form in Figure 1-6.

Leave a Reply

Name (required)

Chris Garrett

Mail (will not be published) (required)

chris@chrisg.com

Website

http://www.chrisg.com/

Great post :)

submit

☑ Notify me of future comments via e-mail

Figure 1-6: Writing a comment.

Comments

You can begin by counting the number of comments you receive after removing junk and spam comments. If, on average, each article attracts ten comments, you know you have made an improvement over when your blog gained only one or two.

Two types of posts you might particularly want to receive are *good feedback* and *considered posts*. If the only comment you ever receive is "You suck," you might not be quite as happy about those ten comments as back when you received two "nice post" comments per article!

Many bloggers also judge quality equally as important as quantity because it is so easy to just post any old rubbish into the comment area (and people do just to get a mention of their own website), but when someone takes time and care to craft a thoughtful comment it can be much more satisfying.

Feedback

Obviously, in addition to comments, people will use your contact form and e-mail to get in touch with you. Many of my best articles have been inspired by reader questions, and it is important to all of us to receive feedback, good and bad, so we know where we are going wrong and what we are doing right.

Interaction

Beyond comments and e-mails, readers can participate on a blog in many ways. Taking part in your blog might include responses to polls, competition entries, and other calls to action. In general, if people do in large numbers what you ask, then you have an engaged audience!

Links

Links are the currency of the World Wide Web. The number of incoming links to your blog can be an indicator of how well you are engaging other bloggers. Incoming links are good for a blog in most cases because of the incoming traffic that follows them, but also because they are a major factor in climbing the rankings in search engines.

They can be monitored in a number of ways.

- **Trackbacks**—If another blogger links to your article you can be notified using a special comment called a *Trackback*, which links back to the original blogger with a small quote of the text used. Though some bloggers hate them due to spammers taking advantage of the free link back, blogs utilize them to further conversations and as notification of what others are writing about you.
- **Search Engines**—To find out who is linking to you, type **link:***domainname* into Google, where *domainname* is the URL of your blog. You can get a good, quick picture of the incoming links that that search engine has indexed for your blog. Browser plug-ins and easy-to-use web services are available that will show you the same thing.
- **Referral Stats**—Most statistics packages offer the ability to track where your readers come from to get to your blog. This shows you the things they are searching search engines for, but also the sites that are linking up.

Search-Engine Results

Getting to the top of a search-engine result for a certain phrase can be the ticket to a flood of traffic and admiration from your peers. Some people take this to the level of a sport, seeing it as a game or competition, whereas other people make an entire career out of it because some search results are worth a great deal of money if you have something valuable to sell. Take a look at Figure 1-7 to see an example search result where Chris's blog ranks top.

Figure 1-7: Chris's blog coming in at the top in an example Google search.

PROBLOGGER BLOG TIP: USEFUL WEBSITES

The following websites and tools are useful for keeping track of your own progress or comparing one blog to another:

- SEO book—http://tools.seobook.com
- SEOmoz—www.seomoz.org/tools
- Alexa—www.alexa.com

EXERCISE

Go back over your list of blogs to read one more time. Do your favorite blogs show any signs of success under the preceding criteria? Do the best have more RSS subscribers, more comments? Can you find them in Google and Alexa?

PROBLOGGER BLOG TIP: STAT ADDICTION

Although monitoring all the statistics mentioned in this chapter can be useful, some bloggers fall into the trap of becoming quite addicted to checking these types of statistics, which can become a pretty competitive and unproductive exercise.

Remember that unlike a lot of endeavors, a blogger doesn't really have competition as such; your fellow bloggers are more normally a source of help, friendship, and traffic rather than adversaries. Plus, it is worth growing a thick skin and keeping your ego in check; sometimes "conversation" can become heated, so keeping a balanced head can be critical!

I, personally, take note of all of these varying degrees of measurements, but it's best not to give them undue attention.

Summary

This chapter examined what a blog is and some of the ways you can use blogging to make money.

Though we do not want you to be pessimistic, we cautioned that it is not something that you will make a ton of money doing overnight, so better hold onto that day job! At the same time it is a great way of earning income, both in terms of the amount of money you can make and the fun you can have doing it.

The remainder of this book goes into detail and shows exactly how to choose a topic for your blog, what you need to do to build your blog, and how to make it a success.

2 Niche Blogging

One of the most important decisions that bloggers need to make when they want to build a profitable blog is what their blog will be about. This chapter introduces you to the concept of *niche blogging* and gives you some questions to ask yourself when you are considering what topic to focus your blog upon.

The majority of bloggers starting out do so by creating a personal blog. These blogs are, in many ways, an extension of the life of the blogger and usually cover a wide array of interests, ranging from life experiences to observations on work, hobbies, relationships, and passions.

Personal blogs can be a lot of fun and are a great place to learn about the basics of blogging; however, having a blog focus on such a variety of topics and delving into your personal life doesn't always make good business sense.

I started out with a personal blog that covered everything from spirituality and church to photography to blogging (and more), and though the blog did become quite popular, after 18 months of running it, I began to notice a number of things that made me consider a new approach:

- **Some readers became disillusioned with the blog.** My blog had a number of main themes, and different readers resonated differently with each one. A few readers shared all of my diverse interests; however, most came to my blog to read about just one aspect of my life. When I focused on a topic they were not interested in, they either ignored the post or, at times, even pushed back. In the end, a number of regular loyal readers became disillusioned with my eclectic approach to blogging and gave up reading me altogether.
- **I began to feel guilty about blogging on certain topics.** Knowing that many of my readers were disillusioned by my scattered approach to blogging, I began to feel more and more guilty about posting on certain

topics and began to dread the pushback that I knew I would get when posting on things that I was interested in, but that some readers were sick of reading about. As a result, I posted on topics that I was less interested in to appease readers and ignored other topics that I'd rather have covered.

I found myself in a rather frustrating position; I was the author of a blog whose readers were increasingly complaining, and which I enjoyed writing less and less. Something had to change.

After a lot of consideration, I decided to splinter my blog into a number of niche blogs that focused on specific topics. This allowed my readers to get the specific information that they wanted and for me to write as much (or as little) on each of those topics as I wanted, knowing that I was writing to people with specific interests similar to mine.

The result was a more natural blogging experience for me and a more useful blog for readers.

10 Reasons Why Niche Blogs Are Successful

Although it is not impossible to build a successful blog by blogging on a wide array of topics, the majority of profitable blogs that I've observed target a defined niche.

Look at the top blogs that you read regularly and you'll find that the majority of them have a defined niche. Some niches are wider than others, but in nearly all cases they've carved out a niche for themselves.

Here are a few of the many reasons why choosing a niche is important for building a successful blog:

- **Loyal readers**—Niche blogs tend to develop a loyal readership because readers know that when they log in to a blog, they'll get relevant information on topics that they have an interest in, rather than random posts on topics that they have no desire to read.
- **Community**—People like to seek out other people who are like them and are interested in the same topics. Many times when you develop a blog focusing on a single topic, you find that a group of like-minded people will gather around it not just to read what you have to say, but also to interact with others who share their passions and interests.

- **Specialist authors**—Authors of niche blogs have the freedom to focus on a topic without feeling guilty about doing so. This can lead to an increase in the quantity, quality, and depth of articles.

- **Brand, credibility, and profile**—Blogging consistently on one single topic increases the chances of that blog (and its blogger) being seen as a credible, trusted source of information in that area. Work this correctly and you can become the "go-to" person in your niche and become known as a specialist or expert in your field. The benefits of being seen as the go-to person are huge if you have a product or service of your own to sell. Instead of needing to look for customers, you'll find that people start to seek you out because of your expertise.

- **Contextual advertising**—Contextual ad networks like AdSense tend to work best on sites that are tightly focused. They serve more targeted and relevant ads when a whole site is on a defined topic—which, in turn, increases the likelihood of those ads being clicked by readers.

- **Ability to sell products**—When you understand a niche well and attract an audience around it, you can create and sell products, confident that they have an eager market and will be purchased.

PROBLOGGER BLOG TIP: SPOTTING NICHES

While you are looking around at blogs, try to identify the niche the blogger is working in and the unique qualities of that niche. You will find variations in approach and conventions from topic to topic typical to just that niche:

- Overall subject
- Target audience
- Advertiser market
- Related niches
- Successful content types
- Design style
- Tone of voice
- News versus tutorial

By thinking about blog niches this way, your awareness will grow, which will help you develop an eye for potential niches in which you could happily work.

- **Direct advertising sales**—Niche blogs are more attractive to private advertisers or sponsors who are looking for content where they can place their ads—content that is relevant and closely aligned to their product or service.
- **Search engine optimization**—Google and other search engines tend to favor sites with a well-defined topic with pages that relate to one another.
- **More posts**—I find that I post more if I have five blogs on five topics rather than one blog on five topics. There is only so much you can write on a blog each day without overwhelming your readership.
- **Leverage to expand into neighboring niches**—One benefit of becoming well-known in a highly focused niche is that you can position yourself to springboard into a neighboring or overarching one.
- **Higher conversion**—If your blog's business model is to sell something to your readers, it is to your advantage to have a blog that has a readership with interests that are highly aligned with your own focus. Trying to be all things to all people is a trap that some bloggers fall into. For fear of losing readers, they allow their content to become unfocused and off topic. Though this might help build readership when it comes to selling a product, your conversion rate will be significantly reduced because a lower percentage of readers will be truly interested in your more targeted product. Niche blogging brings in more qualified prospects.

Choosing a niche for your blog enables you, your bloggers, and your readers to become more focused, and enables you to grow a readership and monetize it more effectively.

How to Choose a Profitable Niche Topic for Your Blog

Defining your niche is important if you want to build a successful blog; but how do you choose one?

The following sections are a series of questions that we recommend you ask yourself as you make this important decision. We've included some practical exercises with each question to help you tackle them more effectively.

Are You Interested in the Topic?

A friend of mine recently explained it this way:

"Probably the best place to start thinking about what your blog should be about is to consider what *you* are about."

In other words, start by identifying your own interests, passions, and energy levels for topics. Although it might be tempting to start blogs based on what other people are interested in or what makes commercial sense, there is little logic in starting a blog on a topic that you have no interest in yourself.

There are two main reasons for this.

- **If you want to grow a popular and well-respected blog, it can take considerable time, and you'll need to take a long-term approach to building it.** Successful blogs don't happen overnight; as a result, it's well worth asking yourself, "Can I still see myself writing on this topic in a year or two?" If you can't, you might need to reconsider your topic.
- **Your readers will quickly discern whether or not you are passionate about your topic.** Blogs that are dry and passionless tend not to grow. Nobody wants to read something that the author doesn't really believe in.

EXERCISE

Take some time to brainstorm possible topics based solely on your own passions and interests. What do you know about? What do you do in your spare time? What do you spend your money on? What topic do your conversations with friends always turn to? What ideas or topics keep you awake at night? What books, magazines, TV shows, and websites do you spend time following? Rate each topic in terms of your passion and interest.

Do You Have Experience or Expertise in the Topic?

This is an important question to consider before you start a blog. Not because you can't start a blog on a topic that you don't have "expert" status in, but because your own experience in the area will determine how you approach the topic.

Take the "make money blogging" niche as an example. I regularly see bloggers starting blogs that claim to teach people how to make money blogging. They present themselves as experts, but the problem is that many of those behind these blogs have never blogged before and don't have any experience to draw upon when it comes to teaching others how to do what they claim they can teach.

The result is that these bloggers often run out of things to write about. Their readers quickly see through the claims of the bloggers, and the reputation of the blogger is damaged.

A better approach for someone just starting out in a niche with little experience would be to start up a blog on the topic that is open about what they do and don't know, and that will document their own learning experience on the topic rather than promote a false claim to know it all and be able to teach others.

These blogs can be quite successful because others at a similar stage often gather around them to share the journey of learning with the blogger. Over time, these blogs can actually transition into "expert blogs" as the bloggers and their readership grow and become more proficient and experienced in their topic.

> **EXERCISE**
>
> List the topics that you know something about. What have you had training in? What have you had experience in? What topics do people always come to you to find information on? What are you currently learning about or wanting to learn more about? Once you have a list, give each topic a rating in terms of your level of "expertise."

Is the Topic Popular?

Although the blogger's interest is important, it's not enough to build a popular blog.

Another crucial ingredient is that others *want* to read about the topic you're writing on.

The law of supply and demand comes into play at this point. You might be interested in your topic and be able to supply great content on it, but unless others are interested in it and are showing demand for it by searching for it, you'll always have an uphill battle in building a well-read blog.

Keep in mind that you are writing in a medium with a global audience of many millions, and as a result, you don't need a topic that *everyone* is searching for, just one that *some* people are searching for.

EXERCISE

Head to a newsagent (newsstand) and take a few minutes to do a little analysis of the array of magazines that you see on display there. What are people into at the moment? Which topics are most prolific when it comes to what people are reading about?

Is the Niche Growing or Shrinking?

The popularity of different topics rises and falls over time.

Ideally, you would want to choose a topic when it is on the rise rather than when it is in decline. This is not easy to do, of course, but predict the next big thing that people will be searching for and you could be onto a winner.

Get in the habit of being on the lookout for what people are into. I constantly ask myself, "What will people be searching the web for in 6 to 12 months, and how can I position myself to be the site that they find when they do?"

Keep an eye on what people are into, what the latest trends are, what events are coming up, and what product launches are on the horizon. Do this online, but also keep an eye on TV, magazines, the papers, and even the conversations you have with friends.

Although it isn't essential to be first to start a blog on a topic, it certainly helps to be early.

EXERCISE

Go to Google Trends (`www.google.com/trends`) and type in some of the keywords from niches that you are considering blogging about. Google Trends charts search volumes for different search terms. It tracks only some words (generally popular ones), but it gives a great trend analysis of whether a niche might be growing or shrinking. Compare two or more niches by separating terms with a comma.

What's the Competition?

One of the traps that some bloggers get sucked into when choosing a topic is to go for the most popular topics with no regard for the competition they might face in those markets.

PROBLOGGER BLOG TIP: NICHE ANALYSIS

When selecting a niche, you want to determine the audience size, the level of competitiveness, whether there is any money to be made, and how well you can populate your blog with content over the long term.

Although many bloggers say there is no such thing as competition in blogging and that we are all friends, it could be too much of an uphill struggle to try to break into an overcrowded niche when other just-as-effective niches are available.

How much competition is too much? You might be surprised to learn that in some cases you actually *want* competition. There are two reasons why you cannot find many competitors for a particular niche:

1. You are a genius and nobody else has thought of writing about your topic.
2. There just isn't enough interest to sustain a blog long-term.

In most cases it will be the second option, but you can test a niche by creating a new category on your personal blog and seeing what kind of reaction you get.

In fact, many bloggers see successful blogs already operating in a niche and decide that if someone else can do it, they should choose exactly the same topic and attempt to emulate them.

A prime example of this is in the gadget blog space where some of the most successful blogs operate (like Gizmodo and Engadget). The problem with starting a blog on gadgets is that thousands of other blogs are already targeting this niche, with some very entrenched and well-established blogs already taking the lion's share of the market. Though it is not impossible to start a successful blog on gadgets, picking a niche with fewer and less-established competitors might be a wise move.

The chances are that if you have identified a niche that you think is "hot" at the moment, someone else will have also. It's supply and demand coming into play again—for any level of demand for information on a topic, only a certain number of sources of information are needed on that topic.

The web is becoming a more and more cluttered place, and sometimes it feels like there are no niches left to blog about. Though this is true in some of the more popular topics, remember that you don't have to go for the topic that absolutely *everyone* is searching for. In fact, sometimes it's some of the less popular topics with little or no competition that are the best earners.

I have one friend, who after years of attempting to do well writing about gadgets, switched to writing about ride-on lawnmowers (a topic he'd been researching for a purchase he was making). He was amazed to find that after just a couple of months of writing on his new topic, it was garnering significantly more traffic (and making quite a bit more) than his gadget websites ever had.

Sometimes it is better to be a big fish in a small pond than a small fish in a big pond.

EXERCISE

Head to Google and search for blogs on your potential niche. See who has been blogging on your topics. How many other blogs can you find on your potential niche? Make a note of them for the next stage of this process.

What's the Competition Neglecting?

This question attempts to find "gaps" that are not yet filled in the marketplace. Though your competition might have the advantage of an established audience, you have the advantage of flexibility and can position your blog very quickly to fill a gap that you might observe in the niche. In doing so, you create a sub-niche within the larger topic.

EXERCISE

When analyzing your potential competitors, you might like to ask some of the following questions:

- What do they do well?
- What are the boundaries of the topics that they focus on?
- What don't they write about?
- How often do they post?
- How long are their posts?
- At what level of reader are they pitching their blog (beginner, intermediate, advanced)?
- What questions are their readers asking in comments?
- What style or voice do they write in?
- How do they monetize themselves?
- What types of posts seem to get the most attention (comments, Trackbacks, incoming links)?
- What is their design like? What do they do well and what do they do poorly?
- What are other blogs writing about them?
- If they have an open or unlocked stats package, what can you learn from their stats? What pages are popular? Where does their incoming traffic come from?

Doing this type of analysis of your competitors will not only help you work out if there are any gaps that you might fill with your blog, but also how you might do it.

The key objective in thinking this way is to develop a blog that is unique and differentiates itself from other blogs.

Will You Have Enough Content?

One of the key features of successful bloggers is that they are able to continue to come up with fresh content on their topic for long periods of time.

Conversely, one thing that kills many blogs is that their authors run out of things to say.

Answering the question regarding whether there is enough content should be done on two levels:

- **Do *you* have enough content within *you* as an author?** This really comes back to the question we asked earlier about your passion, interests, and energy for the topic (so I'll leave it at that).
- **Do you have access to enough other sources of content and inspiration?** Many web-based tools can help you come up with content. Places to check out your topic to see what's happening in your niche include Google News, Digg, Popurls (Figure 2-1), StumbleUpon, and Reddit. Do a search for words in your proposed niche and you will quickly see how much is being written about them in mainstream media and on other blogs.

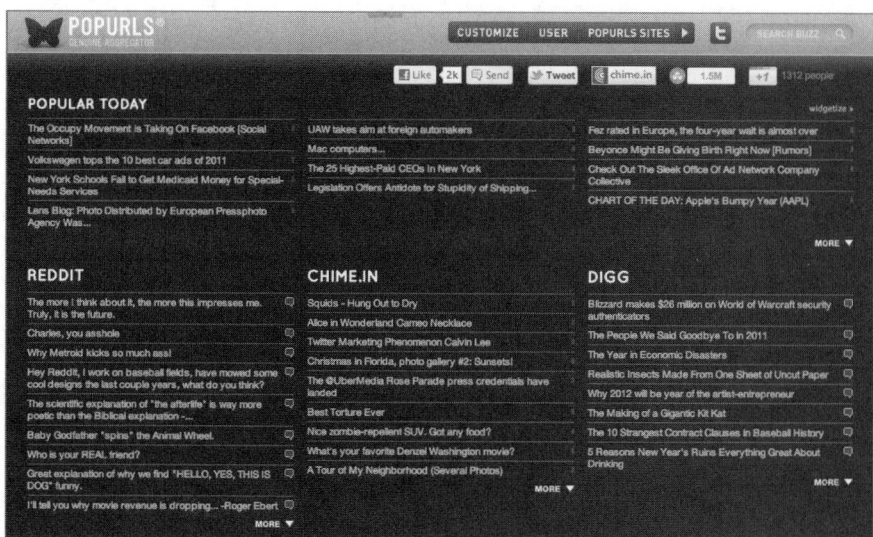

Figure 2-1: Popurls links to sources of information (http://popurls.com).

EXERCISE

Set aside an hour to list as many ideas as possible for posts. If you get three minutes into this exercise and have run out of ideas, it could be an indicator that there's not enough content to sustain a blog for the long haul.

Is the Niche Able to Be Monetized?

If you are interested in earning an income from blogging, you will need to factor in some investigation of whether the topic you've chosen has any obvious potential income streams.

You have many ways to earn money from blogs (we introduce you to many of them later); however, the problem is that not every topic is going to be suitable for every potential income stream.

For example, contextual ad programs like AdSense and Chitika work really well for some topics, but earn hardly anything from others. Similarly, some blogs do fantastically well out of affiliate programs, some are better suited to selling advertising directly to advertisers, and others are better suited to impression-based ads.

EXERCISE

It can be difficult to know how well different income streams will work on a blog before you actually start it and begin to experiment. However, the more digging around and research you do before starting out, the better equipped you'll be to make a decision on which niche topic to choose. You might start by:

- **Looking at your competition**—Check out how other blogs and websites in the niche are monetizing their sites. What ad networks are they using? Are they promoting affiliate programs? If the competition has advertiser pages, how much are they charging for them?
- **Searching for affiliate programs**—Head to your favorite search engine and type in your potential topic and "affiliate programs." You'll be surprised at what will come up when you do this; quite often this will reveal some potential products that you could make some commission on. Try it with a variety of keywords in your search.
- **Searching Google**—Do a simple search on Google for the main keywords of your potential niche and see how many ads appear above and down the right-hand side of the search results page. This is an indicator that advertisers are using Google's AdWords advertising program for these keywords. This indicates a likelihood that there will be advertisers if you use the Google AdSense program to monetize your blog.
- **Checking out Amazon**—Search on Amazon to see if you can find related products that you might be able to link to and make a commission on via its affiliate program.

How Wide Should a Niche Be?

Blogs come in all shapes and sizes. Take a quick look at some popular blogs and you'll find that some have wide niches. For example, Gizmodo (Figure 2-2) covers news on all kinds of consumer electronics and gadgets—it covers everything from MP3 players to digital cameras, through to GPS devices.

Figure 2-2: Gizmodo.com.

Some blogs narrow their niche even further and focus on just one class of product, or even in extreme cases, one brand or model.

Both wide and narrow niches can work; however, while some analysis of the most popular blogs shows that they quite often have a wide focus, it is also worth knowing that they usually are in quite crowded niches (lots of competition) and take a lot of work to maintain (many of the top blogs have numerous bloggers churning out content for them).

On the flipside, don't choose a niche that is too narrow. I once saw a blog start up on a single model of printer. Though this blog had a well-defined niche, its blogger ran out of things to write about after just a week or two.

The take-home lesson is to choose a niche that you can find enough to write about but that won't overwhelm you.

Should You Try Niche Demographic or Niche Topic?

So far we've talked about choosing a niche topic for your blog—something that most successful blogs do. However, there is another type of niche blog that we're starting to see some bloggers develop—one that doesn't focus on a niche topic so much as a niche demographic.

These blogs identify an audience that they want to target and then develop content on a variety of topics that would relate strongly to that group of people.

Let me illustrate with a couple of short case studies.

Gala Darling

When I first met Gala Darling at a blogger meetup in Melbourne, she described her blog to me as a fashion blog that documented her own tastes and decisions in fashion as well as covered fashion news.

A few months after first meeting Gala, we caught up over a coffee to talk blogging and she described her blog Gala Darling (`galadarling.com`, shown in Figure 2-3) in a slightly different way; rather than a "fashion blog," she spoke about it as a "blog for youthful alternative (unconventional, individual, eccentric) women."

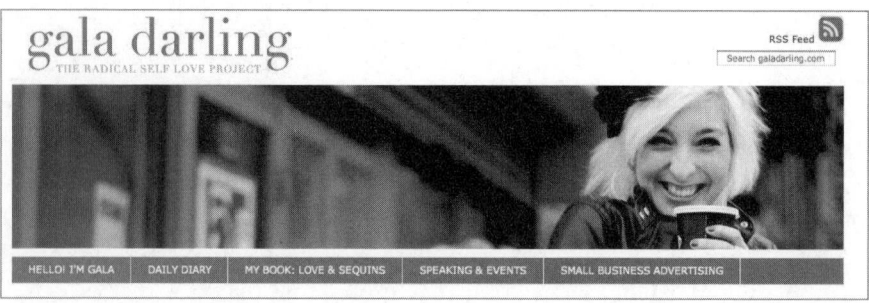

Figure 2-3: Gala Darling.

The way she talked about her blog changed from being one that revolved around a single topic to one that revolved around a certain type of reader or audience.

Fashion still made up a significant proportion of her posts, but so did other aspects (including travel, relationships, shopping, and music) of the lives of her loyal and growing readership. In a sense, Gala is moving toward providing a one-stop shop for her readers rather than just a smaller destination that focuses on one aspect of their lives.

TCGeeks

Chris and I first met Shane Ketterman at the Blogworld conference. He had launched a successful blog called TCGeeks (www.tcgeeks.com, shown in Figure 2-4), which stands for *Tablet Computing Geeks*. As the name suggests, it was aimed at people who were interested in iPads, Kindles, and other tablet-type computers.

What made TCGeeks successful was how Shane went above and beyond the competition. Rather than focusing on the topic, Shane instead focused on his audience. One by one his readers discovered how much passion and care he took over the community he was building, and how deeply embedded in the niche he was.

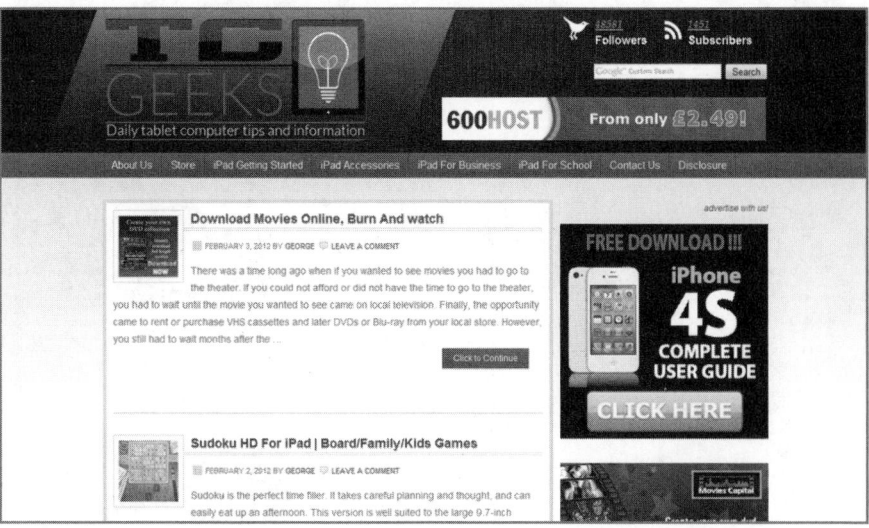

Figure 2-4: TCGeeks.

As you will see in Chapter 6, Shane went on to sell his blog, and part of what gave it the high valuation he received was this focus on his community building.

Sports Networker

Many people now know Lewis Howes as an expert on the social networking site LinkedIn, but in fact he started out in the sports niche. To be specific, he was a professional football player, holding the NCAA All-Division record for the most receiving yards in a single football game.

He founded his website, Sports Networker (www.sportsnetworker.com, shown in Figure 2-5), when an injury permanently put him out of ever playing the game on a professional level, and he had to find a new career direction.

Figure 2-5: Sportsnetworker.

He also went on to found the largest sports business group on LinkedIn with more than 52,000 members and a paid membership site, Sports Executives Association (sportsexec.net). Today his site reaches a network of more than 20,000 sports executives and continues to grow every day.

PROBLOGGER BLOG TIP: THE RIGHT NICHE FOR YOU

You can take two approaches in deciding on your niche: the analytical and the emotional. In most cases our final decision is based on a little of both.

- What type of blog are you drawn to?
- Do you feel excited about working on one topic more than others?
- Are there subjects you just can't stop talking about?
- Do people know you as an "[insert topic here] geek"?

Many of my more successful blogging friends state that if they won the lottery they would still blog; they love their topics so much. Can you think of a subject you could feel that way about?

Remember that professional blogging is hard, takes time, and, especially, needs lots of valuable and unique content. This is so much easier when blogging a topic you are motivated about.

Choosing a Niche

At this point, it's time to choose a topic for your blog. It is highly unlikely that you'll find the perfect topic on all of the fronts discussed earlier.

Although it'd be great to find a topic that you're passionate about that just happens to have massive demand, no competition, and lots of lucrative income streams, the reality is that most topics that you come up with will have at least one weakness to them.

Don't let this get you down; there comes a time when you just need to make a decision and start blogging, because the best way to get the answers to many of the questions in this chapter is to start a blog and see what you learn.

The key is being aware of what the weakness is so that you can work to overcome it.

Tools for Helping You to Choose a Niche for Your Blog

Many tools have been developed that are helpful for bloggers in the process of selecting a niche topic for their blog. The following tools are ones that we use in this research phase:

- **AdWords Keyword Tool**—Sign up as an advertiser with Google AdWords and you get access to a number of useful tools that you can use without actually needing to use AdWords to advertise. One particularly useful tool is the Keyword Tool (https://adwords.google.com/select/KeywordTool), which you need to be logged in to use. This allows you to type in a keyword (or phrase) and will give you an indication of how many people searched for that word in the past month, as well as tell you how many advertisers are competing for that word in AdWords. This gives you an indication of the popularity of the niche and whether there is potential income in it. This tool will also give you other keywords that relate to the ones you enter, which is also useful to know.

- **Google Trends**—Google has a Trends tool at www.google.com/trends (Figure 2-6) that is useful for looking at search volume on Google for different search terms. Though it won't give you specific search numbers and doesn't produce results for every term (it tracks just the most popular ones), it is useful for working out whether a niche is growing or shrinking, and it allows you to compare two different terms to show you how big one is in comparison to another.

- **Google Blog Search**—Google's Blog Search will help you to get a picture of who else is blogging on a given topic.

- **Wordtracker**—Wordtracker (www.wordtracker.com, shown in Figure 2-7) is a popular keyword-research tool with a free trial that helps you to ascertain how many people are searching for different words and how many other sites are competing in those niches.

- **SEOBook**—Aaron Wall has also outlined a great list of keyword-researching tools at www.seobook.com/archives/001013.shtml. Check it out.

Figure 2-6: Google Trends.

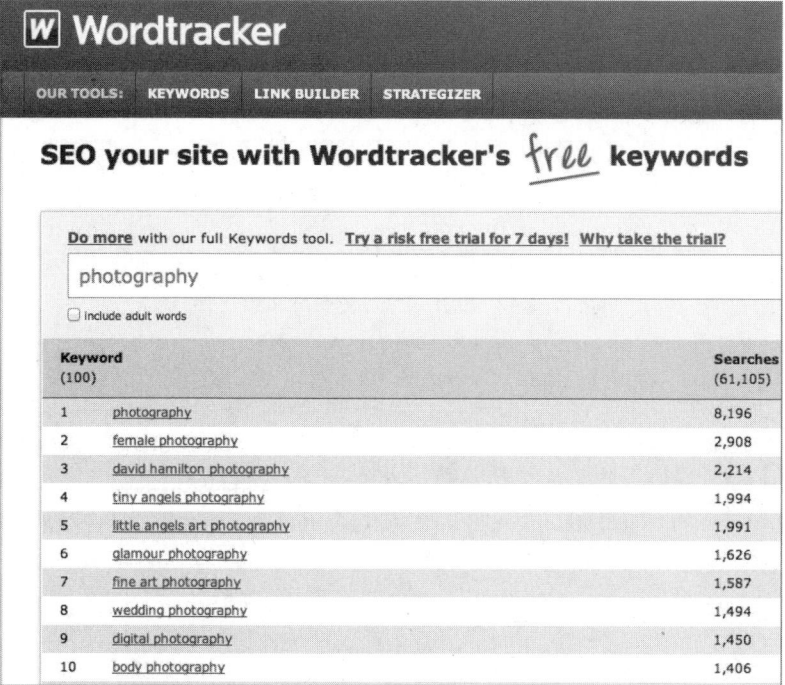

Figure 2-7: freekeywords.wordtracker.com.

Summary

Although the majority of bloggers choose to go with a personal blog when they first start, we hope we have shown that for professional bloggers, a well-selected niche that you are happy writing for can make all the difference to your earning potential.

This chapter looked at the concept of blog niches and gave you an overview of the sorts of considerations that you need to take into account before selecting your blog topic. What you will write about is a much more important factor than many bloggers realize. The subject of your blog, the audience you aim to attract, and, therefore, the market you go into could well be the deciding factor for whether your blog succeeds or fails.

3

Setting Up Your Blog

So far we have looked at what blogging is and what it means to be a professional blogger, and you have investigated what you might want to write about. We are off to a good start. Before you actually start blogging, though, you will need to set up your blog!

This chapter looks at your choices when deciding which blog package to go with, what you need to think about when choosing a blog package, and what the most popular combinations of choices are.

After you have decided on the approach you think might suit you best, you need to actually go ahead and set up your blog so it both works and looks great.

With these goals in mind, this chapter goes step-by-step through setting up a hosted blog and a self-hosted blog.

Choosing the Right Blog for You

"Which blog platform should I use?"
"Should I use a free hosted blog or get my own domain?"
"What are the pros and cons of going with one vendor over another?"
"Could I start out on a free blogging service and upgrade later?"

These are just some of the typical questions that we get asked each day from beginner bloggers trying to decide which blogging platform or tool they should choose.

I'm not going to tell you which blog platform you should use because, as you will see, there are good reasons for choosing most of the available platforms, depending on the goals of your blog and your own technical resources.

Over the years, the choices available to bloggers have grown, while the technicalities involved in blogging have shrunk. This means that now more than ever there really are options to suit every potential blogger. It's now so easy that anyone can have a blog working in five minutes flat.

Don't believe it? Just keep reading!

Blog Platform Choices

As with making any important decision, it is worthwhile to take your time with this decision before jumping in. You'll find many competing blog platforms on the market, all varying in capability, complexity, price, and popularity. Blogger (www.blogger.com) has traditionally been one of the most popular platforms with beginners, as shown in Figure 3-1, but because of that people tend to view Blogger blogs as low-quality.

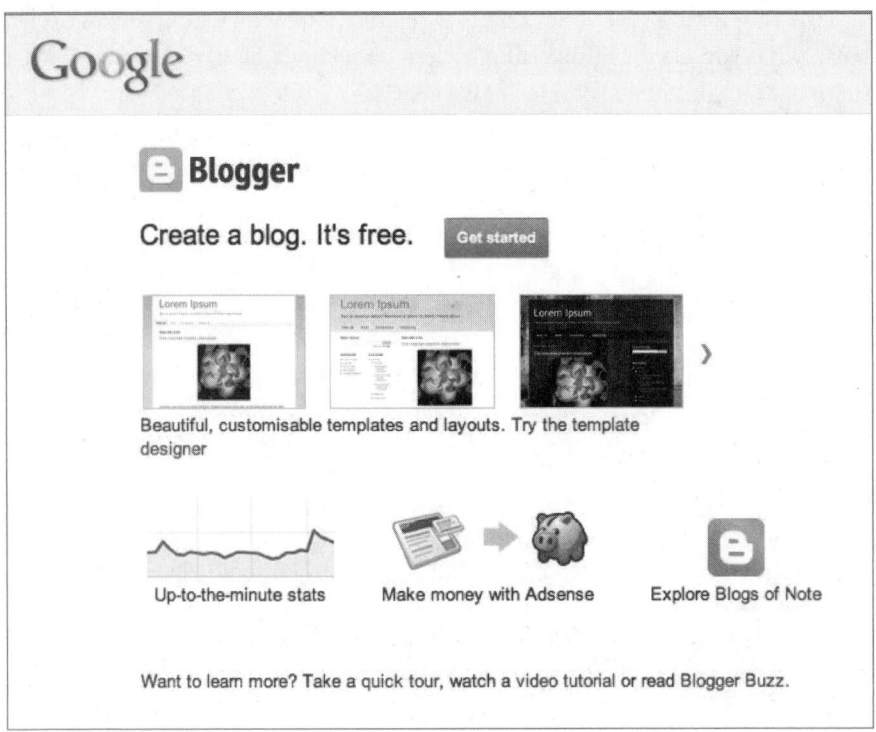

Figure 3-1: Blogger is one of the popular blogging platforms for beginners (www.blogger.com).

Although you can change your blog platform at a later time, and many of them do provide ways to move your content, tricky technical challenges are usually involved and potentially some costs.

Determining which platform suits you is an individual choice, but you can answer some questions to make your decision easier.

What Are Your Goals?

Probably the most important thing to do when starting the process of choosing a blog platform is to consider your aspirations for your blog. Of course, complete first-timers might struggle a little with seeing the future of their blogging, but to the best of your ability, attempt to answer some of these questions:

- Is blogging a passing interest or something you will do long-term?
- What will be the main purpose of your blog?
- Is it for business, or just for personal enjoyment?
- Might you want to show advertisements?

Of course, you'll want to ask many other questions, but the answers to these sorts of questions are worth keeping in mind as you research blog platforms. Some services are much more suited to the hobby blogger and others are more suited to professional blogging applications.

What Is Your Budget?

As with most things in life, blog platforms come with a variety of price points. All hosted platforms offer varying levels of service, and self-installed software varies in price from free to expensive (see Figure 3-2).

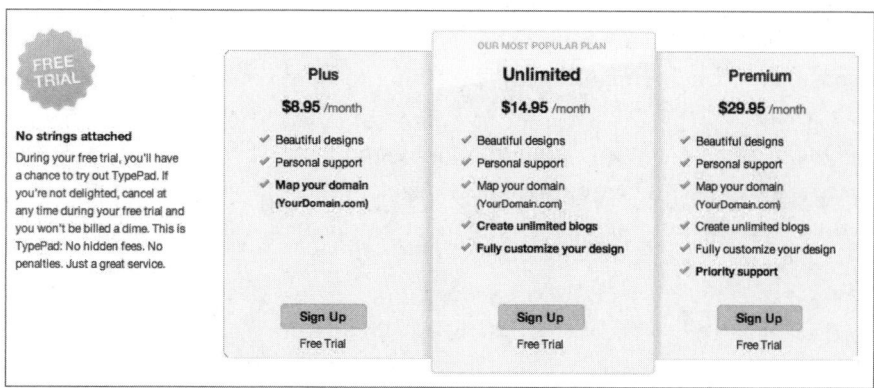

Figure 3-2: TypePad service levels.

Here are three main things that you might pay for:

- The blog software itself or level of service (one-off or ongoing)
- Monthly hosting for your blog
- Your domain name annual renewal fee

There is also potentially an additional cost for custom design and programming depending on your budget and how serious you are. Most people start out with freely available designs and tweak them to suit their own tastes and needs.

Some services, like Blogger and WordPress, offer an all-inclusive service comprising the platform, a unique web address (in the format http://myblog .wordpress.com), and hosting for free.

TypePad (www.typepad.com) offers a similar all-encompassing online service with a monthly fee but more customization options.

Others are downloadable software that you have to install and host yourself. So although they offer the platform for free, you then need to find and pay for your own hosting and domain name and support it yourself. Others still might charge for a license for the platform, depending on how many blogs you have and whether they will have a commercial, personal, educational, or not-for-profit use, and then you need to arrange and pay for your own domain name and hosting on top.

How Technical Are You?

This is a crucial factor to consider when choosing a blog platform. If you've never had any experience in creating a blog or website before and are not a technologically minded person, you can find some blog platforms and setups that will be much more suited to your needs. The other option, of course, is to find someone who is a techie to help you out (either paid or as a friend).

One of the great things about blogging and most of the platforms is that there is a wonderful communal knowledge out there as well as many forums dedicated to helping people get the most out of their chosen platforms (see Figure 3-3).

Figure 3-3: You can find many helpful forums for bloggers.

What Blog Platforms Are Others Using?

Though your blog is your own individual choice and should fit with your own style, it is worth looking around you to see what others, in particular people you know well, are using.

Over the past few years different platforms have come and gone, and you have to suspect this will continue to happen in the future. Figure 3-4 shows the results of a ProBlogger survey regarding what bloggers used for their platforms.

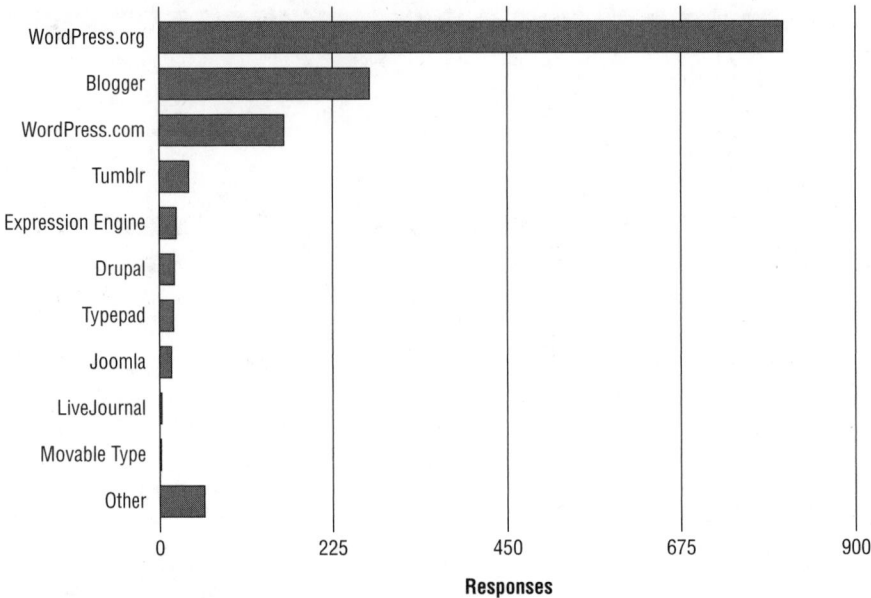

Figure 3-4: A 2011 ProBlogger survey.

By far the most popular platforms right now for pro bloggers are WordPress (both self-hosted and the online service) and Blogger. We have tried other platforms, but now mainly use WordPress.

EXERCISE

Take a look at your favorite blogs; can you tell which platform they are using? Sometimes bloggers will leave a link to the software they use in the footer or sidebar, and sometimes you can tell by the URL (for example, `http://blog.wordpress.com`). Does this software seem to offer you what you need?

Hosted versus Self-Hosted

As previously mentioned, two main types of blogging platforms exist: software you install and host yourself, and online services that handle everything for you. These are often referred to as self-hosted blogs and hosted blogs, respectively.

Hosted Blog Platforms

This is the type of blog that many bloggers start out with, simply because they are quick, easy, and can be free.

Probably the most popular of these systems with professional bloggers are TypePad, WordPress, and Blogger, with only TypePad having a monthly fee.

These systems are *hosted* blog platforms because they "host" your blog on their own domain. After what is usually a pretty easy setup process, they give you a web address (URL) that's usually some combination of their own URL and the name of your blog, for example, `http://blog.wordpress.com`.

Though this is what you get as a default, you are now often given the choice of paying a fee to use your own domain. This is something well worth considering if you are serious about blogging.

Advantages of Hosted Blog Platforms

Using a hosted platform has many advantages. Some of the most immediate are listed here:

- **Cheap or free to run**—Most hosted options are free.
- **Quick and easy to set up**—Most of these types of blogs can be set up with a basic default template within minutes. The setup is usually just a matter of filling in a few fields with your options and choosing a template design. They are ideal if you know nothing or very little about the technological side of blogging. You'll see more on this later.
- **Simple to run**—Once you're through the easy setup process, hosted blogs are usually pretty simple to run. You will obviously need to learn some basics, but these days most blog platforms come with very user-friendly features. Posting is as simple as filling in a few text boxes and clicking Publish.
- **Updated automatically**—If the blog platform changes, it automatically upgrades for you. Instead of having to upload new software onto a server, these updates happen much more seamlessly.
- **Search engines and traffic**—One of the advantages of many hosted blog platforms is that they are hosted and linked from sites that already attract search engine attention and traffic. Some of this "rubs off" on your blog, giving it a little boost.

Disadvantages of Hosted Blog Platforms

Although there are several benefits to having a hosted blog, there are always downsides:

- **Less configurable**—With an online service, the only configuration options you have available are those the service allows you. This may or may not be a problem for you, but in most cases you have fewer choices with a hosted service.
- **Default design limitations**—This can be true for standalone blogging systems, but many hosted blogs end up looking very similar to one another. This is because the default templates get used over and over again, and hosted platforms do not give you complete control over your look and feel.
- **Less ownership**—Another complaint I hear regularly from hosted-blog owners is that they are frustrated by not having ultimate control and ownership over their blog. Although they do own the content, the URL is not technically their own and they are somewhat at the mercy of their platform in terms of whether or not their blog is working.
- **Generic URL**—Some very successful blogs are on hosted platforms, but most bloggers believe that having your own URL is much more professional if you are using your blog in a professional way.
- **Upgrading or moving challenges**—One of the issues of starting out with a hosted platform is that, if there comes a day when you want to move, you have some work cut out for you in retaining your audience and traffic.
- **Non-commercial or lacking monetization options**—Most monetization options assume you have complete ownership and control of your blog site, and some hosted solutions forbid you to create a blog for commercial reasons.

Who Might Use Hosted Blog Platforms?

If you just want a blog and don't care much about having your own unique domain, and you are not too interested in tweaking your blog or getting all the latest and greatest features, hosted options are a completely valid choice.

In fact, it's worth keeping in mind that though some may scoff at hosted blog platforms and say that serious bloggers don't use them, some popular bloggers have used them very successfully or got started that way. For example, three of my favorite blogs cut their teeth on hosted services: Scott Adams and Robert Scoble started out with hosted blogs, and Seth Godin still uses TypePad to this day (`http://sethgodin.typepad.com`).

Standalone Blog Platforms

The other type of blog platform is where you download, install, and host the software yourself.

This is what Darren and I do with all of our blogs these days. You will notice our blogs have their own domains, `chrisg.com` and `ProBlogger.net`, and as I said before, we both use WordPress on our own server spaces.

Though we are fully in favor of people going the hosted route, you do get more control when you host your blog yourself. Of course, this is a double-edged sword!

Benefits of Self-Hosted Blog Platforms

As mentioned before, both hosted and self-installed platforms have their own advantages and disadvantages. Here are the benefits of self-hosted blogs:

- **Full control**—Depending on your ability with the technology and web design, standalone blogs generally are very adaptable. Although I am completely happy with the geekier aspects of blogs, I am not the best designer, so I tend to lean on others for aesthetics.

  Some designers out there manage to create incredibly diverse and clever designs for blogs and provide for download both free and paid themes, so it should be possible to make your blog look fantastic.

- **Adaptability**—One of the things I enjoy about WordPress is the vast array of developers who are coming up with all manner of "plug-ins," which extend the capability of the basic WordPress installation. Many of the other standalone platforms have communities of developers producing similar add-ons.

- **Free platforms**—Although you end up paying for your domain name and hosting, systems like these are usually free to run. Some do have license fees, but most of the popular ones are free to use.

- **URL**—Having your own domain name is great for many reasons. For one, it's easier to remember; second, it's more professional; and third, it is more easily brandable.

Disadvantages of Self-Hosted Blog Platforms

Although both Darren and I have our blogs set up this way, it could be the wrong choice for you for the following reasons:

- **Complicated setup**—Again, this depends on your technical abilities, but when you move into standalone platforms the complexity of setup tends to increase. At the very least it involves arranging hosting and a domain name. There is a wealth of community support available, but for many it is still a daunting prospect.

    One way to simplify the process is to find a web host that provides "one-click installs" of popular packages. You see how much easier this makes things later in this chapter.

- **Cost**—Although the blog platform itself might be free, you need to factor in the ongoing costs of having your own domain name (a yearly fee plus a one-off registration fee) and hosting fees (monthly or yearly). Many great deals are available on these, so it need not cost the world, but if your blog gets a lot of traffic, the costs can go up, and you might want to consider going onto a more professional, and therefore, more expensive plan.

- **Updates**—Most blog platforms go through changes and versions over time. Updating from one to another can be complicated if you don't know what you're doing.

- **Hosting issues**—I mentioned in the cons of the hosted platforms that you have "less control" over your blog and are at the whim of your platform's hosting being up or down. Of course, this is also true for any hosting, because from time to time any hosting solution can have problems.

Whether you use a hosted solution or a standalone solution, it's important to keep backup copies of your files and be aware that things do go wrong from time to time. Choose a reputable company to ensure maximum reliability.

Who Would Use Standalone Blog Platforms?

Standalone blog platforms are ideal if you want a little more control or flexibility with your blogging. They can be configured to look and run very professionally and to be adapted into configurations that are limited only by your imagination.

If you host and control the blog yourself, you truly own it, with all that entails, including being able to sell your blog at some point for a profit.

Of course, just because you go with a standalone blog doesn't ensure you will have the perfect blog. In fact, if you don't have the ability to set up these blogs correctly (or know someone who can), standalone blogs can be messy and unprofessional.

This type of blog is what most people regard as the true professional option, and the majority of the world's top blogs are self-hosted.

Hosted or Self-Hosted—Which to Choose?

To sum it all up, I generally advise people to go with self-hosted just because once it is set up, the hard part is over, and you have more potential to earn money directly with your blog.

If you want to develop a serious blog and have aspirations for it to be used on a professional sort of level (whether as a business or corporate blog, as a blog to build your own profile, or a blog to earn income from advertising), I'd always recommend you go in the direction of a standalone blog.

If you are not highly skilled in this area, it's worth spending a little time or money to get it set up right. You do not need to achieve perfection right away, and with a self-hosted option, the blog can grow with you.

If you use a hosting company that features a one-click install of WordPress to make the initial setup far easier, then you only have to contend with tweaking things to make them how you would like them.

If you want a blog only for fun, as an online diary for your friends and family, or you don't have the time, money, or patience to put into anything complex, a hosted option might work well for you. They are instant (it'll take 5 to 10 minutes to set up), and although they might not have quite the same level of features and they restrict your income potential, the features they do have may well suit your needs.

PROBLOGGER BLOG TIP: GET A FREE BLOG

Regardless of which software you end up using eventually, it might be a good idea to play with some hosted services. It will help you get a clear idea in your head of which features and styles you like and any elements you find difficult to understand. Most online services are either completely free or have free trial periods that should give you plenty of time to work out how your chosen platform needs to work.

Choosing a Domain Name

Having your own domain name is desirable for professional bloggers for several reasons. For starters, if you want to build credibility and a sense of professionalism around your blog, a domain can help. Similarly, a carefully selected domain name can enhance the branding and memorability of a product, service, business, or even person. Domain purchases give the added bonus of e-mail addresses with the same domain (adding to both professionalism and branding) and can, to an extent, enhance your search-engine ranking.

Factors to Consider When Choosing a Domain Name

Just as you have many factors to consider in choosing the name of your child, business, or pet, there can be many implications of choosing names for a website.

What follows is a list of factors to keep in mind as you make the decision. Remember that there are many theories about what is right and wrong in this area and that, despite all the rules that people have, some very successful sites ignore them all!

Also worth remembering is that personal taste comes into decisions like this; what seems a good name to you will often mean different things to different people.

With those disclaimers in mind, take a look at a few areas to consider:

- **What are your goals and objectives?** We often come back to this point because where you are headed is such an important part of thinking about the long-term vision that you have for your blog. Might you want to eventually sell it?
- **What is the topic of the blog?** An obvious starting point, perhaps, but worth considering. Names can reflect the blog's topic or niche.
- **Why are you blogging?** For you, is blogging about having a hobby? Is it about building your profile/expertise? Is it about earning an income via ads? Is it to support an existing business?
- **What style will it be?** Will you be blogging alone or will there be many authors? What length of posts will it have?
- **What tone and voice will it be written in?** Will it be conversational, newsy, rants, professional, or humorous?
- **Who is the intended audience?** Do you want to appeal to businesses, young people, cool people, moms, locals, geeks?

- **What is the source of traffic?** Domains can generate *type in* traffic; this is when people guess at or remember a domain name and type it in to the URL bar rather than search for it. This is why domains like `business .com` and `sex.com` sell for millions.

  On the other hand, domains can have an influence on search engines if the keywords are present in the name.

- **Branding**—Many discussions on domain name decisions talk about choosing between a domain name with keywords in it and domain names that are more brandable or generic. It's worth stating up front that it is possible to achieve both, but I would prioritize memorability and branding over keywords. One example that comes to mind is Engadget (`www.engadget.com`), which has become a memorable and well-branded name that also manages to incorporate the keyword "gadget."

- **Future directions**—Another factor related to defining your goals and objectives is what your blog might look like in the future.

  - **Narrow focus**—I've seen bloggers change their interests over time and be stuck with narrowly focused domains, or want to expand from having a blog to a larger community. Of course, you can get a new domain, but it is less confusing and easier to market if you get it right from the word "go."

  - **Number of blogs**—Consider how many blogs you're thinking of starting on your domain. Take a look at About.com (`www.about.com`) for an example of how it's possible to have one domain with many blogs running off it.

  - **Outdated name**—Don't pick a name that you suspect might date quickly. Picking a name that is time-specific in any way might find you searching for a new domain when it is no longer relevant at some future time.

- **Name length and spellings**—Opinions vary on the ideal length of a domain name. Technically, you can have really long names and still be valid, but it is generally accepted that short ones are better. You want your audience to be able to quickly and easily say, spell, and remember your domain. The longer and harder it is to pronounce or spell, the less likely you will get good word of mouth.

- **Domain endings**—Along with the debates over domain name length come many different opinions over what is best to have at the end of your domain after the "dot." These letters (that is, .com, .net, .org, and so on) are technically called the Top Level Domains (TLDs) and are divided into two types: country code TLDs and "generic" TLDs that signify different types of organizations (in theory, at least).

There is a variety of approaches to selecting which TLD to go for, but unless you are targeting a specific country (for example, .fr for France) or have a particular legal or organizational structure to work within (for example, .edu for education), in general you ought to try for .com first, then try for the others, such as .org or .net.

- **Hyphens**—Another ongoing debate about domain names is over the value of hyphenated names. For example, a friend of the authors has a blog at `http://entrepreneurs-journey.com`. Some people prefer hyphenated names for two main reasons:
  - **Availability**—One of the main reasons for going with hyphens is that all the good names are taken (or at least it can seem this way). Adding hyphens to names gives more options.
  - **SEO**—Hyphens are said by some to identify keywords to search engines more clearly. However, I have doubts as to how effective this is in the wider scheme of things.

  Of course, for every positive there is a negative, and the arguments against hyphens include the following:
  - **Memorability**—Adding hyphens can make it tricky for readers to remember your name.
  - **Difficult to communicate**—Have you ever tried to tell someone a domain name with a hyphen between each word? It can be quite an annoying process.
  - **Increased margin for error**—The more characters in your domain name, the more chance of a mistaken keystroke.
  - **Cheap and nasty factor**—There is a perception that hyphens are spammy. I personally don't mind a domain with one or maybe two hyphens maximum, but domains-that-have-lots-of-hyphens-turn-me-off. Many bloggers have been turned down when requesting links due to their spammy-looking domains, so my advice is to avoid them.
- **Numbers**—Another option to consider when choosing a domain on a topic that is quite crowded is to include a number in it. Once again, this increases your chances of finding a domain with your keyword in it but could add to confusion (do you spell out the number or not?).
- **Keeping it legal**—Think seriously about the legal implications of the words you use in your domain name, and avoid trademarked names

especially. I know of a couple of instances where bloggers were forced into making changes months into new blogs because of legal threats.

- **The "blog" word**—One temptation for many bloggers is to use the word "blog" in the name and URL of their blog. This has the advantage of opening up new options for domain names, but restricts the domain to being forever used as a blog and nothing else.

- **Secure multiple domains**—One piece of advice that many experienced webmasters recommend is making sure that you secure other domain names similar to the one you eventually choose. For example, if you choose a .com domain name it might be worth getting the .net and .org ones if you can, or perhaps even getting plurals or other logical, similar ones. This is not essential but might help you protect your niche in some circumstances.

- **Opinions of others**—Before you buy that domain you've been eyeing, it might be worthwhile to run it by one or two trusted friends (who won't run off and buy it for themselves). It's amazing how focused you can become on finding the right name and how that can cloud your judgment. It's also interesting to see how a name might sound to a person of a different culture. Words mean different things in different parts of the world, and it could help you avoid an embarrassing mistake or just a dorky blog name.

- **Previously used domain names**—It's worth checking to see if a domain has been previously registered. Spammers often buy domain names and then abandon them later once they've used them. This can leave these domains banned by Google, which might get you off to a pretty poor start. On the other hand, people abandon perfectly legitimate sites all the time, and an expired domain could be a bargain when you consider there might already be links pointing to it, or existing traffic.

Registering a Domain

Registering a domain is much easier than choosing one! As you will see, when you order your hosting you can register a domain at the same time. The advantage to this is that your new blog is all set up with the new domain without you having to do any complicated technical stuff. You can order additional domains from your hosting company, too, for the same benefit, although you might find a better deal elsewhere with popular domain companies like Namecheap (www.namecheap.com) or 123-reg.co.uk (www.123-reg.co.uk). Figure 3-5 shows one such service.

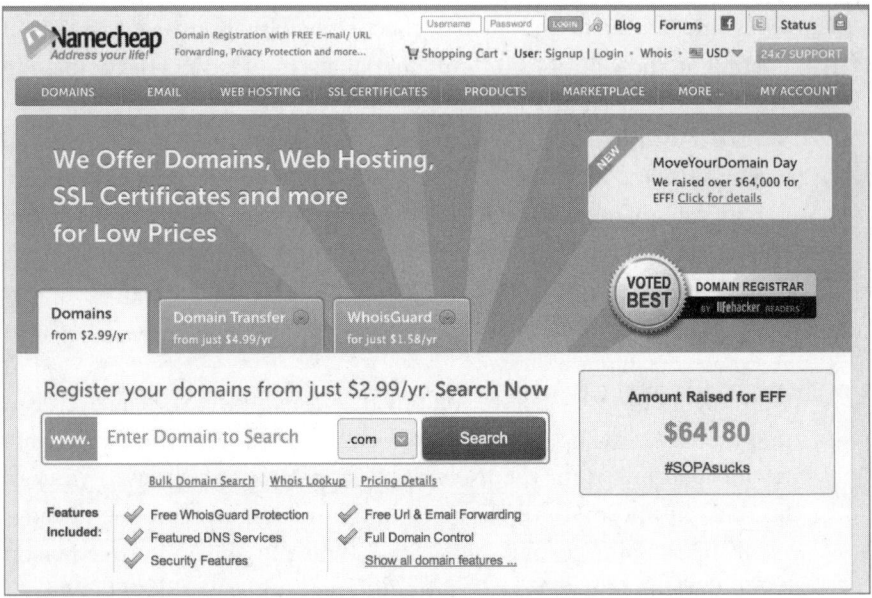

Figure 3-5: Registering a domain independently of hosting.

If you do register a domain with a company other than your hosting one, you will need to have the new domain pointed to your web host so you can take advantage of it. Check with your hosting company for details that you will need to supply to the domain company to do this, or get a technically minded friend to help you out.

EXERCISE

Brainstorm a list of potential blog names and associated domains, and then go through your list with a domain registrar such as Namecheap to see how many are available. When you find a domain that is available, put a tick mark next to the entry. For any domains that are taken, go have a look to see what the owner has done with your chosen domain.

After you have a list of potential domains, rank them in order of preference and get feedback from friends and colleagues about which they prefer.

If you hit on a great domain, snap it up!

Creating Your Blog

We have looked at the different options for building your blog and also some things to consider when selecting a domain name. I bet right now you just want to get on and create a blog already!

First, take a look at how easy it is to create a hosted blog at the `WordPress .com` online service.

Four Steps to Setting Up a Hosted Blog at WordPress

The easiest type of blog to set up is the hosted type, and by following these instructions, you will see just how easy it really is. If you can create a Hotmail or Gmail e-mail account, you can build a blog!

1. Go to `http://wordpress.com/signup` (shown in Figure 3-6).

Figure 3-6: www.wordpress.com.

2. Choose a name for your blog—for example, `blog.wordpress.com`. The first part of your blog's web address will be the username you use to log in. WordPress will suggest a related domain name and offer to let you register it for a fee, or you can continue with the free option.

3. Choose and confirm a password by entering it a second time, then enter your e-mail address, and select your language.

4. Scroll down to view the rest of the page.

5. If you are happy with your selections, click Create Blog (you can also click Upgrade to upgrade to a paid account if you wish) as shown in Figure 3-7.

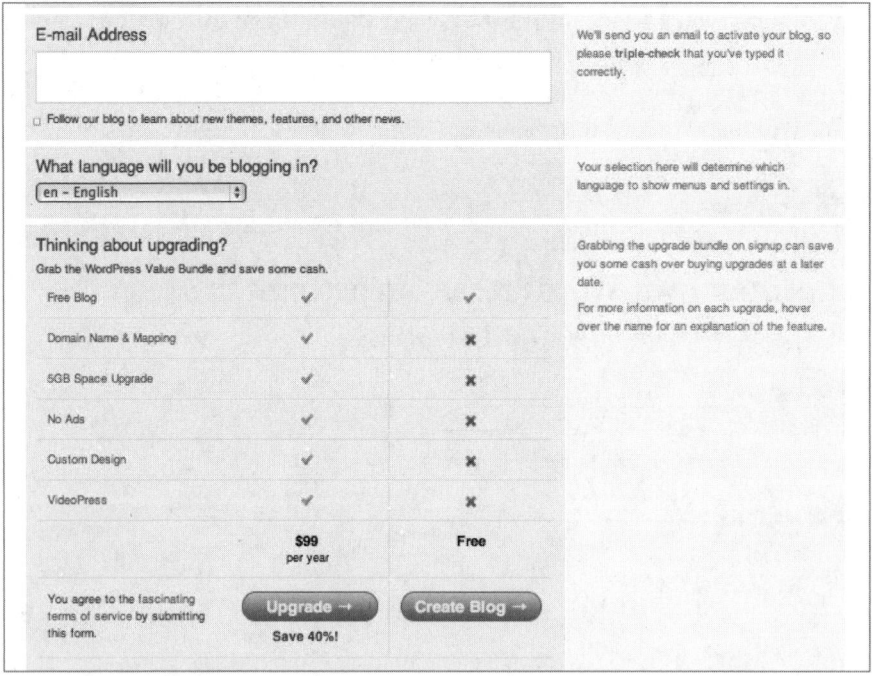

Figure 3-7: Enter your details.

6. Now you need to choose a new look for your blog. Click Appearance ⬄ Themes. You will be able to choose from a variety of different themes (see Figure 3-8). Happy blogging!

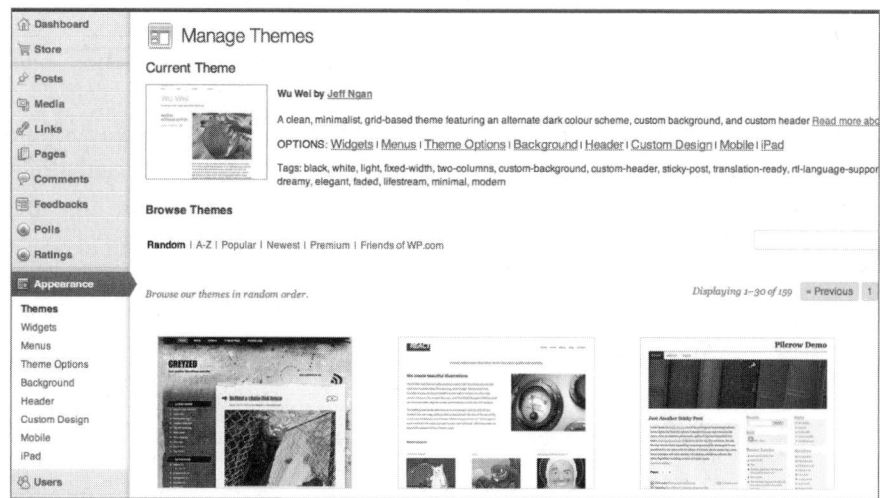

Figure 3-8: Select a theme.

Setting Up a Custom Standalone Blog Using One-Click-Install

The main advantage of a hosted blog is the ease of setup. As you have just seen, you can have a new blog in less than five minutes. For a pro blogger, though, a hosted blog will quickly show limitations, and the pain of moving is far greater than setting up a custom blog in the first place. In this section I show you how easy it can be to set up a custom blog providing you use the right hosting company. What you are looking for is a hosting company that features a Control Panel or cPanel with the facility of a "one-click-install" of WordPress.

Sometimes this feature will be advertised as using one of the branded "one-click install" systems such as Fantastico, QuickInstall, SimpleScripts, and Softaculous.

Before you sign up, you might already have a friend currently paying for hosting. Most of these services provide much more capacity than a single blogger ordinarily needs. Perhaps you can get a contact to host your blog for you? After you have generated some income, though, you would be wise to move to your own account.

Creating Your Blog

To create your blog, follow these steps:

1. First you will need to sign up with a hosting service; for example, HostGator (see Figure 3-9), and decide which package you would like, if you want to pay annually or monthly, and so on.

Figure 3-9: HostGator signup page.

2. Next, you need to choose a domain name (see the earlier section for things to think about). This will be a proper domain in the form `example.com` and you will be able to select other versions from the drop-down menu such as .org.

3. You will be asked to confirm your package and billing cycle, a username and security pin, and then all that is left is to fill in your payment details. How long this process takes will depend on a number of factors, but eventually an e-mail receipt will arrive, followed by an e-mail confirming your new account. Other e-mails may arrive informing you of various other services that are ready to use.

4. At this point, you will have a hosting account and a domain registration. Your domain might not be visible for 24 to 48 hours, but that will not stop you from setting up your blog, and most people find it doesn't take that long.

5. When you log in to your account you should see your "cPanel," and if you scroll down you should find "Software and Services" and, under that, "Fantastico" (see Figure 3-10).

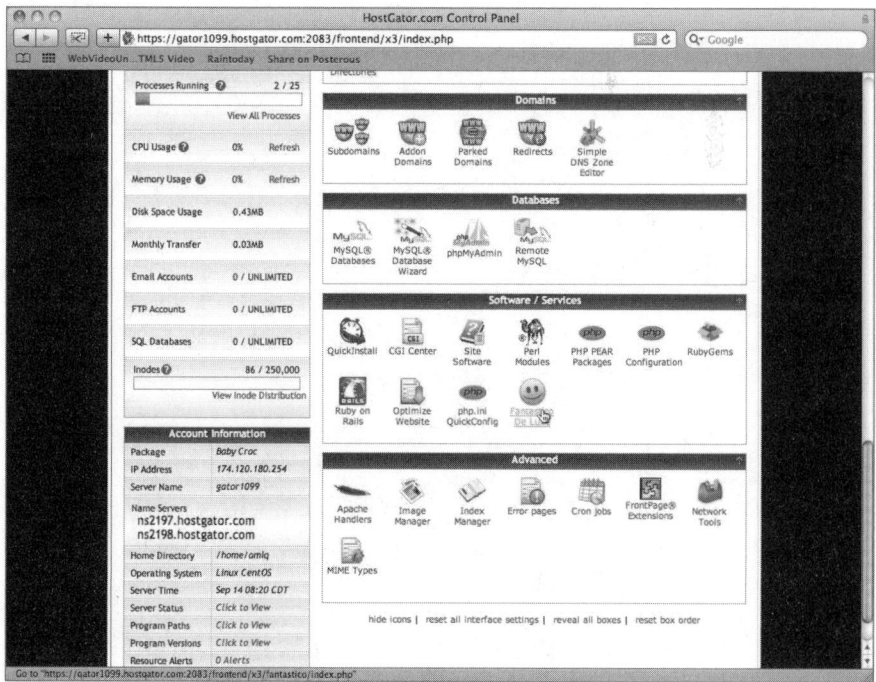

Figure 3-10: One-click installs.

6. Select WordPress from the list in the left column, then click New Installation. This takes you to the installation screen (see Figure 3-11) where you will choose the domain on which you want to install your blog.

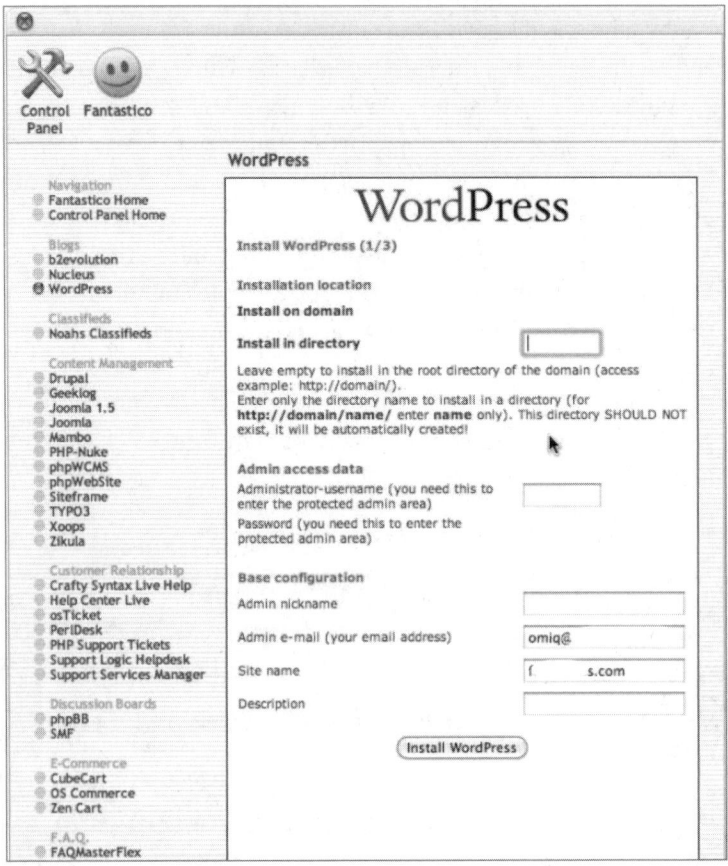

Figure 3-11: Choose where to install WordPress.

NOTE

If you want to install your blog in a subdirectory such as /blog, you can enter a directory name if you want to, but I usually leave it blank.

7. Choose your administrator username and password.
8. Click the Install WordPress button. Your screen will appear similar to Figure 3-12.

9. Click Finish Installation and you'll be taken to the final screen where, if you want, you can enter the e-mail address to which you want your new blog details sent. You can now go to your new blog!

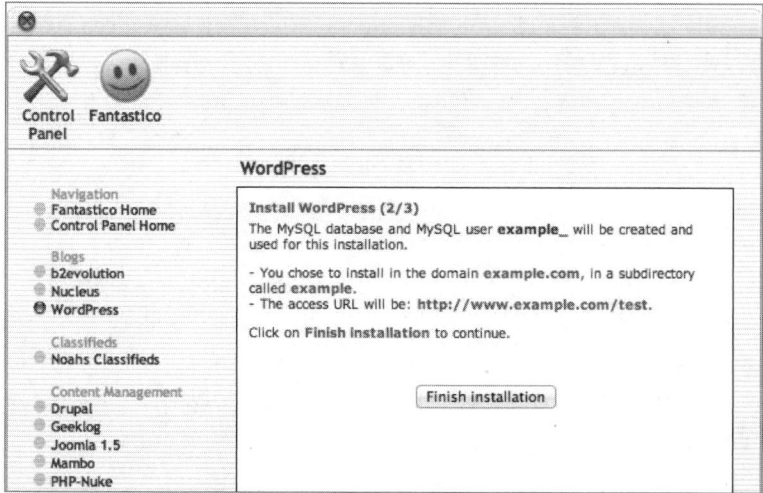

Figure 3-12: Finish Installation.

10. When you visit your domain, you will be taken to the /wp-admin/ folder, which is the location of your WordPress dashboard. Enter the username and password you chose earlier.

11. You should now see a screen similar to that shown in Figure 3-13.

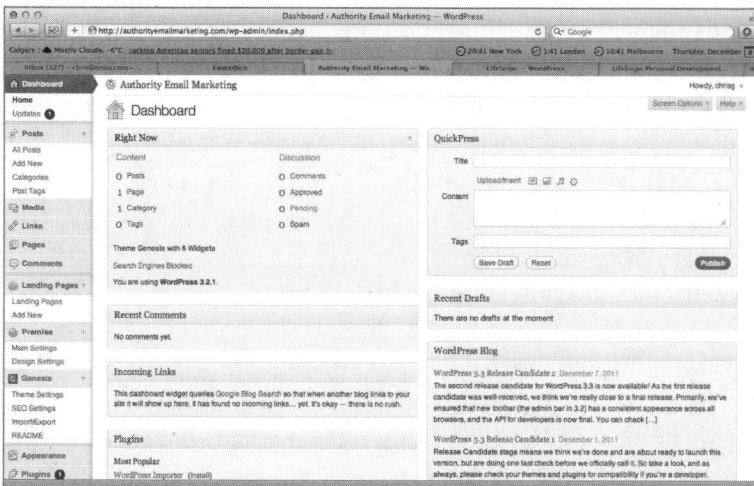

Figure 3-13: The dashboard.

12. You can now select a new theme. Go to Appearance ⌗ Themes. Switch templates by clicking the one you like and activate it.

13. Although your blog is now set up, you might want to look through the Settings menu items to configure your blog exactly how you want it. Pay particular attention to General, where you can set your tagline and date/time settings. Also pay attention to Permalinks, where you can set WordPress to use a friendlier URL structure (for example, `example .com/post-name` rather than `example.com/?p=123`).

EXERCISE

If you have a hosting company account already, check to see if they provide a one-click install of WordPress. Failing that, ask around for recommendations of hosting companies you might want to use. If your friends are no help, you could always ask your favorite bloggers who they use; most would be happy to recommend their choice of hosting company.

If you have not already, go register at the Problogger Book Member's Area and watch the "Fantastico One-Click Install" video:

`http://probloggerbook.com/?/register/bonus`

Enhancing Your Blog

Once your blog is set up you will want to customize it to your specifications. WordPress makes this easier using themes and plug-ins. Both themes and plug-ins are simply collections of files that you upload to your WordPress installation. Themes make your blog look different, and plug-ins add features or functionality not found in the basic WordPress installation.

The method of doing this is broadly the same for both; you have the built-in methods, and the "manual" methods.

To add a plug-in using built-in tools, follow these steps:

1. Log in to your blog admin dashboard.

2. Go to the Plugins area by clicking Plugins in the left-hand menu.

3. Click the Add New link (either under where you clicked "Plugins" or at the top of the screen next to where it says Manage Plugins).

4. Search for a plug-in and click Install.
5. Alternatively, upload the file from your machine using the upload facility.

To upload a plug-in "manually" using FTP, follow these steps:

1. Download a zip file containing your new theme or plug-in.
2. Uncompress to get the actual files the zip file contains.
3. Upload to the appropriate directory of your blog using FTP.
4. Activate plug-ins using the Plugins menu item. Themes are selected exactly as they were using the bundled themes previously.

Plug-ins are uploaded to the `wp-content/plugins` directory of your blog; themes go into `wp-content/themes`.

You can find new themes in Appearance ≙ Themes, or at `http://wordpress.org/extend/themes`, plus there is a list of plug-ins at `http://wordpress.org/extend/plugins`.

One of the first plug-ins I always install is a contact form. This allows site visitors to get in touch via a simple form that will send an e-mail to you on submission. In addition to making you easier to contact, it saves you from exposing your e-mail address to the world. Unlike with a lot of plug-ins, there is an additional step required to implement it, which makes it a good example to demonstrate. Let's go through the process step-by-step now.

Adding a Contact Form to Your Custom WordPress Blog

The following steps show you how to add a contact form to your self-hosted WordPress blog:

1. Search for the contact-form plug-in using Plugins ≙ Add New. For this example, browse the plug-in list by typing **send e-mail** into the search box; it should be the first result. (Make sure you enter exactly: **send e-mail**, including the hyphen).

> **NOTE**
>
> The contact form plug-in I use is called Enhanced Contact Form and is by Joost Devalk, but is no longer being supported or developed.

2. Click Install Now followed by Activate Plugin. Ordinarily, this would activate the plug-in and that would be all you'd need to do. Your contact form, though, needs to live in a contact page—a page that you have to set up.

3. Go to Pages ⌗ Add New, and enter a title; something like **Contact Me** will do. You can enter any page content you like, but you need to enter a special piece of HTML text for the form to show up. For this example, enter the following exactly as shown:

```
[contact-form]
```

NOTE

Obviously this code is specific to the particular plug-in we are using in this example; other plug-ins will have different instructions.

4. On the top the screen you'll find Permalink, the page filename after publishing. Set this to something short, meaningful, and memorable—in this example, use **contact**.

5. Click Publish.

6. Your page is created, but nobody will be able to find it yet because, depending on the theme you are using, it will likely not be linked from anywhere yet. If your chosen theme supports custom menus, you can add it via the Appearance ⌗ Menus panel. If you have not created a custom menu already, give your new menu a name and then click the Create Menu button. Once you have created a custom menu, you should be able to tick the pages you want to appear in your blog navigation menu from the Pages list, then click Add to Menu and then click Save Menu. Choose your new menu in the Primary Navigation Menu list and click Save.

7. If your theme does not allow custom menus, some themes have their own Theme Options panel that allows for custom navigation settings; otherwise, you will need to edit your header template. Go to Presentation ⌗ Theme Editor and edit your header or sidebar depending on where you want to show the link. Look for other page links, such as About, that are already there and add your new one after it. In most cases links are kept in lists, so make sure you add your new link before the closing `</ul>` tag as here:

```
<li><a href="/contact/">Contact</a></li>
</ul>
```

8. Click Update File and take another look at your blog. All being well, your new contact form should show up in your navigation, ready to try (see Figure 3-14)! In the case of the send e-mail form, you'll need to log out if you want to see it exactly as a visitor would.

Figure 3-14: Your new contact form.

Blog Design Considerations

A lot of your blog's initial impact will be from your design. In the preceding section, we just chose a template off the shelf, but you will have much more success if you spend a little thought and effort on providing your blog with the perfect look.

Many people are put off by bad design before reading even a single word of content. A good design can really set off your content, and make your blog appear more cared-for and professional, which can help you get those valuable subscribers.

Before selecting a design for a blog, you need to decide some things:

- **What is your blog goal?** Are you aiming for AdSense profit, to sell products, fame? AdSense templates tend to free up more space for advertising, whereas if fame is your goal you'll want a nice big sidebar area for your "About Me" box.

- **Who is your audience?** Funky? Straight-laced? Cutting-edge? If your target audience is the boardroom, you will need a more conventional design than if your audience is mostly made up of designers. This will influence your graphic and color choices.
- **What specific functions does the site need?** Certain templates have more abilities than others. Some are created to fulfill a certain purpose, such as templates for photo bloggers. Do you need header tabs? Randomized masthead images? Flexible block quotes? Here are some standard features you need to consider and allow space for:

  - Contact details
  - About or bio details/photo
  - Advertising
  - Archives by categories
  - Archives by date
  - Logo
  - Subscription buttons
  - Newsletter signup
  - Search feature
  - Blog roll
  - Recent posts list
  - Links to older key posts

A Word on Color

As everybody knows, color affects mood. What do you want the mood of your blog to be? You will certainly get a different result with a pink blog than a gray one. Colors *mean* something as well as look nice. You know the classics:

- Red = passion, blood, anger
- Blue = conservative, business
- Green = nature, go
- Gray = formal, staid

Carefully consider what ambience you want to project and what possible meanings your color scheme should be associated with.

Customizing a Blog Template

In most cases you will need to make your chosen template look unique. Your blog has to stand out and be unequivocally *yours*.

At the time of writing, the default WordPress template is called Twenty Eleven, and despite being what everyone gets out-of-the-box, it is still pretty nice.

Although major template surgery is beyond the scope of this book (and my abilities!), the main two things people need to change are quite simple: the header image and colors.

Changing the Header Image

Unlike most themes from the past, the Twenty Eleven theme makes it easy to change the header image.

Simply go to Appearance ⌂ Header in your WordPress admin and select the image you want to upload as your header or choose one from those already available (Figure 3-15).

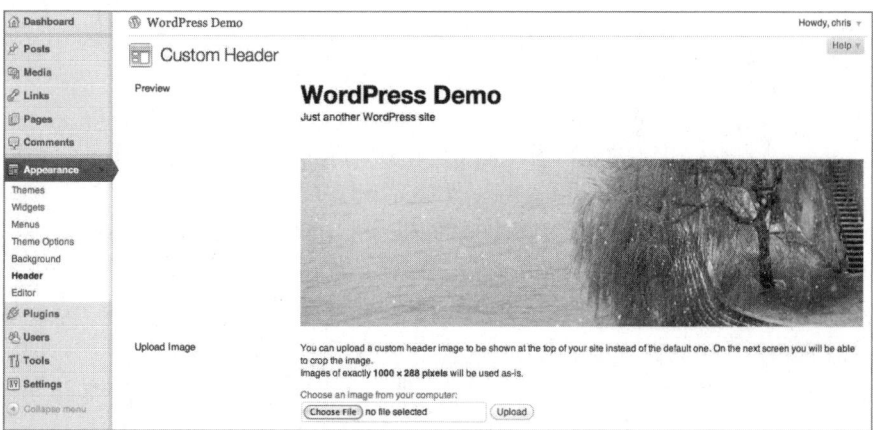

Figure 3-15: Change your header.

Other themes will have varying abilities, so it is worth checking out a few and reading some online reviews of premium themes.

PROBLOGGER BLOG TIP: OUTSOURCING DESIGN

You might struggle to do your own design—this is fine; so do I! Many premium themes are available for purchase, and a good selection of designers are only too willing to take you as a customer. Though top-end design can be expensive, one of the great things about blogging is the community. It is possible to find excellent blog designers for far less than you might expect, especially when it comes to specific items such as header graphics. Ask around forums for recommendations, look at freelance communities like vWorker (`www.vworker.com`), and do not overlook putting out a request on Craigslist (`www.craigslist.org`).

Changing Colors

The other tweak you might want to make is to alter the color scheme somewhat. Again, Twenty Eleven has some built-in features that make this much easier than many themes of the past.

Under the Appearance menu in your WordPress admin you will see Theme Options, Header, and Background. Each of these settings pages allows you to select colors for your header text, background, and links.

Summary

We covered a lot of ground in a short chapter, so hopefully you were not overwhelmed!

The main point we hoped to make with this chapter is that setting up your blog need not be as difficult as it would first seem. Approach it with a feeling of fun and exploration, especially your first blog.

It is worth reiterating that the blog world is full of helpful people on forums and e-mail lists. If any of the information we covered in this chapter confused you at all, the authors and the blogging community as a whole will surely be able to help you out.

4 Blog Writing

Much has been written on what makes a blog successful, but all experts agree that central to all great blogs is one element: great content.

The cry, "Content is king," has echoed through the blogosphere for years; although I think the term ignores other aspects of what makes a blog successful, content is a key ingredient of a successful blog.

What Is Good Content?

Defining good content is a subjective exercise (perhaps in a similar way to defining a good book or a good movie). Good content will vary from person to person depending on their needs, the topic they are talking about, and perhaps even a person's ethics. Not only will bloggers themselves each have a different view on what good content is, but readers tend to also. I know that every time I ask for feedback about what I write about on ProBlogger, I get a real spectrum of responses.

Having said this, there are some things that can be said about good content, and this chapter attempts to unpack some of them. At most points along the way there will be debate, but hopefully you can mix and match the elements and identify what works for you.

So without any more introductory remarks, let's get into it with the first element of writing quality content.

Usefulness and Uniqueness

Let me start the exploration of good content with a fairly obvious, but important, statement:

> For a blog to be successful, your content needs to be useful and
> unique to your readers.

It isn't rocket science, but two questions that bloggers need to continually ask themselves are, "Is my blog useful?" and, "How is it different from other blogs?"

Back in the days when I studied marketing, I remember sitting in lecture after lecture getting more and more frustrated as I listened to instructors drum into us the same thing time after time. Although they said it in different ways, the lesson that they communicated was largely the same in every instance and boiled down to this:

"Start with the customers—find out what they want, and give it to them." This is a good lesson for bloggers also.

I would also recommend that you start with yourself as a blogger and blog out of your own passions, experiences, and knowledge, but it is essential that you be aware of your readers and that you create content that will add something to their lives.

Give them something useful and unique.

What Is Useful Content?

Useful content to me is different from what it is to you, but could be any of the following:

- **Entertainment**—Increasingly, blogs are used for entertainment. People are going to them for laughs, gossip, and fun conversation.
- **Education**—Some blog readers are primarily interested in learning something about a given topic.
- **Information**—Many successful blogs are built on the thirst that readers have to be informed on an issue, product, or topic.
- **Debate**—Some blog readers want a place where they can have a good old-fashioned dialogue, debate, or even a fight over an issue.
- **News**—Many blog readers just want to be kept up-to-date with the latest news on a topic.
- **Community**—People have a desire to belong. Many successful blogs tap into this and are all about connecting people interested in exploring a topic. Quite often the topic is secondary to the actual relationship built on the blog.

To learn more about how to build a community around your blog, visit Chapter 8, which covers how to build a sticky blog community.

Each blog has the potential to be useful in a different way, and it would probably be unwise to start a blog that tried to be all of these things at once (although many blogs do a variety of these things at once).

Research Your Readership

The best advice that I could give on developing useful content is to research your readership (or potential readership). If you already have a blog, do this by surveying your readers (either formally or informally) or by asking for feedback.

I regularly ask my readers for questions, and much of what I write emerges directly from these queries.

Another quick tip for finding what questions your readers are asking is to check the referral statistics of your blog to see what words people are typing into search engines (SEs) to find your blog. A great little tool for this is Google Webmaster Tools (www.google.com/webmasters/tools), which tracks how people arrive at your blog and identifies questions being asked by your readers in search engines.

If you don't have a blog already, you'll need to work a little harder to research your potential readers. Survey friends, follow the comments sections of other blogs on your topic to see what readers are asking there, and look in forums and online discussion groups that cover your topics, where there is usually a lot of question asking going on.

As you do this you'll begin to put your finger on what people want and what you might be able to provide to meet those needs.

Who are your favorite blogs attracting? Why is that? Spend some time thinking about who you want to attract to your blog and the kind of work, lifestyle, and needs they have.

Unique Content

Another factor to consider when thinking about good content is uniqueness.

Technorati (http://technorati.com) tells us that a blog is being created every second, and that tens of millions of blogs are in existence today. This presents bloggers with the challenge of building a blog that stands out from the crowd.

I see blogs every day that provide "useful" content, but that have no readers simply because people are finding that information in other places.

Distinguish Yourself

New bloggers trying to break into a niche where others are already blogging should surf through the other blogs and websites in that niche and do some analysis on what sort of content those blogs and websites are producing.

In most niches, you'll find that sites are all presenting very similar information in pretty much the same voice, tone, and style. As a new blogger on the topic, you have a choice: you can either replicate what they are doing and try to do it better (difficult because they will already have loyal readers, and unless you're brilliant at it you're unlikely to convert these readers over to you), or you can distinguish yourself in some way from what others are doing.

This might mean focusing on a slightly different topic (perhaps a sub-niche), but could also mean writing in a distinct voice. (Take a look at Manolo's Shoe Blog [http://shoeblogs.com] for an example of a blogger who has grown a cult audience by writing about an odd combination of topics as an anonymous blogger writing in the third person.) It might also mean writing in a different genre of posts. (That is, if everyone else is writing newsy posts, you might like to write more opinion-type posts.)

Bring together the elements of useful and unique in your content, and you will be one step closer to a successful blog.

Writing Tips for Bloggers

Writing for the web—and more particularly, on blogs—is very different than writing in other mediums. This section explores some practical tips for writing effectively as a blogger.

Scannable Content

Web users are known for not staying on web pages long and for skimming through content rather than reading it word for word. This is even more the case when readers read through their RSS feeds. Rather than reading each word on a web page, web users scan pages for information, looking for keywords, phrases, and visual cues.

As a result, it is very important to learn how to write content that is scannable.

Here are a few tips and techniques you can use for working *with* your scanning readers instead of against them:

- **Lists**—This will be no surprise to ProBlogger readers—I'm pretty big on lists, and my stats show me it's my posts with bulleted or numbered lists in them that get linked to and read *a lot* more than similar-length posts written in an essay style. You can see an example in Figure 4-1.

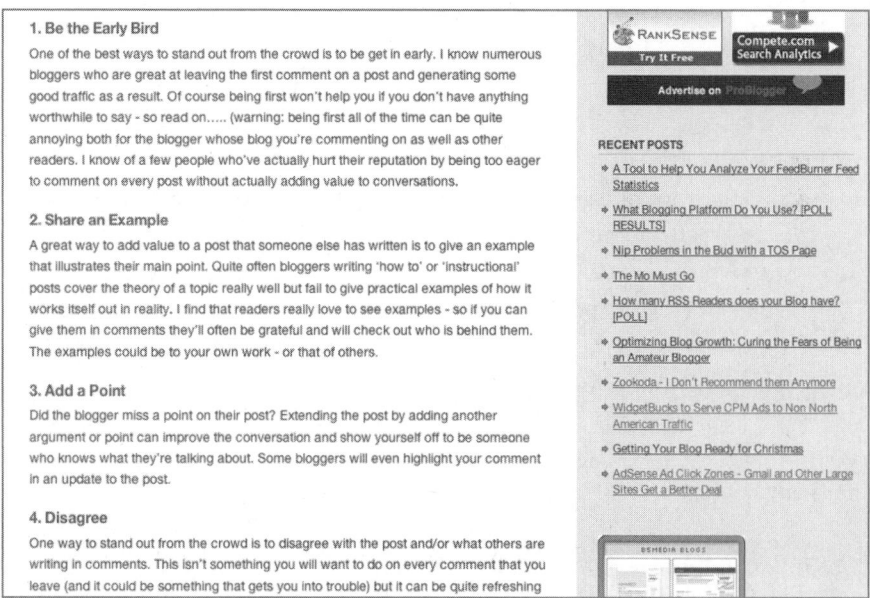

Figure 4-1: Lists make it easier for readers to scan content.

- **Formatting**—Use **bold**, CAPITALS, *italics*, <u>underlining</u>, and other formatting techniques to emphasize points. Don't go overboard, because you run the risk of frustrating your reader. Do be careful with underlining because it is also commonly used to indicate that text is a link. Also consider changing font size, color, and style to draw your readers' eyes to your main points.
- **Headings and subheadings**—Using headings midway through posts helps with post structure, but headings also are great for drawing your readers' eyes down the page and helping them find important points and the elements of your article that will most interest them.
- **Pictures**—Clever use of pictures in your posts can grab attention, emphasize points, and draw people down into your post. In a largely text-driven medium, images give your post visual points of interest. I've tested how readers react to pictures in posts, and pictures are particularly effective at the top of posts to get people reading, and worthwhile to break up the text in longer posts and to draw the eye to action items.
- **Borders/block quotes**—Boxes around quotes and key points can similarly get the attention of readers.
- **Space**—Don't feel you have to fill up every inch of your screen; rather, create spaces because they help readers not to feel overwhelmed and, again, tend to draw readers' eyes to what is inside such spaces.
- **Short paragraphs**—Web users tend to get lost in large blocks of text; break text into smaller bites, and you'll find that people continue to read a post longer.
- **Don't bury your points**—Make your main points as clear as you can, and get your main point across in the first few sentences rather than bury it in your conclusion.

Work hard at producing content that can easily be scanned, and you'll find that your readers will stick with you, even through the longest of blog posts.

PROBLOGGER BLOG TIP: MAKE IT EASY

No points are awarded for making your content complex, and your readers will not respect you more if you use longer words. In fact, the reverse is probably true. Remember, your reader might have poor eyesight, be distracted, or be in a rush. The easier you make your blog to read, the more readers you will attract.

Using Titles Effectively on Blogs

My mom drilled into me at a young age that first impressions are important. Outside of the design of your blog, perhaps the best way of creating that good first impression is through your post's title.

Well-written titles are important on many fronts, including the following:

- **Grabbing attention in search engines**—Go to Google and type in virtually any word you can think of, and you'll often find millions of results. The interesting thing is that for most search results in Google (and other search engines), there is very little for readers to go by in deciding which result to click on. There is a title, a short excerpt, and a URL. The most highlighted of these is the title, and I believe it is a key to getting search-engine-referral visitors.

- **Getting RSS readers' attention**—In a very similar way, titles can grab the attention of those following your blog via RSS feeds in news aggregators. News-aggregator readers tend to scan the titles of posts for things of interest rather than reading full text, stopping to read and visiting the posts that pique their interest. Figure 4-2 gives an example of this technique.

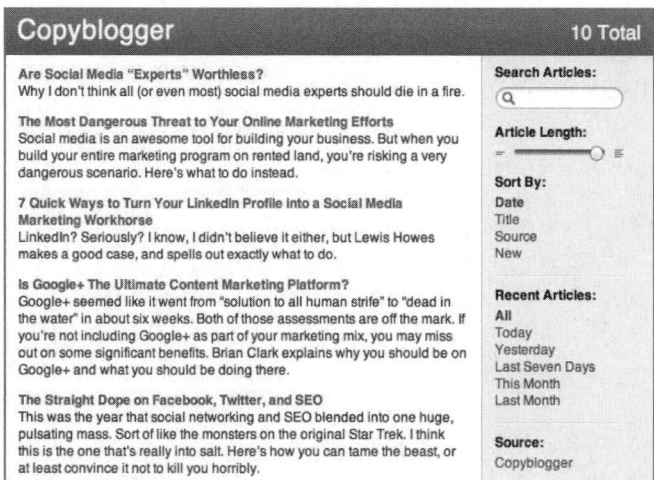

Figure 4-2: Skimming a feed reader.

- **Getting attention in social bookmarking sites**—The same principle is true in social bookmarking sites like digg (http://digg.com) and delicious (http://www.delicious.com), which have the potential to send your site many thousands of visitors based almost solely upon the title of your post.

- **Loyal readers**—Good titles also impact the way your loyal readers interact with your blog. As I've already mentioned, web users scan pages, and one of the best ways to make them pause as they roll their eyes down your site is to capture their attention with a good title that intrigues them enough to slow down their frantic web surfing and actually read some of the content that you've poured time and energy into.

- **Search engine optimization**—Though many factors contribute to how search engines rank a page of your blog, one of the most powerful onsite factors is the words that you use in the title of that page. By default, most blogging platforms include your title in the title tags of your post's page and the URL structure of that page; both of these factors contribute to that page's search-engine ranking. Add to this that other bloggers often use your title to link to you (a very powerful thing), and your titles become a very important factor in ranking well and generating traffic in search engines.

The title of a post is like an advertisement for it, and it can mean the difference between it being read or not read, so creating great titles is a skill we highly recommend you learn.

How to Use Titles Successfully

Successful bloggers use many strategies to draw attention to their posts with titles. There is no real right or wrong way, and as with many aspects of blogging, what is a good title is subjective.

Ultimately, the goal of your title is to get people to read the first line of your post. To do this, consider some of these techniques:

- **Keep it simple**—Most research that I've seen about titles argues that the most effective titles are short, simple, and easy to understand. Though breaking these rules can help grab attention (see the next item), they can also confuse, frustrate, and put a glazed look in the eyes of potential readers. Shorter titles are also good for search engines; keep it under 40 or so characters, and you'll ensure the whole title appears in search results in Google.

- **Grab attention**—Good titles set your posts apart from the clutter around them and draw readers into your post. Attention might be achieved using tactics of shock, big claims, controversy, or even confusion. Though these tactics do work at getting people in, it should also be said that they can do more damage than good if the rest of your post doesn't live up to the promises your title makes. By all means, try to grab attention—just don't trick your readers into thinking you'll provide them with something you can't give them.

- **Meet a need**—An effective title draws people into reading more because they feel you've got something to say that they *need* to hear. Indexes like del.icio.us illustrate just how effective this is. Quite often the articles that get to the top of the list are "how to..." or "tutorial"-type articles that show readers how to solve a problem or need that they might have.

- **Describe**—Some readers are drawn into a post by a cryptic title that doesn't tell them much about what they'll be reading, but the majority of readers need to know something about what they'll find if they read further. Titles should describe what readers will get in the main post. They don't need to give away everything in the post, but being descriptive definitely helps.

- **Use keywords**—As I mentioned earlier, titles are a powerful part of SEO. If you want to maximize their power, you need to include the search engine phrases and keywords that your audience is searching for. This, of course, is challenging when you are attempting to keep it simple and to also grab attention and intrigue, but it can be done. Words at the start of titles are thought to be more powerful than words at the end when it comes to SEO.

Take your time with writing post titles. Many bloggers pour a lot of effort into writing engaging and interesting posts, but then just slap any old title onto it without realizing that in doing so they might be ensuring that their post is never read.

Treat your title as a mini advertisement for your work. Take at least a few minutes before hitting Publish to not only make sure your post is in order, but also that your title is going to do everything it can to maximize the chances that people will engage with what you have to say.

A great place to learn more about crafting your titles is copyblogger (www .copyblogger.com, shown in Figure 4-3), which has a wealth of information on writing good copy for blogs.

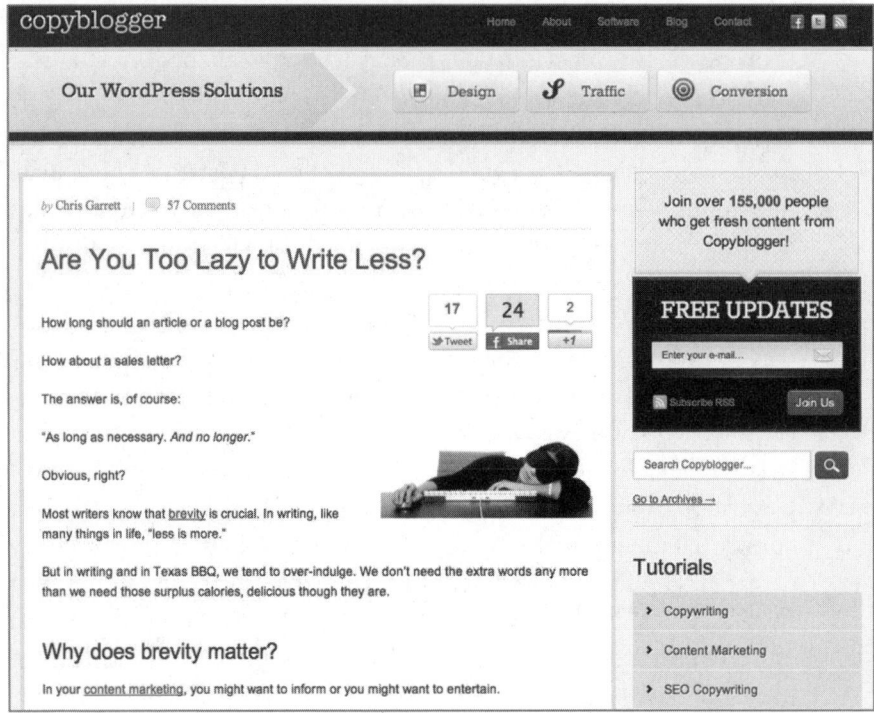

Figure 4-3: Go to copyblogger for examples of titles.

PROBLOGGER BLOG TIP: STEAL IDEAS!

Copywriters have a sneaky strategy for learning from the best writers. They steal ideas! No, this is not about plagiarism, but using what they call a *swipe file*. Whenever they come across a particularly effective headline, introduction, or turn of phrase, they take note of it for future inspiration.

Chris has posted a swipe file of 102 Headline Templates in the Problogger Special Book Buyer Bonus Download area:

```
http://probloggerbook.com/bonus
```

If you have not done so already, sign up here. Make sure you type the address exactly as shown:

```
http://probloggerbook.com/?/register/bonus
```

Opening Lines Matter

The purpose of a post title is to get readers to read the first line of your post. However, to get people to read your full post, your opening lines are also crucial.

Readers will make a judgment as to whether your full post is worth reading based upon how it starts, and they will continue reading *if* you succeed in connecting with them on one of a number of levels.

Opening lines should pique interest and curiosity, highlight a need that your reader has, show a benefit of reading on, and/or make some sort of promise to entertain, inform, teach, or offer something of value.

You don't need to do all of these things in the opening sentence of each post you write, but if you want your readers to reach the bottom of your posts and to be persuaded by what you write, you'll need to work hard early on at hooking them on some level.

Post Length—How Long Should a Blog Post Be?

The optimal length of a blog post has been hotly debated by bloggers for years, and you have a number of factors to consider when thinking about it, such as the following:

- **Reader attention span**—It is pretty well documented that the typical web reader has a short attention span when it comes to reading content online. My own investigation into length of stay on blogs found that average blog readers stay 96 seconds. That's a minute and a half to communicate to your readers. As a result, many webmasters purposely keep their content length down to a level that is readable in short grabs.
- **SEO**—There is a fairly strong opinion among those considered experts in search engine optimization that both extremely short and extremely long web pages are not ranked as highly as pages that are of a reasonable length. Of course, no one really knows how many words are ideal in the eyes of Google and its fellow search engines, but the general opinion seems to be that a page of at least 250 words is probably a reasonable length. Similarly, many advise keeping pages less than 1,000 words.
- **Topic/genre**—The type of post that you're writing will often determine its length. For example, when writing a review of a product, you'll

generally write a longer post than when you write a news-related post where you link to something someone else has written.

- **Comprehensive coverage of the topic**—Ultimately, this has to be the main criterion that bloggers go with. Write enough to comprehensively cover your topic and then stop. Long posts for the sake of them are not a wise move, but neither are short ones that don't cover the topic well.

My personal preference is to mix up my post length from post to post. I try to write one long post per day to give readers something meaty to chew on, but I also mix in short newsy posts most days.

Post Frequency—How Often Should a Blogger Post?

One of the common pieces of advice that I see given to new bloggers is that they should write frequent posts on their blog. This is good advice, but in my experience it's not quite as simple as that.

I think posting frequency is an issue that bloggers need to consider carefully on a number of fronts:

- **Writer burnout**—Every year, I do a 24-hour blogathon to raise money for a charity. Although I enjoy the process a lot, I find that it generally leaves me quite burned out—physically as well as in my ability to write. This is an extreme example, but it happens if your posting frequency is too high over a sustained period. The constant drive for high quality and relevant content is something that takes its toll on a blogger. Post too often and the quality of your writing could suffer.
- **Reader burnout**—Too many posts can also leave your readers burned out. I recently asked ProBlogger readers for the reasons that they unsubscribe to blogs, and "too many posts" was among the top reasons. I know from personal experience that if my news aggregator shows more than 20 unread posts on a blog, I'm less likely to read each post in full and will unsubscribe from it if I can't keep up.
- **Reader participation**—Post too often, and you'll not give your readers enough space to have good conversations in the comments of your posts. Each time you post, you push recent articles further down the front page of your blog, making them less likely to be seen and responded to by readers. Also, there are only so many conversations that your readers can

have at once. Post too many times per day and they'll feel overwhelmed and give up attempting to participate.

- **Search engine and RSS referrals**—One of the reasons to consider increasing your posting frequency is that the larger the quantities of quality content that you produce, the more open doors you have into your blog via both search engines and your RSS feed. Although you risk frustrating readers with high post levels, it generally leads to higher traffic.

- **Blog topic**—I'm a firm believer that there is no "one size fits all" approach to posting frequency on blogs. One of the main reasons for this is that different topics tend to lend themselves to different styles of blogging. For instance, a blog like Engadget (www.engadget.com) has a very wide topic (consumer electronics/gadgets). This topic covers a lot of subcategories, and to do it justice it needs to post a high number of posts (20 or more per day). Its readership knows this, and I suspect a lot of them want it, because they are attempting to keep up with a wider industry. Gadget lovers are also quite often information junkies who are usually tech-savvy and able to consume larger amounts of information. Other blogs with tighter topics would not be able to sustain such a large number of posts because there is only so much to write about on any given day.

- **Visitor type**—I've already touched on this a little (in saying gadget fans are often information junkies), but another way that your visitor type can impact posting frequency is the source of the visitor. For example, at ProBlogger I have a much higher readership that comes via RSS subscribers and bookmarks than on my digital-camera blog, which is largely visited by search-engine users and those coming from my e-mail newsletter. As a result, it is not as crucial that I keep my posting level down to a reasonable level on my photography blog, because it's not likely to impact many people. In fact, having more posts can be helpful because it means there are more landing points for SE traffic.

- **Post length**—Another observation that many people make about some of the most highly visited blogs is that while they post a lot more frequently than other blogs, their post length is shorter, making the high number of daily posts less annoying.

- **Momentum**—Posting too much can burn out your readers, but not posting enough can be just as frustrating. If readers subscribe to your RSS feed, or newsletter, or bookmark you, they are actively inviting you to communicate with them. When you don't, it can be quite annoying. On weekdays, I have a once-per-day blogging minimum for my own blogs. Other bloggers establish a weekly rhythm and find that it works for them, but I like to produce something daily, which builds an anticipation and momentum with readers that helps to grow the blog.

- **Rhythm and consistency**—When it comes to post frequency, it is important to find your blogging rhythm and stick to it. Though readers don't want you to be monotonous in terms of *what* you write, I've found they do quite often want it in terms of *how* you write—and more specifically, in *how often* you write. People want to know what to expect; they buy into things that they know fit in with their own rhythm of life, so if you start out writing daily but then increase the frequency to hourly, you'll probably find people reacting against it (and the same goes the other way around).

Posting frequency will vary from blog to blog, and you should experiment with different ways of doing it as your blog develops. If you are just starting out, attempt to post to your blog four or five times a week while you're finding your feet; over time you'll find a rhythm develops that suits you and your readers.

> **EXERCISE**
>
> Take a moment to think as a reader. How often do you like your most visited blogs to update? Do you visit each blog every day? Have you ever found a blog you liked that posted too often? Not often enough?

Keeping Posts Granular

One topic per post—we've already spoken in this book about choosing a niche topic for your blog, but another strategy of many successful blogs is that in addition to having an overarching niche topic, they tend to have each post focus on a more tightly targeted topic.

On some levels this is a fairly natural and logical thing that most bloggers do, but occasionally I come across a blog post that seems to want to answer every question known to humankind in a single post. The result can be a long, unfocused, rambling post that doesn't really go anywhere.

Instead of feeling you need to stuff everything into one post, a strategy that often works better is to be more granular in the way you post (that is, break it down into grains). This structure is quite similar to that of a book, which has an overall topic, chapters, and then sections. Each post will not cover the whole category (unless your categories are very small), but will cover an element of it. Tightly focusing your posts on different elements of your category will help you round out your whole niche topic.

In effect, you end up with a blog that can be shown visually like Figure 4-4.

Figure 4-4: Blog granularity.

These categories having the following hierarchy:

- **Niche topic**—Your overall blog has a niche topic or focus—something we talked about earlier.
- **Categories**—Within the niche, you have categories that break the overall topic into smaller parts. (For example, at ProBlogger, I have a category for blog design, writing content, and blog tools.)
- **Posts**—Your categories will then be broken down even further into posts.

This hierarchy is important for the following reasons:

- **Readability**—Some of your readers will not be interested in the whole niche that you are writing about, but instead will want to look at only part of it (one or two of your categories). Category pages become, in effect, like a mini blog within your whole blog, which can help readers find and follow the elements of the topic they are interested in.

- **Ease of use**—We've already talked in this book a number of times about how people don't stay long on websites and that blog readers have short attention spans. Granular posts help with this. They are shorter and punchy and go directly to the point.
- **SEO**—Pages with single topics make it easy for search engines to work out what your post is about. This helps them to rank you accurately for the topic you're writing about. Also, search engines like information that is clustered together and linked to other information like it. This is one of the reasons that niche blogs work well in search engines. Categories help this further, with category pages often ranking well in SEs. They also help the SE bots that come to scan your site to get around easily (important for getting your whole site indexed).
- **Contextual ad relevancy**—Similarly, having only one topic helps contextual ad systems like AdSense determine what you're writing about and serve relevant ads for that topic.
- **Ease of writing**—This is more of a personal reflection than anything, but I find it easier to concentrate on one topic at a time. I'm much more productive in this way.
- **Granular does not equal short**—One of the criticisms I've seen of the idea of granular posting is that some people like longer posts. I would argue that granular posts need not be short at all. Some of my most popular posts are tightly focused on a single topic, but are quite long.
- **Utilizing a series of posts**—One option for those bloggers who find it difficult to write in a granular style is to break their longer, general posts down into a series of posts. In fact, I quite often start out writing a post on a topic and find that it'd be much too long and diverse to be read all at once. We cover how to write a series of granular posts later in this chapter.

PROBLOGGER BLOG TIP: KEEP IT SIMPLE

Granularity is just one way that keeping your blog simple can benefit you and your reader. So many bloggers try to overcomplicate things when simple and easy can be just as effective, and it keeps your stress level down!

20 Types of Blog Posts

One of the traps that I see some bloggers fall into is that their blogs often become quite one-dimensional in terms of the types of posts they write.

Mixing up the types of posts that you write can add variety and character to your blog, which will help to keep readers over the long haul.

There are many types of posts that you might like to use; here are 20 to start experimenting with:

- **Instructional**—These tell people how to do something. I find that posts that contain tips or that are tutorials generally are the ones that are among my most popular. One of the main things that people search the web for is to find help in overcoming a problem. Position yourself to answer these problems, and you can build a nice source of traffic over the long term.
- **Informational**—This is one of the more common blog post types, where a blogger simply gives information on a topic. It could be a definition post or a longer explanation of some aspect of the niche that you're writing on. This is the crux of successful sites like Wikipedia.
- **Reviews**—Another highly searched-for term on the web is **review**. Every time I'm considering buying a new product, I head to Google and search for a review on it first. I know that I'm not alone. Reviews come in all shapes and sizes and on virtually every product or service you can think of. Give your fair and insightful opinion and ask readers for their opinion; reviews can be highly powerful posts that have a great longevity.
- **Lists**—One of the easiest ways to write a post is to make a list. Posts with content like, "The Top Ten ways to...," "7 Reasons why...," "5 Favorite...," or "53 mistakes that bloggers make when..." are not only easy to write, but are usually very popular with readers and can be successful at getting links from other bloggers.
- **Interviews**—Sometimes, when you've run out of insightful things to say, it might be a good idea to let someone else do the talking in an interview. This is a great way not only to give your readers a relevant expert's opinion, but to perhaps even learn something about the topic you're writing. One tip if you're approaching people for an interview on your blog is to not overwhelm them with questions. One or two good

questions are more likely to get you a response than a long list of poorly thought-out ones.

- **Case studies**—This is where you walk readers through an example of something that you're writing about. These are useful posts for readers because they are real-life situations and often have practical tips associated with them.
- **Profiles**—These are similar to case studies, but focus on a particular person. Pick an interesting personality in your niche and do a little research on that individual to present to your readers. Point out how this person reached his or her position and write about the characteristics he or she has that others in your niche might like to develop to be successful.
- **Link posts**—This is a favorite form of blogging for many bloggers, and is simply a matter of finding a quality post on another site or blog and linking up to it. You usually also include an explanation of why you're linking up, a comment of your own take on the topic, and/or a quote from the post. Adding your own comments makes these posts more original and useful to your readers. The more original content the better, but don't be afraid to bounce off others in this way. These link posts are powerful because they not only give your readers something good to read, but they can also get you noticed and help you build relationships with other bloggers.
- **Problem posts**—Another term that is often searched for in Google in conjunction with product names is the word *problem* or *problems*—that is, where people are searching for help on a problem that they might have with something that they own or are trying to do. Problem posts are similar to review posts, but focus more on the negatives of a product or service. Don't write these pieces just for the sake of them, but if you find a genuine problem with something, a problem post can work for you.
- **Comparison posts**—Life is full of situations that require you to make decisions between two or more options. Write a post contrasting two products, services, or approaches that outlines the positives and negatives of each choice. In a sense these are review posts, but are a little wider in focus. I find that these posts do very well on some of my product blogs where people actually search for "X Product comparison to Y Product" or "X versus Y" in search engines.
- **Rants**—Get passionate, stir yourself up, say what's on your mind, and tell it like it is. Rants are great for starting discussion and causing a little controversy; they can also be quite fun if you do them in the right spirit.

Just be aware when you write passionately about a controversial topic that others are likely to comment in a similar way. Rant posts lead to flaming in comment threads and to people saying things in the heat of the moment that they later regret, and that can impact their reputation. Proceed with caution.

- **Inspirational**—On the flip side of the angry rant (and not all rants have to be angry) are inspirational and motivational posts. Tell a story of success or paint a picture of "what could be." People like to hear good-news stories in their niche because it motivates them to persist with what they are doing. Find examples of success in your own experience or that of others and spread the word.

- **Research**—In the early days of ProBlogger, I wrote quite a few of these posts where I'd carry out surveys or gather statistics on different aspects of blogging. Research posts can take a lot of time, but they can also be well worth it if you come up with interesting conclusions. Present your findings with a nice chart and with useful statistics, and you'll often find other bloggers in your niche linking up to you.

- **Collation posts**—These are a strange combination of research and link posts. In them, you pick a topic that you think your readers will find helpful and then research what others have said about it. Once you've found their opinion, you bring together everyone's ideas (often with short quotes) and tie them together with a few of your own comments to draw out the common themes that you see. These posts are often quite interesting to readers, but can help you build relationships with others bloggers who you quote and link up to.

- **Prediction and review posts**—We see a lot of these at the end and start of the year when people do their "year in review" posts; they look at the year ahead and predict what developments might happen in their niche in the coming months. Prediction posts often cause interesting debate.

- **Critique posts**—Numerous bloggers have made a name for themselves by writing strong critiques of other people, products, or companies. Though sometimes these posts border on being "attack posts" and have rant-like qualities, a good constructive critique can be an effective way of making an impression on others. People like to hear opinions, and although they might not always agree with them, if they are insightful, constructive, and respectfully written posts, they can lead to you growing your reputation in a niche.

- **Debate**—I used to love a good debate in high school; there was something that I quite enjoyed about preparing a case either for or against something. Debates do well on blogs and can be done in an organized fashion between two people, between a blogger and "all comers," or even between a blogger and… themselves. (Try it; argue both for and against a topic in one post. You can end up with a pretty balanced post.) Probably the easiest way to do this is simply to ask your readers a question with two or more alternatives and see what they've got to say. Be willing to share your own opinion to get things going.

- **Hypothetical posts**—"What if" or hypothetical posts can be quite fun. Pick something that could happen down the track in your industry and begin to unpack what the implications of it would be. "What if Google and Yahoo! merged?" "What if Canon released an update to XYZ camera?" These posts can actually position you well in search engines if the hypothetical situation actually happens.

- **Satirical posts**—Well-written satire, parody, or humor can be incredibly powerful and is brilliant for generating links for your blog. Keep in mind that sometimes these types of posts will be misinterpreted and people can react strongly.

- **Memes and projects**—This is an idea that spreads—an *idea virus* as Seth Godin would describe it. In blogging, this is seen as an article or topic that gets copied from one blog to another, usually with a link back to the originator. Write a post that somehow involves your readers and gets them to replicate it in some way. Start a poll, an award, a competition, or ask your readers to submit a post/link or run a survey or quiz. These types of posts add an element of interactivity to your blog and sometimes can go viral through the blogosphere.

This is not an exhaustive list, but rather just some of the types of posts that you might like to throw into your blog's mix.

Not every one of these will be suitable for all blogs or bloggers, but using more than one format can definitely add a little spice and color to a blog.

EXERCISE

Next time you read a blog post, try to identify under which category from our list the article falls. How has the author added her own unique spin? Are there any tips you can take away?

10 Steps to Writing a Successful Series on Your Blog

One effective way of building momentum on a blog is to write a series of posts that build upon one another and explore a topic over a number of days.

Writing a series gives readers a reason to come back to your blog over a period of time, but it also enables you, as a blogger, to create multiple bite-sized posts on a larger topic, making the writing process easier and yet still comprehensively covering the topic.

Though writing a series can seem like an overwhelming task at first, it needn't be. Here's the workflow that I use to create one:

1. **Identify a topic.** This is, of course, key when it comes to developing a successful series (as it is with single posts). As I reflect upon most of the series of posts I've written at ProBlogger over the past year, it's interesting to see that in virtually every case the series has started in my mind as a single post that grew into something bigger. The key is to make sure you choose a topic that is large enough to warrant multiple posts (you don't want to write a series just for the sake of it), but manageable enough not to overwhelm you. Some topics are so large that they could almost be a blog in and of themselves.

2. **Write a list.** When I make the decision that a topic is big enough for a series, I start with a brainstorming session and compile a list of the main points that I want to make. These lists generally start out as bullet-point lists of keywords and phrases written up either in a text document or a notebook. Once I have a list of the main points, I then go back and add a few descriptive sentences to each one to describe what I want to say. It's amazing how many of these sentences make it into eventual posts. I find that once I'm on a roll, a lot of it just flows and I can end up with a list of 10 or so ideas pretty quickly. The list is rarely the final list of points that I end up publishing (some don't make it and others are added), but it does form the basis for my series, with each point usually ending up as a post of its own; remember, we're aiming for granular posts.

3. **Set targets.** At this point I set myself some goals for the series and establish boundaries for it. Looking at the list, I can generally tell how many posts I'll need to complete it, which in turn helps me decide how long it will run. I usually try to run them for a one-week period (starting on a Monday and ending on a Friday), but have been known to run them over longer and shorter timeframes.

4. **Set up draft posts.** With these details settled, I then take the list I've created and whatever I've written for each post so far (often just a few keywords and a sentence or two) and copy and paste them into some draft posts on my blog. I give each one a draft title (often changed later) and just leave them each there as drafts for me to work on in the coming days.

5. **Pick a series title.** The name that you give your series is a very important factor in its success, and I would recommend that it be something you give serious consideration to. The title of your series is an advertisement to readers and will draw them into it. Readers decide on first impression whether they will read a post, and they do the same with a series. If you don't capture their imagination with the first post of your series, they are unlikely to read those that follow. The way to pick the title for a series is pretty similar to the process of choosing one for individual posts, and is often a combination of something that is catchy and something with some good keywords in it (for SEO purposes).

6. **Announce the series.** Up to this point all my work is in private, but I put the pressure on myself now by announcing the series with an introductory post. This serves a number of purposes, including letting your readers know what to expect. (It creates some anticipation.) It also makes me accountable for finishing what I've started. There's nothing like telling your readers that you'll be writing X number of posts on a topic to keep you motivated and accountable for the task. Encourage readers to subscribe to your feed at this point in order to follow your post.

7. **Write an introduction to the series.** The announcement post should also include an introduction to the topic as well as where you'll head over the coming days. (You may want to name the actual topics you'll cover.) The other thing that this post does is to help highlight the "need" that the series will help to address. I'm a firm believer that the most successful series of posts that I've written have been popular because they meet some sort of need that people have, so help readers to see why tuning into your blog in the coming days is important.

8. **Write a post per day.** My workflow is to write posts in a series on a daily basis. Some bloggers prefer to write them all in advance, but I like to keep them fresh and to not only build upon what I've written the previous day, but what readers have written in the comments on those

posts. I also find that writing a lot of posts all at once can be a little too overwhelming; breaking it down into bite-sized pieces is much more manageable for me.

9. **Interlink your posts.** I see a lot of bloggers attempting to write blog posts as a series but not joining their posts with links. Though your current regular readers can follow your post by logging on each day or reading it in RSS, future readers of your blog might not have as much luck. They often come in via a search engine to a middle post in the series and if you haven't linked to the rest, they will have to go searching for it. You can interlink your posts easily enough by linking to them all on the introductory post to your series and by linking back to that introduction at the beginning and end of each post (telling readers that they'll find the full series there). Alternatively, you can link to the preceding and next post in the series in each post, making it like a chain from one to the next.

10. **Finish your series well.** Though it might sound obvious to finish your series, I think it's important to do this well. If you don't have a definite end, a series can fizzle toward the end and some readers will feel that they've been left hanging. Summarize the series and the main points and invite readers to add their own points, sharing what they think you might have missed.

Learning the art of creating a good series is something that can bring a lot of life to your blog. I try to do one at least once a month, and I find that readers generally respond to them very well. They work particularly well if they are teaching-oriented, practical, and connected with a real need that your readers have.

At ProBlogger, my most effective series have included the following:

- Blogging for Beginners
- 31 Days to Building a Better Blog
- Battling Bloggers Block
- 7 Days to Rediscovering Your Blogging Groove

In each case, the series was very practical and connected to a need felt by my target audience—bloggers.

EXERCISE

Brainstorm some potential series topics for your blog. Which subject areas can you write consistently about over a number of days? Now take the most promising ideas and sketch out the contents in bullet points. Before embarking on any series, it is a good idea to have a roadmap of the key points you will cover.

Building an Interactive Blog by Encouraging Comments

The beauty of blogging is that it is conversational in nature. As a blogger, you start the conversation and others respond in comments on your blog or in posts on their own. Work with this and write in a way that invites others to participate, and you'll grow a more dynamic blog. Here are a few quick tips on getting more comments for your blog:

- **Invite comments**—It sounds too easy to be true, but people are more likely to comment when you ask them to. Give a call to action to comment, and people will.
- **Ask questions**—Including specific questions in posts definitely helps get higher numbers of comments. This is particularly the case when the question is asked in the title of the post.
- **Be open-ended**—If you say everything there is to say on a topic, you're less likely to get others adding their opinions because you'll have covered what they might have added.
- **Interact with comments left**—If you're not willing to use your own comments section, why would your readers? If someone leaves a comment, interact with them. Doing so shows your readers that their comments are valued, it creates a culture of interactivity, and it gives the impression to other readers that your comments section is an active place that you as the blogger value.
- **Be humble**—I find that readers respond very well to posts that show your own weaknesses, failings, and the gaps in your own knowledge rather than those posts where you come across as knowing everything there is to know on a topic.

- **Be controversial**—There's nothing like controversy to get people commenting on your blog. Of course, with controversy comes risk and the potential for being attacked, so use with caution.
- **Reward comments**—Reward good comments by highlighting them on your blog. Drawing attention to your readers who use comments well affirms them, but also draws attention of other readers to good use of your comments section.
- **Establish boundaries**—Occasionally, the comments section on a blog can descend into something of a squabble. Establish boundaries up front on what is and isn't acceptable in comments. You even might like to post this as a comment policy. Ultimately, it is your blog, and the rules you set are up to you to decide. Having boundaries helps your readers to know what is and isn't acceptable and can help you in your comment moderating.
- **Shape your blog's culture**—I am increasingly aware that bloggers set the tone for their blog's "culture." It is important to note that readers usually take your lead when it comes to the tone they use in comments. If you write posts in an angry and personal attacking style, expect to see this reflected in your comments section. If you model a more inclusive and friendly style, the majority of your readers will follow your lead in this also.

Don't get too down if people don't comment on your blog with great frequency. Even the most popular blogs tend to attract only about a one percent commenting rate on them! Persist with the preceding techniques, and you'll build a blog that not only grows in traffic, but one that truly engages people and develops a culture of community.

EXERCISE

Make a note of blogs you frequent that manage to create a vibrant community feel and those that barely manage to generate any comments at all. Can you see anything in common between them? Which ways do the bloggers draw you in?

Summary

There is no doubt about it: Blogs are all about content. Without great content you will not attract an audience, and you will never achieve your blogging goals.

The topic you write about is only the start; you need great headlines, formatting, and an appropriate type of post for the subject to bring your readers into the community you are building and keep them engaged. Hopefully after reading this chapter, you have ideas about how to make this happen in your blog.

5 Blog Income and Earning Strategies

There is no single right way or wrong way to earn money from blogging. If you compare the approach Darren uses with the one I use, you will see quite a distinct difference. Cast your net wider, and you will be hard-pressed to find two bloggers who make money identically. This is a good thing!

The opportunity is there for any blogger to make some money, and to do it in a style that works for them. Each blog and each blogger is different. The opportunities vary depending on your own abilities, the opportunities presented by the niche, and even your own specific audience.

Though not every blogger will achieve the huge paydays that some bloggers achieve, many bloggers are doing quite nicely through the tactics I describe in this chapter.

Time to Make Money?

The first decision you have to make is obviously whether you even want to try making money. Many bloggers swear off any sort of commercialization of blogs, and others try and do not like it.

I'm going to assume you do want to make money off your blog. The two questions then become:

- When?

and

- How?

When to monetize is a question with no correct answer. Ask around and you will get many answers, none of which help very much.

There are two dominant camps of opinion on this question, both of which have their own merits:

- **Run ads from day one**—The idea here is if you're thinking of running ads eventually, you might as well integrate them from the start. The reasons you might want to do this include the following:
  - **Reader expectations**—Starting a blog with no ads and then adding them later means running the risk of disillusioning readers whose expectations are that the blog is and always will be "ad-free." Some readers feel very strongly about this, and changing the rules mid-stream can cause problems. Start with ads from the beginning, and you set the expectations from the start and don't cause any upset later.
  - **Consistent design**—Running ads from the beginning of your blog keeps everything consistent, which is good from a reader-comfort and branding point of view, and also means that you don't need the hassle or expense of a redesign later on to accommodate ads.
  - **Earnings**—Darren's blogs were ad-free for months until he implemented AdSense; he regretted his delay later, after seeing what he could have earned. Put ads on your blog from the start, and you'll begin to see some money right away. Of course, it might not amount to a lot, but you could be pleasantly surprised.
  - **Ad-optimization experience**—It takes time to learn how to tweak ads. Most of us learn best through personal experience rather than by just reading about it. The great thing about starting early with advertising is that you can experiment and try different techniques without too many people seeing the mistakes that you make along the way. This means that by the time the traffic does start to come in, you can have your ads optimized to take advantage of it.
- **Establish readerships and then run ads**—Rather than put ads in right from the start, there is an equally valid argument for keeping them off until you have built an audience. This argument is basically that if you

put ads on your blog too soon, you could potentially turn people off your blog because it will look too commercial or like too much of a money grab.

The thought is that you can gradually add advertisements later once you've established some trust, gathered a sizeable readership, and have built up lots of good-quality links that serve to enhance your search-engine visibility.

As mentioned earlier, Darren launched this way initially and his most recent blog, Digital Photography School (`www.digital-photography-school.com/`; see Figure 5-1), was only lightly monetized at launch, which I am sure helped him gather his huge audience.

I have personally used both approaches, as I will explain later.

Ultimately, the decision to add advertising to a blog is a personal one, and neither approach will work for everyone.

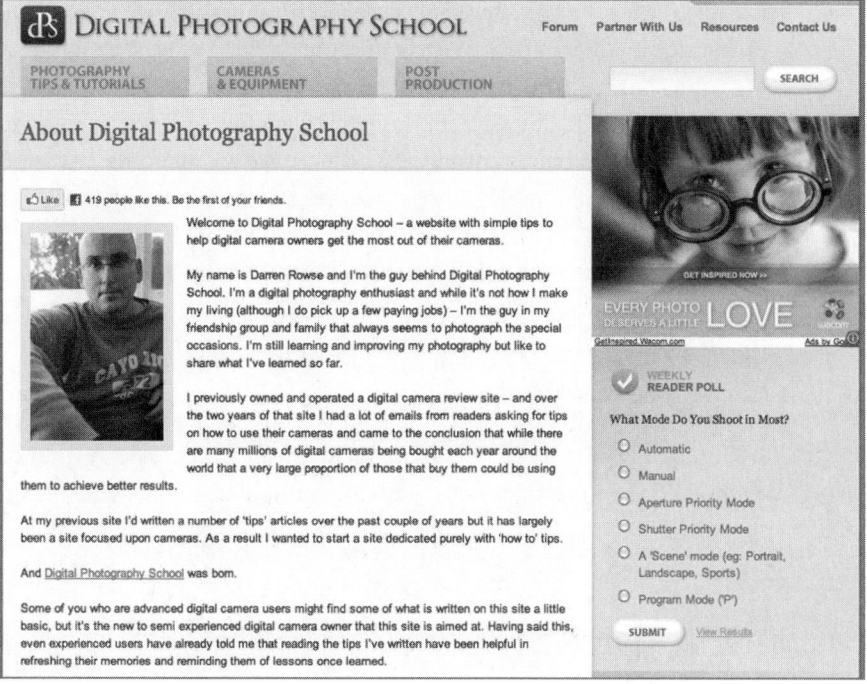

Figure 5-1: Darren launched his most recent blog with little monetization.

Factors to Consider

How do you know whether to hold off with the ads or put them in place right now? When deciding which approach to use, consider the following:

- **How commercial is your niche?** I used to own a photography blog all about a type of camera called a DSLR. People who follow the topic tend to be heavily into equipment and therefore ads are not just tolerated, they are practically encouraged, so right from the start I featured advertisements and affiliate links in reviews. Other niches may be very anti-commercialism and therefore you'll need a lighter touch.

- **Is it worth it?** You might find the only advertising you can show from the start is the poorly paying, untargeted AdSense. If you are getting only one or two clicks a day at some tiny amount per click, you might find there is not much point in adding advertising until you have an audience and the content to allow you to earn from it. In most cases, you can use your advertising spots to show affiliate ads or advertising for friends to make your blog more attractive to potential paying advertisers, but it is worth considering as part of your decision.

- **Will ads detract?** If your primary monetization strategy is to use indirect methods or sell your own product, you might want to concentrate on using your blog real estate for those channels. Also, you have to consider how tacky the advertisements tend to be in your niche. People are much more likely to overlook ugly advertising in an established blog than a new one. You don't want to damage any fledgling trust you are building with off-putting ads.

Again, choosing whether to show ads is a personal decision that's driven as much by financial pressures as personal taste. Luckily, there is no right or wrong answer, and the presence of ads is no longer held in as much suspicion as years ago.

Monetizing Directly with Advertising

Advertising is by far the most popular monetization method that bloggers use. After deciding to show ads, your next decision is which type.

The most popular advertising system with bloggers is Google's AdSense, but several other advertising system options are available, including:

- AdGenta
- Blogads
- Intela (CrispAds)
- DoubleClick
- Text Link Ads (note the warning later in this section)
- Vibrant Media (IntelliTXT)

In fact, many types and varieties of advertising exist, from banners to links to textual ads to pop-ups. It is easy to be overwhelmed and not know which to try first. The best idea is to focus your efforts on one or two types at a time and take the advice of other bloggers as to what is working for them.

Although there is a great variety of advertising types, in general they fall under the following headers:

- **Banner advertising**—These are the traditional graphical ads showing text and pictures. These can be bought and served up by an advertising system or can be bought as a private deal between the advertiser and blogger. Banners have been around for a long time in Internet years, so they are very familiar to web users. You can see some examples of banner ads in Figure 5-2.

Figure 5-2: Some example banners.

- **Textual advertising**—Textual ads do not have graphics, just text and a link. They are extremely popular with advertisers, especially when served up *contextually*; that is, when the ad is automatically matched to the content it sits next to. This makes them ultra-targeted; for example, someone searching for "red widgets" would see ads for "red widgets" in the page. Textual ad programs like AdSense are very popular with bloggers mostly because they are simple to use. Implementing this type of advertising just involves pasting some code into your templates. Everything else, from finding advertisers to showing ads, is done for you. Contextual ads best suit blogs that have some sort of commercial angle with many associated products and services being advertised. They are not so good with "general" multi-topic blogs or opinion-based subject areas. See Figure 5-3 for some sample text ads.

Figure 5-3: Examples of textual ads.

- **Product-based advertising**—A recent type of ad system has arrived that aims to promote specific products from retailers or auctions. The best known of these is Chitika's eMiniMalls. These systems, either contextually or based on the blogger's tweaking, target readers with product selections showing thumbnail images and pricing. For product-heavy niches these systems can work well, but as with all of these ad types, testing and tweaking is required. Figure 5-4 shows what these ads look like.

Figure 5-4: Chitika shows a product-based ad.

- **Text-link ads**—For a while, selling links was an increasingly popular way to sell ads. The beauty of these is that they don't take up much room, and depending on the system you choose to run them, you can have control over which advertisers you accept and reject. Advertisers loved the system because the links influenced and improved Google and other search-engine results. Many bloggers were using links as their main income generator. Unfortunately, Google made a big public fuss about its disapproval of text links and giving out penalties, driving the sales underground and scaring off many bloggers. Selling links is not something we recommend unless you are sure you know what you are doing.

- **RSS ads**—A popular way for people to read blogs is via RSS. As a result, publishers and ad providers have been keen to find ways to place ads in feeds. These attempts have been met with a variety of success levels. Though you do not hear of too many people making big dollars with RSS ads as yet, they are an area to keep in mind. Appearing in the feed makes them complementary to any onsite advertising, plus it allows you to make money off the people who never visit the blog itself.

- **Sponsorships**—Another form of advertising that a smaller number of bloggers are using is sponsorship. The nature of the sponsorship can vary from deal to deal, but in most cases it consists of showing banners for a certain amount of time, showing logos in the header or sidebar, or being mentioned in competitions or reviews as being a supplier of a product.

EXERCISE

Make a note of the blogs you know that run advertising, which type, and how many ads they display. Do you find yourself distracted or put off by these ads? From your list, which blogs do it well and which blogs go too far?

Ad Payment Types

Some ads can pay simply to be present for a certain amount of time regardless of any other metric. Then there are ads that are paid according to more strict criteria. Three popular performance-based payment types are currently in use:

- **CPC**—CPC stands for *cost per click*. Payment is on a *per-click* basis, so the blog publisher gets paid a certain amount for each click of an ad.

- CPM—CPM stands for *cost per thousand* views and means the blog publisher gets paid a certain amount for the number of times an ad is displayed. Each display is regarded as an *impression*.
- CPA—CPA stands for *cost per action* or *cost per acquisition*, meaning the blog publisher gets paid a commission if the ad makes a sale, signup, or generates a lead.

Finding Advertisers

The advantage of automated systems is that, in theory, they bring advertisers to you, but this is not always necessarily the case; plus some of the best deals are those you arrange yourself. For a start, there's no middleman taking a cut.

The key to getting advertisers is to make your blog attractive, and then approach likely prospects with a good pitch.

Preparing for Advertisers

Step one to getting advertising is to put your house in order.

Having an "Advertise Here" Button and an Advertising Page

This is fundamental. If advertisers are to know they can advertise on your blog, you need to show them, plus you need to have all the required information at hand. Provide an easy way for advertisers to contact you, and, if they are not already visible, display your rates. Make an attractive image that links to your "advertise here" page and put this image where it can be seen.

Clearly explain who you are, what your site is about, and why you are an authority on your topic. The key is to answer why anyone should care enough to purchase an ad. Answer "What's in it for me?" Figure 5-5 shows an example and is part of Darren's advertising page.

Showing Them What They'll Be Buying

If you currently have no paid placements on your site, put up *house ads*, which are banners for products or sites from your own company. Alternatively, you can place your partner ads in the same spot you would run a paid spot should it sell. *Partner ads* are advertisements for partners—where either no money changes hands or a sales commission is given the partner for an instance when someone clicks that ad then buys the product.

Advertise on ProBlogger

Become a Premium Sponsor ProBlogger and have it seen by hundreds of thousands of web entrepreneurs and influencers.

ProBlogger is viewed by hundreds of thousands of readers every month and is one of the few blogs around that is **almost exclusively read by bloggers**.

Your Message Here

As a result it represents a unique opportunity for those wanting to give their product or service the chance of being sneezed quickly throughout the blogosphere in a viral manner.

Figure 5-5: Part of a sample "advertise here" page.

Giving a Freebie

Create a free advertisement on your site to get attention from the target company or its competitors. Politely ask the company how well the ad works out (for example, total clicks, any purchases, and so on). You might find that once you start delivering traffic, the company is willing to pay for the spot to maintain the stream of new visitors.

Showing off Your Stats

You need to show at least the basic information, such as monthly unique visitors and page views, on your site. To many advertisers, traffic numbers are key. Keep working to update these stats as you build traffic. Be ready to share your numbers and back them up with graphs from multiple stat packages as evidence.

Any other information that might be useful to advertisers is also well worth displaying, such as gender and age demographic information. Demonstrate that you know your audience well and appeal to their market. If you do not have this information at hand, put together a survey or get more detailed statistics from comScore (http://www.comscore.com/) or Quantcast (http://www.quantcast.com/).

Darren often tells potential advertisers the keywords and phrases for which he ranks in Google. Compile a list of words that you rank for that you can pull out next time you're talking to an advertiser. If people search the web for information on products that they sell and they end up on your site, you have a valuable and unique selling point.

Keeping Your Blog on Topic and Professional

If you are not writing on topics that attract a specific audience, advertisers won't know if they are a good fit for your site. Talking about random topics, ranting about your drive to work, swearing, bashing every product you can think of, and other unpredictable behavior will scare away advertisers.

Putting Together an Advertiser Pack

Not all advertisers want to read your advertising page, plus it looks more professional to have comprehensive information available rather than a brief overview page. Compile your stats, rates, advertising options (that is, what you offer), reader demographics, and any other relevant figures into a professional-looking document that you can e-mail to interested advertisers. Include your contact details, references, and testimonials from other advertisers if you can get them.

Niches Sell

Most of us will never directly compete with the broad mainstream publications that are out there. Don't try to fool advertisers into thinking that you're bigger than you are; use your niche status as a positive and sell the fact that you can speak persuasively to a narrow and highly-targeted group of people. This makes the money an advertiser spends much more effective: "Spend $1 on a big site, and you might reach a lot of people who are mildly interested in your topic; sell $1 on our site, and you'll reach people who are *obsessed* with your topic…"

Finding Advertisers

Once you know your angle, the next step is to find and approach potential advertisers. You can do so by:

1. **Starting close to home**—Have a look at your own blog; are there people advertising on it already? If you have Google AdSense running on your blog, then Google is already serving up advertisers for you. Why not contact the advertisers directly and do a deal?

2. **Checking out who is advertising on blogs similar to yours**—Click a few and find the contact details. Send a polite and brief e-mail asking if they'd be interested in advertising on your blog as well. Include introductory information to get them interested, along with a link to your advertising page, and mention your advertiser pack without sending it to them right away.

   Companies that already advertise on blogs are going to be a lot more open to advertising on your blog than companies who have not yet tried this kind of advertising. By the same logic, those who are already advertising elsewhere online will be more likely to try advertising on blogs than those who do not yet do any web advertising. Look to see who is buying Google AdWords for your common niche searches.

Now that you know the products and companies in your niche, make a wish list of every company you would love to see advertising on your blog, and start contacting them. In the end, selling advertising is a numbers game, and the more frogs you kiss, the better chances you have of turning up a prince.

Approaching Advertisers

Whereas some advertisers will contact you after reading your "advertise here" page, others you'll need to directly approach, so it is a good idea to create a standard letter to contact advertisers. There is no one-size-fits-all solution here, but you can follow these general guidelines:

1. Introduce yourself and quickly explain why you are e-mailing them.
2. Explain why you chose to contact them, with an emphasis on what *they* have to gain.
3. Give brief details about your blog (traffic, subscribers, topic, audience).
4. Tell them about the advertising options (location on the site, max number of advertisers, monthly price).

Do not overdo it. Potential advertisers should be able to decide pretty quickly if they are interested or not. If they reply, then you can fill in all the fine details. Keep in mind that all the information I mentioned should be contained in two or three paragraphs, tops. If you send an essay to potential advertisers, they will just trash it as spam.

EXERCISE

Brainstorm potential advertisers who might be interested in your blog. As you go around reading blogs, also take notes on who is advertising and—from looking at other "advertise here" pages—what they might be paying. Are there any "likely suspects" who tend to advertise a lot? What are the going rates in your niche?

Taking Payments

You might have everything else in place, but if you cannot take payments or, more important, if advertisers cannot pay *easily*, you will end up losing deals.

PayPal (www.paypal.com) is generally the best option, because it allows you to accept cash transfers and credit card payments; however, PayPal is not currently available in all countries.

How Much to Charge

How much you should charge depends on what an advertiser would expect to pay and how much value you provide.

Advertisers, of course, will want to see a return for their investment. This might be in the form of a sales increase or increased exposure. Make sure, therefore, that you do everything in your power to ensure your blog demonstrably delivers.

Remember that some pretty cheap advertising options are available and you will need to be competitive. Provided you reserved a good spot for the sponsors (sidebar or header, preferably), you could start by charging $0.50 CPM (50 cents per 1,000 page views). With this pricing, a blog generating 100,000 monthly page views would earn around $50 a month for that one advert.

Start low to attract early sales and then build your prices steadily upward. Super-popular blogs can earn a higher CPM, sometimes as high as $10, but it takes time and a great deal of credibility to get there.

You can easily check whether you are charging a suitable rate by using AdSense on the places where you want to sell direct advertising. Analyze how much you would gain with AdSense, and adjust your rates accordingly. Alternatively, you can check similar sites' "advertise here" pages.

Be flexible regarding the terms, perhaps even offering free test periods. Make advertising agreements on a month-to-month basis. People don't like to commit to something they are not completely confident in. Encourage longer-term deals with a discount.

Ad Formats

Which ad format to show is mostly a question of what advertisers are willing to pay for! If you look around, though, most bloggers are using the small, square, 125-pixel banner size like Darren's, shown in Figure 5-2 earlier in this chapter.

Over the past year or so, the 125-by-125-pixel advertisement has emerged as the most common size for advertisements. Some of the more prominent blogs using these small square ads include TechCrunch, ReadWriteWeb, John Chow dot Com, as well as many others.

The 125-by-125-pixel ads are an attractive option for bloggers and advertisers for the following reasons:

- **Fit**—Blog designers like the way they fit nicely into sidebars in a square or vertical line.
- **Multiple ads**—This format gives the option to sell multiple ad units in a space often reserved for one larger ad (four 125-by-125 ads fit into the position of a *skyscraper*, which is a large rectangular ad). This provides options and also potentially more revenue.
- **Price**—Advertisers like the fact that this format is often cheaper than a larger ad, so they can have these smaller versions of their ad appear on multiple blogs for the same price as one larger ad on a single blog.
- **Frequency**—More and more often, affiliate programs are offering publishers 125-by-125-pixel ads to promote their products. We look at these programs in detail in the section "Affliate Programs." Bloggers can use these in their unsold ad spots, making good use of their space and making their ads look more popular.

Some ad formats work better in some industries than others; each niche and industry has its own preferences for ad unit sizes. Many larger advertisers have ad agencies on their payroll that might prefer more traditional ad sizes, with some clients not set up to sell anything else.

The best idea is to look around to see what ad types sell well in your niche before deciding which types you should offer.

How Many Ads to Display

Before filling your blog with ads, consider the effects of having too many ads:

- **They detract from your content**—Displaying too many ads is bad for readers because they can crowd out actual content and put off new visitors to your blog. Some blogs have so many ads that their content is pushed way down the page and effectively hidden.

- **They cheat the advertiser**—From an advertiser's point of view, too many ads on a page dilutes the conversion that advertisers get; if an ad is one of four, it has a much higher chance of being noticed and clicked on than if the ad is one of ten.

Look around your niche to see where blogs place ads and how many they have. Take particular note of any blogs that seem "overdone." In most cases you will see an ad in the header and maybe four or so small ads in a sidebar. Much more than that, and your blog risks looking more like a racing car than a content site.

Optimizing Advertising

To get the best performance out of your advertising, you need to have advertising where visitors can see it without causing annoyance and distracting from the content. This means balancing highly visible placements and ad formats with your regular readers' comfort.

In general, this means putting ads *above the fold*; that is, above the bottom of the browser window, where you wouldn't need to scroll to see it. Ads tend to get more clicks if they are embedded in content, but make sure they do not obstruct legibility.

With services like Google AdSense, you can test color variations, and it is well worth experimenting. Some bloggers do well with ads that are blended into the color scheme of their blog, and others say they get better results when ads stand out and contrast with the rest of their content. Although ideally you might get more clicks from camouflaging your ads as site navigation, this is a pretty crummy trick to play on your readers and might even get you into trouble with the ad service.

Monitor any changes you make to see if you improve or reduce performance, and get advice from other bloggers about what works for them.

Other Direct Forms of Income

In addition to advertising, you have a few other ways to make direct income. Let's take a look at some now.

Affiliate Programs

Affiliate programs involve taking a commission for referring a customer to a product. Probably the most common of these for bloggers is the Amazon Associates program that now has tens of thousands of products to which you can link. Darren uses this to great effect on his photography blog (see Figure 5-6). Other affiliate programs that represent many different companies and products include LinkShare, Commission Junction, and ClickBank.

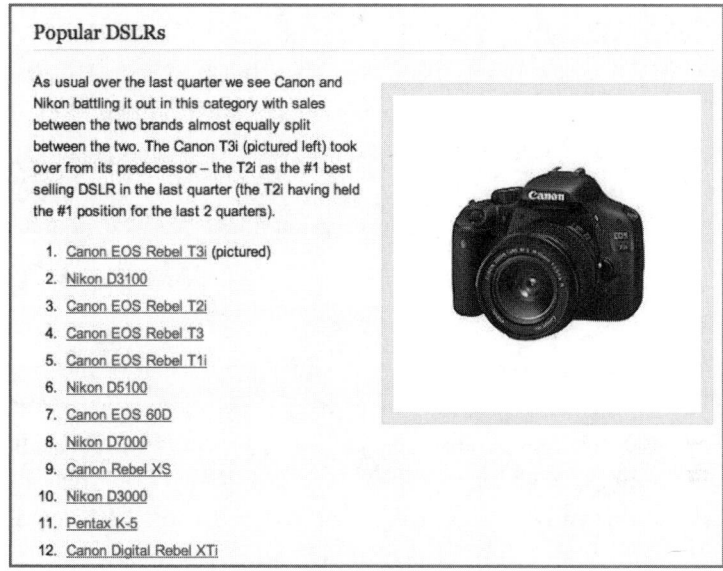

Popular DSLRs

As usual over the last quarter we see Canon and Nikon battling it out in this category with sales between the two brands almost equally split between the two. The Canon T3i (pictured left) took over from its predecessor – the T2i as the #1 best selling DSLR in the last quarter (the T2i having held the #1 position for the last 2 quarters).

1. Canon EOS Rebel T3i (pictured)
2. Nikon D3100
3. Canon EOS Rebel T2i
4. Canon EOS Rebel T3
5. Canon EOS Rebel T1i
6. Nikon D5100
7. Canon EOS 60D
8. Nikon D7000
9. Canon Rebel XS
10. Nikon D3000
11. Pentax K-5
12. Canon Digital Rebel XTi

Figure 5-6: Darren uses Amazon links on his photography blog.

EXERCISE

List good quality products that you have bought recently that match your niche. Sign up for Amazon Associates so you can provide links to them. Search the top blogs in your subject and related areas for reviews to get an idea of the products you could feature on your blog.

Tips for Using Affiliate Programs on Your Blog

Affiliate programs take some work if you want to get the most out of them, but they can be lucrative if you match the right program with the right blog/topic.

You must be careful when using affiliate links, because, in effect, you are recommending a product. If you suggest your readers purchase a lousy or disreputable product, you can expect to lose your good reputation very quickly. Also, the Federal Trade Commission (FTC) in the U.S. has strict rules governing affiliates. For a start you need to disclose your affiliate relationship and be careful about any claims you make about a product's performance.

Here are some tips for getting the most out of affiliate marketing on your blog.

Consider Your Audience

Put yourself in your readers' shoes and consider what they might be looking for as they surf by your blog. Are they shopping for specific products? Might they be looking for related products or accessories? What would trigger them to purchase? Start with your reader in mind rather than the product. If you take this approach you will end up doing your reader a favor as well as making a few dollars on the side.

Authenticity

You have literally hundreds of thousands of products and services you can recommend to your readers, but making money from them is not as simple as randomly adding links from your blog. Readers come back to your blog day after day because something about you resonates with them. Don't recommend products you don't fully believe will benefit them. If you have doubts, say so.

The best results I've had from affiliate programs are where I give an open and honest appraisal of the product, including both its strengths and weaknesses. You might think that this isn't a wise move and that to make maximum sales you should give every product a glowing review; however, sales consistently prove otherwise. People want to know what they are buying. Consider your own experience of shopping at Amazon or anywhere else that displays reviews.

Wherever possible, choose products and companies with a good reputation and quality sales pages.

Link Deep

We always say to bloggers we're consulting with that they should learn something from contextual advertising when it comes to affiliate programs. The secret of contextual ads like AdSense is that the advertisements match the content. The same is true for affiliate programs. A banner to a general page on every page on your site won't be anywhere near as effective as multiple links throughout your blog that advertise products that are relevant. So if you're writing an MP3 player review, link directly to a page selling that particular product.

Traffic Is Important

Although it's not the *only* factor, traffic levels are key when it comes to making money from affiliate marketing. The more people who see your affiliate links, the more likely you will be to make a sale. Consider how you might direct traffic on your blog toward pages where they are more likely to see your affiliate links.

Track Results

Most affiliate programs have some type of tracking. See what is selling and what isn't. Watching your results can help you plan future affiliate efforts. Keep track of what positions for links work well, which products sell, what wording around links works well, and so on, and use the information that you collect as you plan future affiliate strategies.

PROBLOGGER BLOG TIP: AFFILIATE LINKS

There has been a lot of debate over the years about affiliate links, but in general, if you link to a product you genuinely would recommend regardless of any commission, I don't think you will go too wrong. In reviews now, people expect to be pointed to a place where a product can be bought. Where your audience is particularly sensitive to affiliate links, you might want to draw attention in the post that although your links go through your affiliate link, you would recommend the product either way, and provide a general disclaimer in your footer or about page. Some affiliate programs have their own disclosure requirements, so it's best to check the small print of any affiliate program you join.

Donations

Rather than sell something via ads or affiliates, you can ask for small donations. A very small number of blogs have a history of making good money with donations—Jason Kottke and Leo Laporte come to mind. Jason Kottke (`http://kottke.org/`) went full time as a blogger in 2005 thanks to donations from his readers. Leo Laporte runs a successful podcast network (`http://twit.tv`) that generates income via advertising and also audience donations.

To be successful when asking for money from readers, you'll want to have a large and loyal readership that gets a lot of value from your work. Most bloggers just don't have the critical mass or the cult following to make it work very well, but you could make a few dollars.

I once experimented with a "Buy Me a Coffee" button. Although I never disclose my earnings out of principle, I did get a bunch of donations through the plug-in. It averaged out to a few donations every couple of days after the initial spike. Providing you write posts that people like to reward, I can see donations competing income-wise with AdSense.

Although I did not take the donations route for long, here are some of my positive findings regarding them:

- **Reward goes to good content.** People are willing to reward bloggers when they see value in your writing.
- **There seemed to be some pent-up demand for a concrete way my readers could thank me.** For this reason alone it might have been worth keeping it or finding some other outlet for gratitude.
- **The most rewarded posts were of the motivational kind.** There seems to be a correlation between donations and "feeling good" posts, which makes sense to me. On the other hand, the messages I received implied that donators were people who had been reading the blog for a while— so the blog as a whole matters as much as the single post from which readers clicked.
- **You can't get better encouragement than someone sending you money out of their own pocket!** If somebody gives you cash, you know you are on the right track somewhere.
- **It's useful to have a PayPal button around your blog.** A couple of people used it to send me unrelated payments.

Sounds good, right? So why did I not leave the button on the blog? Here are some not-so-positive findings:

- **The notice given the donation may have been due to novelty.** I noticed a big batch at the beginning, but that trailed off.

- Some people have judged it as "begging." I don't see it that way, but your readers might. The majority of people who sent me money were genuinely grateful for what they had read.

For me it was just a matter of taste. I would encourage anyone who is interested to try it, but for my own blog I don't think donations work because I make sufficient income from my products and services.

Classifieds

Some blogs do very well using classifieds, such as Darren's ProBlogger Job Board (http://jobs.problogger.net; see Figure 5-7). If you have a sizable audience that needs to advertise jobs, personals, sales, or want ads, then it might be worth a try.

Figure 5-7: The ProBlogger Job Board.

Merchandise

This will not work for every blog, but services are available, such as CafePress (www.cafepress.com), which allow you to create merchandise like T-shirts, mugs, and so on with your own logos and designs. With the right topic and/or audience, you might sell well, with the added benefit of each customer acting like a walking billboard for your blog.

Subscriptions

One of my favorite monetization strategies is charging a subscription fee rather than a one-off payment. You make a sale once but get paid over and over. It's the gym membership model.

Some bloggers do this with private forums, like Darren's `http://problogger .com` membership site, whereas others offer online training courses, like Chris's `www.AuthorityBlogger.com` course. It's well worth investigating.

The problem that some bloggers face is that some topics you think would work as membership sites already have free content available. To make your blog succeed, you must have some sort of premium/exclusive content and/or real expertise on your topic.

Indirect Income-Earning Strategies

Rather than work to make money from advertising and other direct means, another profitable blogging route is to make money indirectly. Indirect monetization tactics rely on you demonstrating your experience, expertise, and personality through your blog. This section looks at the popular indirect monetization options.

Freelance Blogging

Freelance blogging is a great way to earn money from blogs. Rather than working on your own blog, people are willing to pay to have someone blog on their behalf.

Though it isn't a passive income, it does earn reasonably well, predictably, and is itself a form of marketing, so doing a good job often leads to more work. When starting out, you might be at the lower end of the pay scale, but as you build a reputation you can earn more than 10 times your starting fee.

It's not just about the money; it is also a lot of fun—especially if you enjoy writing and variety. I started out very much in the technical and geeky topics, but now I find myself writing about all sorts of things, from clients as diverse as a micro stock photography company to a software developer. I am in a lucky position that these jobs now come to me; in the past that was not always the case.

So where to look for leads?

- **Using your own blog and your own audience**—Put up a page saying you are available for hire and refer to it in your sidebar and posts. Those people who read your writing regularly are the most likely to want to hire you, because they already know and like your work and there is some trust built up. By extension, any guest postings you do have the same potential. Though readers will not see you as often, putting a small reference to your freelance availability in your attribution line could garner some leads. See if you can get some guest-post spots on likely blogs.
- **Asking around**—Work outward from your blog to people who know you. Put the word out that you are looking for writing work. This isn't begging; you can really help someone else with your writing skills or just by saving them time. Friends of friends and word of mouth is where I get half my work, so this is a really effective method. When you are down, it is hard to sell yourself, so it really helps if someone is doing it for you.
- **Working the forums**—Your writing doesn't have to appear only on blogs to get noticed; blogging forums are also a good place to get your name out there. Good forum posts and a friendly, helpful nature could be all you need to get either paid work or guest spots that lead to paid work. As before, mention in your profile your availability.
- **Applying to online job ads**—There are lots of online job boards; you can start at the following locations:

      http://www.freelancewritinggigs.com
      http://jobs.problogger.net
      http://craigslist.org
      http://jobs.freelanceswitch.com

Once you get word out and really start looking, you will see there are writing opportunities all over for a hard-working blogger.

What Blog Owners Look For

Someone might hire a blogger for many reasons, but the most common are:

- To increase traffic, visibility, and search-engine rankings

- To build credibility and authority
- To supply constant content to keep visitors returning
- To increase sales leads and repeat customers

When site owners are looking for a blogger to write for them, they have the following criteria in mind:

- Can they write original and interesting articles for the topic?
- Does their style suit the property and audience?
- Are they able to write all required types of content?
- Will I get more value back than what I pay out?

The first three points all cover the craft of writing. If you can show ability in your writing samples, the job of getting the gig is half done. Usually, though, there are several other writers in the running, so the last point is where the choice is really made.

If you are looking to get paid blog-writing gigs, you have to have a good archive of posts that you can point to, plus evidence of value over and above just the writing. Here are some tips:

- **Create your own blog**—Demonstrate you can do the job that needs filling.
- **Vary your standard posts to show off your capabilities**—Have a collection of newsy posts, review posts, opinion posts, essays, and tutorials. If there is a certain blog you want to write for, try to match exactly the sort of content they like, their style, and tone of voice.
- **Show you have high-value skills**—Examples are basic SEO and promotional experience.
- **Get known in forums**—With intelligent blog comments, people are more likely to hire you if they know who you are.

The question to ask is, "Why me? Why would someone select me over some other blogger?" If you can answer that convincingly, you will have no trouble getting paid blogging gigs.

Why Freelance Blogging?

For the blogger, the benefits come down to increased exposure and pay. Payment can be per-post, word-count-based, or on a retainer. Obviously, all fees come down to negotiation, expectations, article length, complexity, and blogger experience. If you are just starting out, do not expect to get more than $20 a post, but for a proven blogger in a competitive niche, with lots of research required, you can earn 10 or 20 times that amount.

The arrangement can work very well for both the blogger and the client, provided everything is clear from the start, and the responsibility for making sure this happens is on the blogger.

Some example questions you might need to agree on beforehand are as follows:

- Who is in charge and what is their goal?
- How will the goals be measured?
- Will your performance affect the contract?
- Which topics should be covered?
- Are there verboten topics?
- What is the schedule?
- Will you e-mail copy or post it live yourself?
- How will you be paid and when?
- Will it be a fixed-term or rolling contract?
- Who owns the content?
- Are you being paid just to write or will there be other tasks?
- Do they have a stock photography account or will you have to supply images?

Normally, all this can be cleared up with a single conversation, but it's always best to get these things in writing.

Magazines and Books

Once you make a bit of a name for yourself online, you can use this experience and reputation to get jobs and contracts writing for print. It's about being seen as an expert in your field and having something original to say.

You will find that publishers are more receptive to having an idea pitched to them by someone who has already managed to gather an audience, and they might even seek you out.

This book you are reading right now came about because of one popular blog!

Many blogs already have large amounts of content ready to be pulled together into a book. It isn't only publishers who are looking out for writers;

sometimes already-signed authors get bogged down trying to complete their own book or need to fill a gap in their expertise. After Chris's technical articles became popular, he was approached on several occasions to join authors to collaborate on books that wouldn't have been completed otherwise.

Although books obviously provide more prestige, magazines and newspapers work on a faster schedule and can be just as lucrative, or on occasion more so. To land these gigs, e-mail editors for their submission guidelines. Again, like books, sometimes the work comes to you. Manolo from Manolo's Shoe Blog (http://shoeblogs.com) landed a writing gig in *The Washington Post Express* after he was discovered via his blog.

Speaking

Once again this is dependent upon the topic you're writing about, but some bloggers end up with all kinds of opportunities to speak at conferences, workshops, and seminars on their topic of choice. Sometimes they are freebies, other times the conference will cover costs, and on other occasions there are speakers' fees. If you are lucky, you might even have an opportunity to hear both Darren and me at various conferences!

Consulting

When you are perceived as an expert on a topic, you will find that people naturally come to you for advice and some of them are willing to pay for it. A good deal of my income is from consulting work, and I am fortunate that this work comes to me rather than me having to go out and seek it.

Some niches are probably better positioned than others for their bloggers to get into paid consultancy work, of course. The key is to demonstrate expertise and experience every day in your blog and to build trust. If you show that you are reliable and can help, you have won half the battle.

Potential customers will not know you have services to offer unless you tell them. I have a link in my navigation (see this in Figure 5-8) that leads to a services page showing example offerings along with pricing. A particularly nice bonus for me is that anyone buying, say, an hour of phone consultancy, will pay in advance through a PayPal button, meaning I get far fewer non-paying customers now.

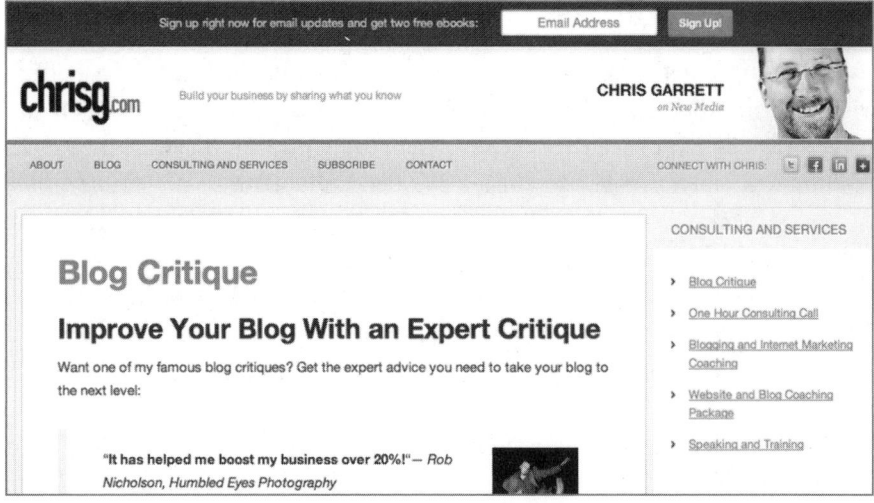

Figure 5-8: Chris's consulting and services link shown in the blog navigation.

PROBLOGGER BLOG TIP: SELL YOUR SERVICES

Could you make some money selling your own services? Many people over-look marketable skills and experience they have developed. It's not just writers, designers, and programmers who can benefit from providing work this way. Things you do every day might be just the solution someone is looking for. In fact, once you have your own blog up and running, you might find people want to know if you can help them do the same thing! Take some time to think of possible services you can offer.

Employment Opportunities

Even if you are not a freelancer, blogging can be an excellent addition to your resume. If you can demonstrate expertise and experience, you could get hired by your dream employer. PR blogger Steve Rubel was hired by a larger PR firm. We have to believe that Steve was offered the job because of the profile he'd built from blogging. Bloggers are increasingly being targeted by companies because of their demonstrated abilities in their field of expertise. Of course, bloggers have also lost their jobs because of what they had written!

Selling e-Resources

I wasn't sure whether to classify this as direct or indirect (and depending on how you do it you could probably go either way), but some bloggers are leveraging the expertise they have in an area by putting together their own "e-products" such as e-books, online courses, and videos.

Darren has sold e-books from both his ProBlogger and Digital Photography School blogs, and Chris sells e-books directly to his `www.chrisg.com/` audience, and also through third-party collaborations, such as Wordtracker.

Chris also runs courses, such as his Authority Blogger online course, and also teleseminar- and webinar-based courses where you can hear and interact with him live.

The key to selling digital products is to attract an audience with a clear want or need and to solve their challenges. You will find it much tougher to write your e-book or course and then try to find a market for it!

You can see examples of e-books in the Problogger Book Member Download Area:

```
http://probloggerbook.com/bonus/
```

If you have not already, sign up here (make sure you type the address exactly as shown):

```
http://probloggerbook.com/?/register/bonus
```

Networking and Business Partnerships

One of the benefits of blogging about a niche topic that interests you is that you will begin to connect with others who have similar interests and expertise. As you interact with them, it's amazing to see the opportunities that arise for working together.

Summary

Both Darren and I make money from blogging in our own ways. We are living examples that it is possible to not only make a good living, but also have fun doing it!

Whichever way you choose—direct, indirect, or a mixture—I hope this chapter offers an approach to making money by blogging that is right for you.

6 Buying and Selling Blogs

Over the past couple of years, we have seen some high-profile blogs changing hands for some tidy sums of money—upwards of five figures for well-known properties.

It started with domains and traditional websites, but now blogs are carving a market unique to website sales.

The most publicized sale probably was that of Blog Herald, www.blogherald.com, which has been bought and sold a couple of times. One of the blogs I helped found, Performancing (http://performancing.com), also attracted a lot of attention and speculation when it changed hands in early 2007.

Though the sums involved often surprise people outside of the blogging community, once you start thinking of blogs as a business asset it is easy to understand how they will start to become traded as such.

As more people hear about the money being made, of course they are piling in to see if they can get their share, too. This chapter is all about how you, too, can buy and sell blogs for profit.

Introduction to Buying and Selling Blogs

Buying and selling blogs is like any form of property trading. You have buyers, sellers, brokers, and even people who buy to sell (flip) online properties. Just like buying and selling physical property, there are risks, scams, and fraudsters, so do your research before getting involved.

Why Sell?

The first question we have to address is, why would someone sell a blog they have put so much effort into building up? For a number of reasons:

- **Profit**—As you might expect, this is the most common reason. People are willing to pay good money for a well-developed blog. In fact, you can get fair money for a not-so-well-developed blog as a fixer-upper! A growing number of people are using blog sales as their primary source of professional blogging income.

  A lot of the private sales I've been privy to have been in cases where an owner has been made an offer too good to turn down, but there are also many cases where the owner needed cash and needed it fast.

- **Too much work is involved**—What about cases where money was not the primary motivation? Well, a percentage of bloggers try it for a while until they decide one day it is all just too hard. Some give up, others try to recoup some compensation for the time and money they have sunk, and some don't want to see the blog go to waste. Take my photography blog, DSLRBlog (`http://dslrblog.com`), for example. I started the blog with the intention of learning photography, which I did, but I soon found it was becoming hard work to keep it running. My friends, who were initially helping me with it, lost interest. One day I was made a very healthy offer, which I joyfully accepted.

> **NOTE**
>
> It is sad to see someone take what you have built and change it in unrecognizable ways, but it is better than leaving something that you put so much work into to rot.

- **Changing life priorities**—When you set out to start a blog, you think it will go on forever, but as we all know, life has a habit of changing. What with families, careers, businesses, and so on, all it takes is one event to change your mind and priorities. It doesn't have to particularly be a catastrophe; it could be a job offer or a new baby. Not many people would choose to continue to blog over such commitments!
- **Bragging rights**—This is also a factor that comes into play. What would you prefer as a story: "I tried and failed," or, "I built it and sold it"?

Whatever your reason, selling your blog is probably the more financially prudent exit strategy compared to not renewing your hosting fees and letting the blog fade away.

Why Buy?

We can understand someone selling a blog; it seems perfectly reasonable. A transaction requires two parties, though. Why would someone buy a blog rather than start a new blog of their own?

Advantages of Buying a Blog

There are many advantages to buying a blog rather than building one. The main advantage is time. Starting a blog and building up traffic and an audience take a lot of time and effort; a purchase is probably the only practical shortcut available.

Buying gives you a head start, especially if you are entering a market with a lot of tough competition. Though there are instances of blogs gaining traction very quickly, nothing can compete with the immediate effect of taking ownership of a mature property.

Traffic, even with the best techniques, takes time and skill to grow and attract. You can buy traffic, through advertising and paying consultants, but an existing blog might have ideal traffic already and at a more affordable price.

When you are buying a mature blog, in addition to the obvious assets such as design, programming, and subscribers, what you are also buying is a proven concept. Research has been done for you, and you already have an indication of how successful the blog will be.

What you also might be buying is potential. Just like in housing deals, people buy blogs in order to refurbish them and sell them at a profit.

Having said all that, much like when looking at offline franchises, you might want to buy a blog that turns a predictable profit, where everything has already been worked out, and you just want to keep it running and reap the benefits.

Disadvantages of Buying a Blog

Although it has many benefits, buying an existing blog is not always entirely free of problems. The following is a list of some of them:

- **The cost**—Starting a blog is cheap but buying a blog can be expensive. If you only look at dollar value there would be no competition; you have to look at it as an investment. Like all investments, value can go up or down, and history is not always a reliable indicator of future performance.

- **You're the new guy**—Even with the best deal, you might be starting over with an existing audience. How this goes depends on your approach and how open-minded the readers are. Blog subscribers do not always take to new writers; after all, the new guy is not who they signed on to read. Loyalty here is both a boon and a bane; it is hard-won and easily lost. In many cases it is a good idea to keep the old writer(s) on long enough to transition, or longer if you can work out a deal all parties are happy with. It helps everyone, not just the audience, adjust and settle in.
- **The risk**—In most financial deals there is an element of risk. Will it all go wrong? What happens if you buy something broken or misrepresented? Could the seller run off with your money? These worries put a lot of people off trying but all you can do is try to mitigate any risks you identify.

Research is key. Look into the seller and the site. Just like a car, a blog has many interdependent moving parts. Knowing how they work is essential, or at least knowing an expert who will help you. On the surface everything could look nice and shiny, while under the hood there could be problems. Getting third and fourth opinions could pay dividends, but you never truly know what you have bought until it is yours.

Deciding to Build or Buy

Whether you choose to build or buy usually comes down to a combination of three things:

- **Resources**—How much time and money do you have at your disposal? If you have all the time in the world, you can save your money and do things yourself. On the other hand, if you are up against a deadline you will have to spend money to save time.
- **Expertise**—Do you have the experience and expertise on hand to make a successful blog? Can you take the risk of getting it wrong? The only proven blog is an experienced blog, and, for most people, the only way to get an experienced blog is to buy one.

* **Control**—This might seem a strange thought, but it does have a big impact on people in quite surprising ways. When you buy any site, you are inheriting a lot more than bits and bytes. Your only chance to make something entirely your own is to build it yourself. If you buy a blog, you buy its baggage too. Buyers—just like buyers of a pre-owned home—must be prepared to do some work to make the blog feel like theirs. They should also be prepared to be routinely compared against the old owner.

Buying to Sell (Flipping)

As already mentioned, a growing number of professional bloggers are looking to blog sales as a way to earn a profit. The income can be very good, plus many bloggers are more enthusiastic at launch than they are when in maintenance mode, so they can be continually working on new or refurbished blogs with full enjoyment and then offload them when they begin running out of steam.

The key to making money from buying blogs to sell is simple: *Have a market of likely buyers before you buy a blog to flip.*

At first this might not make sense, but think of the alternative. Do you want to put the time, money, and effort into a purchase only to find you have no buyers? That is a surefire way to lose on any deal. You need to know that if you can do a good job, you are certain to find a buyer.

Before getting into the buying-to-sell game, routinely review the buying and selling sites to see what types of blogs tend to do well and which find fewer bids. What characteristics stand out to bidders in your niche? How are the sales publicized and where? Your niche will have its own trends and habits, so get to know the winning formula for your favorite topics.

Who are the likely candidates for a blog purchase?

* Competitors
* Companies in your niche that are looking for traffic or growth
* Bloggers looking to expand their audience
* The losing bidders at a similar auction

Taxes on blogs you buy and sell are a potential minefield, so definitely get advice. In fact, even if you're sure there is no risk of getting into any financial trouble, you will probably find it useful to get an accountant's take because you might find he or she can help.

Always deal with the chief decision maker when buying or selling to make a profit, usually the CEO or owner. When buying and selling blogs as a business, you can't afford to have your time wasted by people who are just testing the waters or who have no authority to make a deal. Time is money.

> **PROBLOGGER BLOG TIP: BUILD A BUSINESS MINDSET**
>
> The skill of evaluating blog values is useful regardless of whether you want to actually get into buying and selling. Those bloggers who train their business brains tend to do better overall because they have the ability to see their efforts both in terms of building an asset and creating an audience and content.

Blog Sales Basics

The basic theories behind buying or selling a blog are a lot like buying or selling any property, but blogs probably have most in common with business sales or investing. There is value in the property itself as an asset as well as the potential for future revenue.

Both buyer and seller need to analyze the value they perceive in the blog. What inherent value does it hold right now? What value *could* it hold?

Value can be found in the money a blog generates, the content that has been created, the traffic it attracts, any resale value, and the potential it holds.

Investing in an Older Blog

In general, the older the blog, the more attractive it will be, not only because older sites are more favored in SEO circles, but also because an older blog has history. You would hope that a blog that has been around a while has hit a good formula and will have a lower risk going forward. With all the ups and downs in search engines and blog reputations, any blog that has stood the test of time and grown an audience is a premium over blogs that are new.

When looking at an older blog, the main things to check out are stability and trends. In general, you want to see steady audience, content, and traffic growth. Be wary of random spikes and dips; these point to risky or erratic behavior. Also be aware that, just like with cars, a blog that has had one careful owner is a better gamble than a blog that has changed hands a lot.

Investing in a Newer Blog

Young blogs under, say, six months old can be bargains, but their lack of track record makes them much more of a risk. They are easier to pump up to look like a good buy when in fact they have little substance or value. In a new blog you are better off looking at the value purely in the assets, such as design, domain, and technology. The rest is too easy to game.

Having a Game Plan

Go into any deal knowing your overall game plan. Will you buy to hold or buy to flip? Are you looking for monthly income, an income you can improve, or just to make money on the sale itself? Each goal will have differing tactics; for example, if you are looking to flip, you must be more aggressive in gaining a lower purchase price and be absolutely sure you can add value. As the saying goes, "You profit when you buy, not when you sell."

In any case, don't buy at the height of a blog's value; you *sell* at the peak. Work out how much more you could make by adding value both when buying and selling, but do not allow this to cloud your mind when it comes to gaining a discount.

When you are looking at exchanging large amounts of money, consider using escrow. Much as you want to keep things friendly, do you really want to risk a lot of money on someone you don't know?

Now, the question, when buying or selling, becomes how to work out how much the blog is worth.

Valuations

How you arrive at a valuation is very important. The other party or parties will value the same blog very differently—you can count on it! This is not just because they will take a different approach to valuing the property, but because valuations are subjective and largely depend on what you are in the deal to achieve. The same blog being bought for monthly income will attract a different price if it is being bought just for the domain, or as a refurb, and so on.

There is no standard way to value any site. Just like when valuing a business, the most common valuation method is based on a multiple of monthly income while taking other factors into account.

Even if you don't want to sell right away, you should still know the value of your blog. Bloggers often want to know value for ego purposes, too—it is a way to score yourself and compare against other blogs in your niche for sport!

Audience

Audiences and niches are important to a valuation. If your audience is super-targeted and high-value, full of rich people who spend a lot, your blog will garner a higher price than if you have a small, unidentifiable audience of freebie hunters.

Registered users, e-mail subscribers, well-frequented forums, and RSS counts have high value. In fact, e-mail lists can be sold off separately. Loyal, engaged users are extremely sought-after.

Even related niche audiences still vary in value. For example, the "making money" and "blogging" niches may overlap, but you can make more profit from people who want to make money than from the general "blogging" audience. Knowing which niches return higher revenue is important in deciding which blogs are a good buy.

Content

Every blog needs good content—that is a given. It is hardly worth buying an empty blog unless you particularly like the domain, template, or some special technology. If that is the case, you might be better off hiring a freelancer. When purchasing a blog, you need to look at the whole package; when selling, you need to make that package as attractive as possible. Here are some things you need to consider about content:

- **What went into its creation?** No matter how you look at it, great content is expensive in terms of talent, ideas, time, and money. Therefore, content should have value. Pinning down a dollar value, though, is very hard to do. My approach is to consider how much effort it would be to create and what result the content is currently achieving; for example, a simple "me-too" article versus something remarkable that gains hundreds of links and visitors.
- **What is the quality of the content?** Because many freelancers are willing to work for pennies, content is often seen by some as a commodity.

This is simply not true; great content is worth a premium because it is what your visitors will come to see.

- **Is it quality material?** If you have to choose between quantity and quality, always go for quality. It always makes me wonder why sites containing millions of "computer-generated" pages (that is, spam) still sell; $1,000,000 \times \$0 = \$0$!

- **What's the content source?** Where the content was acquired is as important as the quality. You need to know you have ownership of what you are buying. Do not even consider buying a blog if you even suspect it has plagiarized, automated, or free or private-label articles. A blog full of stolen or duplicate content is too much of a liability to be worth it.

- **Where will you find new content?** In the excitement of buying a blog, you can often overlook where new content will come from. Can you write well on the topic? Will the existing bloggers stay on? How much will you need to pay them? Can you find replacement bloggers? All these questions and more need to be answered.

Search Rankings

Companies will often buy blogs that rank in phrases that are important to them. This is often more cost-effective than other solutions.

This might seem counter-intuitive—how can purchasing a blog at several thousand dollars be more cost-effective than investing the same money into ranking their own site, which already exists? Well, for a start, you get instant and guaranteed results, but secondly, a red-hot SEO expert would probably charge thousands of dollars in consultancy fees on an ongoing basis.

If a company buys a blog that ranks on the same page as its own site, the company will then get two search results, thereby doubling the chances of a click.

Although a top ranking on Google is often listed as a selling point, you do have to consider whether that result is worth anything to you. In SEO circles there are search results, and then there are *valuable* search results. Valuable rankings are often called search rankings for *money terms*—that is, phrases worth money. A result that never gathers any clicks is not worth considering.

Never buy a blog because it "ranks for many phrases." This is meaningless unless those keywords are much sought-after. Bottom line—a search phrase is useful only if (A) people actually search using those keywords and (B) you can do something valuable with the traffic.

Traffic

A blog that attracts thousands of visitors month after month is extremely valuable. You want long-term, verifiable traffic, and diversified from a reliable source.

Ideally, you want a lot of traffic from many sources and spread over several places on your blog. A single source or a single hero article increases the risk that your traffic might dry up or be fake.

> **NOTE**
>
> Keep in mind that I did not say you want just *any* "traffic." Sellers will inflate their traffic figures. Sometimes traffic is misleading because of the way the stats are gathered or because they have been artificially pumping the traffic.

Here are some ways to get an accurate idea of what traffic is like on a blog:

- **Get the stats**—You need to see reliable stats, not just the blog's log analysis. If the only stats available are from logs, get a copy of the logs and analyze them yourself. When in serious negotiation, ask if you can put your Google Analytics code into the blog so you can watch traffic yourself.
- **Discount traffic spikes**—Traffic spikes (see Figure 6-1) should be separated out from your calculations. Very often you will see blogs listed with "20,000 unique visitors a month" only to find that 19,990 of those unique visitors came directly from one mention on a popular site. It's likely those people will never visit the site again and will not subscribe or take any other action. Social media and referral hits are worth having in the future (when done right), but past spikes should not be taken into account in your valuation. If visitors are blog nourishment, one-off traffic spikes are empty calories!
- **Look for targeted traffic**—In addition to sustained and diverse traffic, you want to look for blogs with targeted traffic. Non-targeted traffic has fewer monetization options; in fact, the main choice is impression-based ads, whereas there is a world of opportunity when the traffic is targeted.

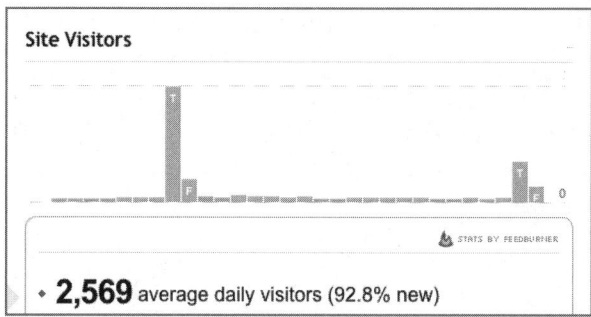

Figure 6-1: Traffic spikes can make blogs look more popular.

● **Look for paid traffic**—Paid traffic, though not as attractive as free, is not a bad thing provided the blog still turns a profit and you get all the required details, deals, and If you are on the selling side, keep these points in mind. High traffic levels are a selling point, but only if your buyer can believe you.

Inbound Links

Many blogs that are bought for SEO benefits are purchased simply for the inbound links they have attracted. A good spread of quality natural links, featuring no link-farmed, fake, or bought links, is a valuable prospect. Aim for both deep links and links pointed at the homepage, with varied and well-targeted anchor text. Essentially, find blogs that search engines would favor.

Brand

Branding can work both in your favor and against you. A respected and famous brand can be worth a lot of money, but readers might also be loyal to the old owner, or the brand might have peaked, with no room for improvement.

Is the blog a draw because of its archive of useful content or because of the blogger's personality?

If you are selling, cultivate the brand awareness carefully, and long before you put it up for sale, recruit fellow bloggers and depersonalize. That way the changeover will not be such an audience shock.

Profit

If the blog shows a profit, this will get the most attention. Profit is both directly and obviously valuable, but it is also a proxy metric for other signs of quality;

after all, a blog with zero visitors or content is not going to make a great profit!

Under no circumstances should you take revenue figures; you need to split the profit out to know that you are not taking on a liability. Only profit makes sense, unless you are happy to buy a blog laden with debt, advertising costs, and no way of making your costs back!

After determining the site's current level of profit, you need to determine the following:

- How hard is that profit to earn?
- Can *you* earn that?
- Where does the profit come from?
- How have profits changed over time?—Get a monthly breakdown.
- How easy would it be to grow that profit?
- What other potential products and revenue sources are available?

As with traffic, you want the income to be diversified, easy to work, and not reliant on any "special deals" that are lost with change of ownership. Given a choice between a blog that makes money with various advertising channels and only one or two hours' work a week and an e-commerce site with low-margin physical products shipped out of a warehouse, I would choose the former.

Design

Is the design off-the-shelf or custom? Does it look good? A free design or bad design is worth nothing, whereas a brilliant custom theme has resale value entirely separate from the blog. Many designers make reasonable cash selling good blog themes. Of course, if the theme is based on a premium theme framework, it is worth looking into the licensing small print as well as how easy or expensive the theme is to upgrade when new versions are released.

Domain Factors

We talk about domains elsewhere (especially in Chapter 3 and 7), but when valuing a domain you must be aware of how domain sales have gone over the years to know what to look for. Domains *can* sell for millions, but usually do not.

First, a `.com` is better than any other extension, without exception. After the extension, consider the name itself, its snappiness, brandability, and pronounceability. Is it short, snappy, easy to say, and easy to recall? Shorter names are also rarer. I believe all the three-letter `.com`s are taken and most of the four-letter ones too. I was lucky to get my four-letter company name!

Many SEOs like to have the keyword in the domain, and the world's most expensive domains tend toward dictionary words such as `poker.com`, `business.com`, and `sex.com`. This is because these domains have a potential for type-in traffic and instant recall rather than needing a great amount of promotion.

Calculating a Blog's Value

Blog sale prices are impossible to predict accurately. Ask ten different bloggers to value the same site, and you will get ten different answers. A blog's value depends entirely on the buyer. Valuations can be affected by all sorts of variables, from why and by whom it is being bought, to today's economic headlines, the parties' moods, and how drunk they are!

Blogs are worth what someone is willing to pay; that is all we can tell with certainty.

My approach is to look mainly at profit. A multiple of profits is a fair approach and easy to work out:

Annual Profits = 12 × Monthly Repeatable Profit

For your own purposes you also can work out additional asset values for things like the design, subscribers, and any interesting technologies you would be gaining ownership of. If these assets are worth more than the asking price you might buy just to get access to them, or if the blog doesn't work out you might still recoup some money through sales:

Assets = Design Value + Subscriber Value + Technology Value

Is the blog worth a premium because of its content or traffic? Some blogs are bought based on traffic alone, valuing each individual unique monthly visitor at so many cents to come to a total value:

Premium = Flagship Content Value + (12 × Monthly Free Traffic Value)

So for your own use you might use the equation:

Bid = Profit + Assets + Premium

As I say, it is all subjective and you should never make a high first offer; consider this calculation as your maximum!

> **PROBLOGGER BLOG TIP: LEARN THE MARKET**
>
> In real estate investing, the advice is to learn your market. The same is true with virtual real estate, too. With houses you would get to know an area, the type of property, and some of the people involved; with blog sales it is good to hang out at the popular blog sales sites and see what prices they go for, which sell, and which languish with zero bids. This helps you develop a "sixth sense" for blog valuations before you spend time looking at the numbers.

Buying a Blog

Shop around and watch some auctions (see Figure 6-2) from the sidelines before diving in. When you are buying a blog, always remember that the listing details are not a replacement for due diligence! Never take the owners at their word. There is nothing there to enforce the truth on the part of the seller, so be extremely cautious and suspicious of anything claimed.

Find out as much as you can. Why are they selling? Do a background check on the seller using Google, www.archive.org/, and domain tools such as http://whois.domaintools.com/, and see if they are selling in multiple locations.

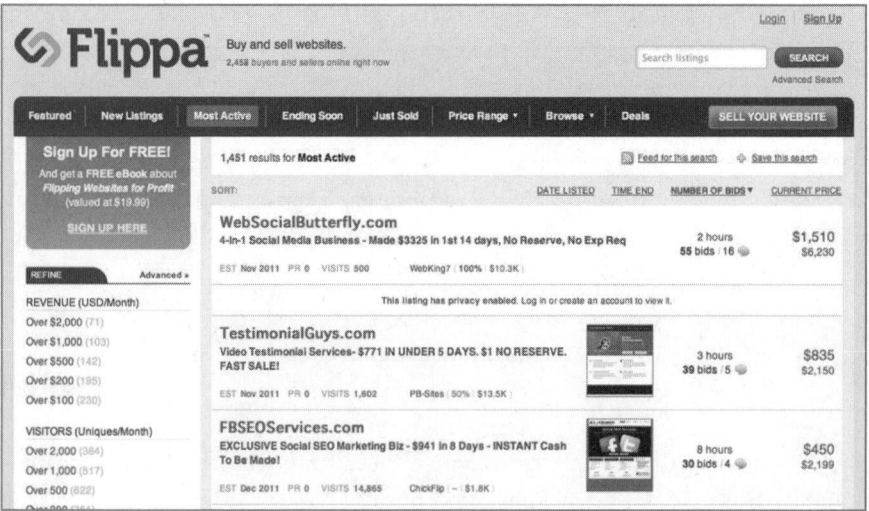

Figure 6-2: An example list of auctions.

Don't get caught up in the excitement of an auction. The "winner" doesn't win anything; an auction is still a purchase, not a competition. Some auctions happen very fast, whereas others take their time. The only way to guarantee a purchase is to pay the "Buy It Now" (BIN) price, which, of course, potentially means paying a higher price.

Don't be afraid to contact the seller with questions. Do not be embarrassed or shy—there is no such thing as a stupid question where your money is concerned.

In general, it is believed that the first to mention a figure usually loses, but of course sellers are not going to low-ball their own price. It is possible they are willing to take less if offered.

Raise your bids slowly and only in small increments. A common beginner's mistake is to unnecessarily raise bids too high too fast.

When the sale goes through, ensure that everything has your name on it, everything is backed up, and that you have all logins, passwords, URLs, licenses, and so on, including the following:

- Domain transfer
- Business name
- Hosting
- Database, software licenses, and code
- Subscriptions
- Feedburner
- Newsletter subscribers

Never join an auction unless you have a plan. What will you do with it if you win? Have your top price in mind and don't go over it. Always be prepared to back out if things don't feel right.

EXERCISE

Find some blog-for-sale listings and see which excite or interest you and which do not. Try to determine the aspects that draw or repel you. This is useful knowledge for when you take the plunge yourself.

Selling Blogs

When you are selling your blog you need to get the highest fair price you can achieve while not giving away too much insider information, which could be used to rip off your ideas. It is a delicate line to follow and is best formed by watching other successful blog sales.

In general, you want to be open, polite, and cooperative. Anything else will make buyers smell a rat. Any evasiveness will be taken as a danger signal and a risk that at best lowers your price and at worst ruins the sale entirely.

Maximize value ethically by giving the blog a makeover in every department, just like if you were putting your home up for sale.

Non-competes can be popular; a lot of buyers do not want to purchase your blog only to see you a week later try to poach back your audience. A non-compete is basically a legal agreement that blocks you from competing with the property that you just sold, usually specifying a time frame after which the market is fair game for you again. If a buyer demands a non-compete you might be able to use it in the negotiations, but just be sure of what you are signing on for.

> **NOTE**
>
> Be warned: Non-competes can be specific and short-term or so vague you might find your blogging days are over!

When the price is significant, consider getting legal advice. A short book or "some-guy-on-the-Internet" is no replacement for a good lawyer.

If you do not like the idea of sales or negotiations, ask around on the blog forums for recommendations of experienced brokers. In many cases this can work out well for all parties.

Where to Sell Your Blog

The following are the best venues for selling your blog:

- **Online Auctions**—The most popular way to sell small- to medium-size sites is through auction at sites like Digital Point (http://forums.digitalpoint.com) and SitePoint (www.sitepoint.com) (Figure 6-3).

These venues are popular and respected. Surprisingly eBay (www.ebay .com), although the world's best-known auction marketplace, is a bad place to get a good price for a blog as a seller and is rife with dodgy deals.

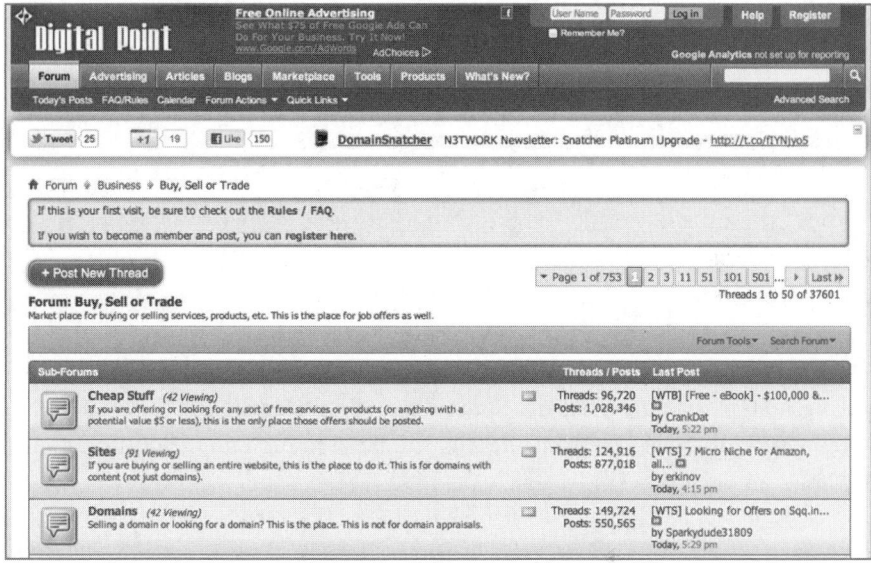

Figure 6-3: Digital Point marketplace.

- **Sales forums**—Performancing (http://performancing.com) has a free sales forum for smaller deals, as do many other popular blogs.
- **Direct, private deals**—These are where the big money is made. Word-of-mouth networks allow sales to be made without the time pressure of an auction, but, on the other hand, they can be protracted and complicated negotiations.
- **Contacting a potential buyer directly**—This is always an option, as is getting an offer to buy out of the blue. If you want to sell and are open to casual offers, consider telling your friends and readers that your blog is on the market.
- **Blog networks**—An option many people do not consider is to approach blog networks. Blog networks grow by acquisition mostly and might even want to hire you to maintain them.

EXERCISE

Imagine you have $50,000 to spend on buying a set of blogs. Go to the sites listed here and create a virtual portfolio. List the blog name and the price you would be willing to go up to. Revisit the sites when the auctions are over to see how well your estimates compare. Would you be happy with your purchases?

```
http://forums.digitalpoint.com/forumdisplay.php?f=52
http://business.listings.ebay.com
https://flippa.com
```

How to Sell Your Blog

Once you know you want to sell and have an idea how much you would accept, the next step is to do a listing. Some of the Blog Herald auction details are shown in Figure 6-4. The basic details you need to include in addition to any graphics are as follows:

Blog Herald - Industry Leading Blog - 2K/Month - PR7

URL: http://www.blogherald.com

Age of site (months): 36

Monthly revenue: 2000

Revenue details:
Typical monthly revenue streams:

Adzaar: $300
Adbrite: $100
Blogads: $250
Fastclick: $50
Google/ YPN; $400-600
Direct ads: average $100 per month
TextLinkAds: $200-300
Affiliate: 50-100$/month
Performancing: $325 gross (direct ad sale)
Other: $200-400

Monthly page views: 750000

Traffic details:
750K+ Pages/month
200K visitors/month
75K+ uniques/month

Description:
The Blog Herald is **the** industry leading blog news site. It has grown a reputation in the 3 years it has been serving the blog community as the place to go for blog-related news.

Typical readers include professional bloggers, journalists, analysts as well as regular bloggers who are just curious

---

Figure 6-4: Blog Herald auction details showing revenue and traffic.

- Blog name + URL
- Date started
- Description
- Hosting and software details
- Average monthly unique visitors, page views
- Inbound links according to Yahoo! and Google
- Monthly profits
- Posting frequency
- Auction end date
- Payment method
- Support offered

Determine a "Buy It Now" price to allow a buyer to end the auction with a purchase immediately. Something like 4× the annual profit multiple is not out of the question. You do not necessarily have to post a BIN right away. Starting bids are usually something like a 1× multiple.

EXERCISE

Create a listing for your blog as if you are about to sell it. Can you put to hand all the necessary information? If you were to sell your blog now would any of your bullet points raise a red flag in the mind of a potential purchaser?

Like many online community interactions, blog auctions attract the trolls and abusive idiots. Get ready to catch some heat as people use your listing for their own amusement and as an excuse to knock and insult from the safety of anonymity.

PROBLOGGER BLOG TIP: RAISE YOUR VALUE

Valuing a blog does not necessarily need to be done only when you are ready to sell. It is a worthwhile habit to get into every few months. Seeing the growth in your blog value can be incredibly motivating! Is your blog growing in value? How can you improve the value of your blog? What aspects are holding you back and what do you need to work on?

Blog Sales Case Studies

We have spoken to many bloggers who have bought and sold blogs since the first edition of this book. Many reached out to us because they were overjoyed at the figures their blog sales achieved; however, there have been some interesting developments in how those blog sales came about and the aftereffects of the transactions.

Here are a few examples to illustrate what it is really like to sell your blog.

Shane Ketterman

We have already mentioned Shane and his blog, TCGeeks, a few times in this book.

Shane (shown in Figure 6-5) started TCGeeks, (www.tcgeeks.com), a site aimed at people who are interested in tablet computing—things like iPads and Kindles. Shane had built up a considerable momentum by the time he sold his site and was earning a decent income, but was starting to lose interest in the subject and wanted to pursue other passions. This was compounded by the major shock of having Google change how it ranked its search results (due to the "Panda" search algorithm update), which lost the site a great deal of traffic and revenue and caused Shane a major amount of stress as he attempted to shift strategies and recover from the setback.

Figure 6-5: Shane Ketterman.

One day he received an unsolicited approach from someone describing himself as a website broker, a middleman who would take a percentage in return for setting up a deal.

Shane told me, "I was really nervous. I had just quit my day job and felt like I was looking over a ledge and had to decide to jump or not. I was also nervous about selling because there are all kinds of 'what-if's' like what if it didn't do well after the sale? What if the buyer backs out? What if they destroy the brand I built? And of course, I was nervous about working with a broker."

Shane's sale did go through, and he received a five figure sales price—twice the yearly revenue—a terrific result given that the site was still recovering from the loss of traffic and that it was only 12 months old.

The sale went (mostly) smoothly, but it could have come off the rails at one point, strangely, because the site suddenly received *too much* traffic! Shane explained, "A week before the sale was to be finalized, one of the articles I had written got lumped into some other articles mentioned on the Huffington Post (www.huffingtonpost.com/). So it crashed the server and my hosting company shut it down completely. I had to work for three days to get it back online and convince the buyer that it was just a fluke."

Most of the money from the sale went toward Shane's personal income, because he chose not to go back to his job but to keep pursuing his passions instead. He now blogs at http://shaneketterman.com and has several new projects planned.

Gayla Baer

Gayla Baer, unlike Shane, sold her site out of necessity rather than as a result of a random contact. One morning she awoke to find her entire basement flooded due to several days of non-stop heavy rains.

"I was in a place of complete despair and [had] no clue as to how I was going to pull out of it. I was literally watching everything I'd worked for floating in the flood waters around me. A friend had told me my answers were as far from me as my knees were from the floor—and that's exactly what I did. I prayed. Then I read my ProBlogger book.

"As I read about selling blogs, I realized I was sitting on some fairly nice, prime online real estate and I was going to take a shot at selling one of them. I followed the plan as described by Darren and Chris and composed the perfect pitch. Once I was comfortable with the wording and presentation, I e-mailed the proposal to seven people/companies who would likely have interest in my particular niche. With a quick prayer and a click of my mouse, the wish was released and the waiting began. Within 2 days, the first bid came in at $75,000 and by the end of the week, I agreed to accept a bid of $95,000."

As well as helping Gayla recover from a disaster, the blog sale meant the start of a new life for her and her family. "I embraced a new level of confidence and escaped an abusive marriage. I placed a sizable down payment on a beautiful home where my kids and I would move five months later. I did invest a small portion in projects I've worked on with my mother, who lives in Canada.

It's nice to have a mutual project that keeps us feeling close even when we're thousands of miles apart.

"Today I freelance and consult. I live in an area of Indiana that was hit hard by job loss from the auto industry shutdowns. I've been very blessed to work from home since shortly after becoming a single mom to toddlers. I enjoy helping local people discover their own entrepreneurial spirit and find ways to earn a living that keeps them home with their families more."

You can find out more about Gayla and her story at her site `www.gaylabaer` `.com/`.

Patrick Meninga

Patrick Meninga's site, The Spiritual River (`www.spiritualriver.com/`), was familiar to me because Patrick was a member of my community, so I had followed his journey from the sidelines for a while. What I did not know until Patrick e-mailed me, however, was exactly how much his site was worth!

The Spiritual River (Figure 6-6) was launched as a blog and community for people concerned about drug and alcohol addiction. This is a niche with a great deal of immediate need, and also a large market of high-priced products and services.

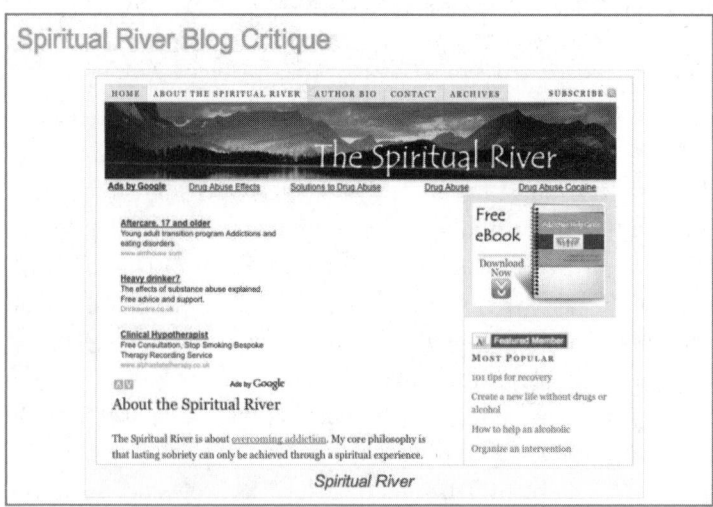

Figure 6-6: The Spiritual River.

In a blog critique, I advised Patrick to diversify from using AdSense as his dominant monetization method. Patrick started taking direct advertisement sales and one of his advertisers appreciated the traffic they were receiving so much that they approached him to buy the site, which was not even up for sale at the time.

At first Patrick was stunned and not sure if selling would be wise—after all, it was his major source of income. After agreeing with his parents and financial advisor that the amount offered ($200k) was a life-changing amount of money, he went ahead.

Based on this experience, Patrick has launched a new site, Make money with no work.com (www.makemoneywithnowork.com).

Deb Ng

Deb Ng is not only a friend but a popular and well-known person in the blogging world, not least because of her role as Conference Director for BlogWorld Expo and as a book author, but many people know her from her community for freelance writers, Freelance Writing Jobs, also known as FWJ (www.freelancewritinggigs.com), which she sold in 2010 (Figure 6-7).

Figure 6-7: Freelance Writing Jobs (FWJ) at the time it was sold.

Deb would post regular updates with writing jobs and opportunities, and a community grew up to support freelance writers from absolute beginners to successful professionals.

Selling was not an easy decision for Deb. "I worked hard at creating a helpful community for freelance writers and the freelance writing community responded in kind. I don't know that I ever meant for FWJ to become a full time job, but it did. Not only did it pay the bills, it enabled me to hire about ten freelancers so new writers could learn from the best, and [so] veteran writers [could] commiserated and shared with the rest. FWJ became my life and my brand. Thanks to FWJ, many clients found me and I made so many friends. This blog changed my life for the better and I don't know where I'd be now without it. It's my most valuable experience."

After making the decision to sell, Deb received around half a dozen offers and chose to sell to the company she felt had the best chance of making the site work. Rather than focus on the sales figure, she wanted to make sure her community and bloggers would be well treated in the transition.

As well as focusing on the BlogWorld conferences and her book writing, Deb has a new community at Kommein (`http://kommein.com`).

Unexpected Results

While some of the case study stories in the previous sections are inspiring, especially because of the sales figures these blogs managed to attract, you must also be aware of how it feels after the excitement has subsided:

- **Shane Ketterman**—"I think the biggest surprise, in all honesty, was the feeling of loss. I had been in this mode for so long of 'blog all day long' and 'get no sleep' so I started feeling a bit lost. I also had this odd feeling that something was being taken away that I had built myself."
- **Gayla Baer**—"The sense of loss has been an on [again] and off again struggle. With the downturn in the economy and being the lone provider for my twins, there have been numerous times I feel the sting of regret. It's at those times I push that sense of loss aside and focus on the realization that if I did it once, I could do it again, eventually."
- **Deb Ng**—"I always liken a blog sale to a real estate transaction. For example, when you're getting ready to sell your house, you might make it less about you. Perhaps you take down family photos, and you paint your rooms a more neutral color. You might also start removing the more personal aspects of your blog as well.

  "Just as many homeowners don't plan on the emotions they might encounter after viewing their home long after the new owners move in, former blog owners might also experience strong emotions after watching the new blog owners make decisions they might not necessarily agree with. There's no worse feeling than watching a blog you built from scratch tank in the search engines after it was number one. It's also hard to watch a new design go up, even if it's not a terrible design. It's closure, but it's also a reminder that something that was once so personal isn't yours anymore. If a blog loses traffic and community engagement, it's not pleasant for a former blog owner to see. I stay away from my former blog because I want to remember it as it was."

I (Chris) have sold a few websites over the years and the impact has ranged from none at all through to a significant feeling of loss. Selling your blog could be a great financial decision, and might well be the right decision for you, but don't overlook how emotional it can be.

Summary

We have covered a lot of ground in this chapter, and as you can see from the case studies, blog sales can be both exciting and nerve-rattling, but the basics are, in fact, simple sales. Just keep in mind that a blog is worth only what someone is willing to pay for it. Both the buyer and seller should keep that in mind; that way neither will feel cheated.

Income is the most reliable valuation method, but not every blog makes a profit, so other factors come into play and people are willing to buy blogs for more than just revenue alone.

Being successful at blog selling takes good sales and negotiation skills, but most of all, if buying or selling, be careful and look out for potential scams.

7 Blog Promotion and Marketing

Going from zero to a decent-size audience is one of the hardest parts of blogging. Although some people seem to hit their stride effortlessly and instantly, getting an audience is something most of us have to work on.

Content is critical; it is the foundation of a good blog, but you still need more than that. Some people will tell you *all* you need is good content; unfortunately, reality is a little more complex, and I wouldn't suggest trying the "build it and they will come" formula. As I like to say, content might be king, but without posh clothes and an army to back him up, what is a king but an arrogant bloke in a funny, shiny hat? Success in blogging means having great content backed by solid promotion—at least until your audience is big enough that your readers' word of mouth does the promotion for you.

A blog is not going to make you much money if nobody reads it. After writing content, promotion is probably the second most important activity of a blogger. This chapter takes you through how you can attract readers and, equally important, how to keep them.

Building Readership

As I said in the introduction, content is critical. After all, that is what people will come to your blog looking for. There is daily, run-of-the-mill content; there is foundation or pillar content; and then there is flagship content.

Building a Content Magnet

Anyone who has visited my chrisg blog (www.chrisg.com) and downloaded my free e-book is familiar with the term *flagship* content. Essentially, it goes above and beyond mere blog posts and works as a draw to your blog. It attracts people, because it provides a resource, a reference; something remarkable that is worth talking about.

When launching your blog, in addition to flagship "attraction" content, you need a good foundation of solid evergreen content. Darren calls this content pillar articles. A *pillar article* is usually a tutorial-style article that aims to teach your audience something useful. Generally, they are longer than 500 words and have lots of practical tips or advice. This evergreen type of article has long-term appeal, stays current (it isn't news- or time-dependent), and offers real value and insight. The more pillars you have on your blog, the better.

Do not rush this part; all the other traffic techniques depend on you having something useful to visit. If you think about it, what use is driving tons of visitors to something that is incomplete or not valuable?

While promoting, try to keep your blog fresh with useful posts. The important thing here is to demonstrate to first-time visitors that your blog is updated reasonably often, so they feel that if they come back they will likely find something new and worthwhile. If they think they have exhausted your blog's usefulness on the first visit, they will not bookmark or subscribe to it.

You don't have to produce one post per day all the time, but it is important that you do keep updating while your blog is brand new. Once you get traction, you still need to keep the fresh content coming, but your loyal audience will be more forgiving if you slow down to a few posts per week instead. The first few months are critical, so the more content you can produce at this time the better.

PROBLOGGER BLOG TIP: NOTICE POSTS YOU NOTICE

Half the battle of getting a blog off the ground is to have not just "good" content, but *compelling* content. So, next time you stop to read an article, ask yourself why. What was it about this particular article that caught your eye? How had the author presented it? Analyze the headline, where you found it, and most importantly, how you can integrate these lessons into your own blogging.

Blog Relations

Word of mouth is critical in promoting blogs. You need your blog to be memorable and spreadable. The first thing to sort out is your blog name. As discussed earlier in the book, use a proper domain name if you can, because the easier your URL is to remember, the more likely it will be recalled. Try to get a .com if you can because that is the most widely understood domain, and focus on small, easy-to-remember, catchy domains rather than fuss about having the correct keywords.

> **NOTE**
>
> For more and very detailed advice on the dos and don'ts of selecting a blog name as well as how to set up your blog, see Chapter 3.

Consider some of the blogs you know and love—ProBlogger, Copyblogger, BoingBoing (Figure 7-1), chrisg.com, and so on. These blogs have memorable names rather than being stuffed with search phrases like make-money-online-blogging.com.

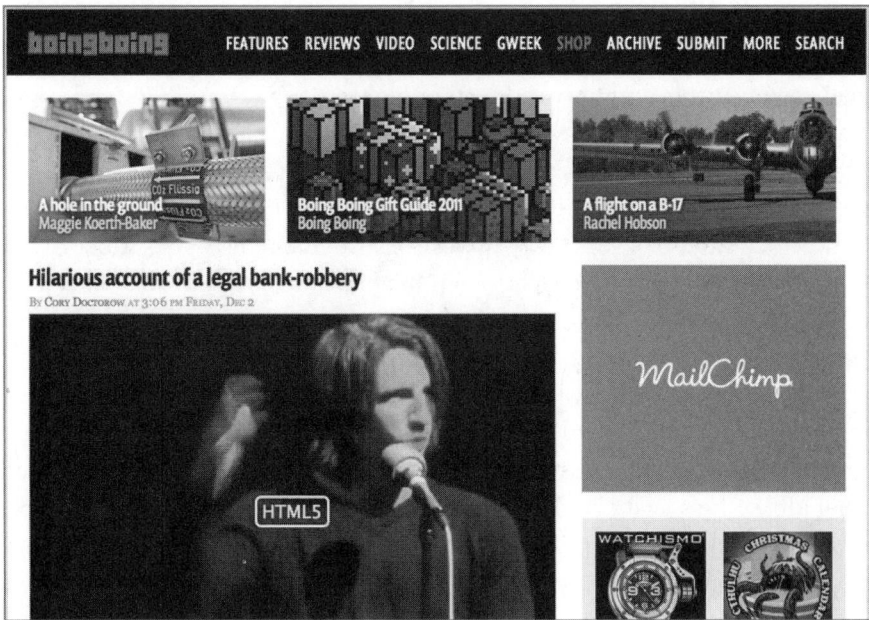

Figure 7-1: www.boingboing.net.

Comment and Link Generously

As soon as you have five to ten pillar articles, start commenting on other blogs. You should aim to comment on blogs focused on a niche topic similar to yours because the readers there will more likely be interested in your blog.

Most blog commenting systems allow you to have your name linked to your blog when you leave a comment. This is how people find your blog. If you are a prolific commenter and always have something valuable to say, people will be interested in reading more of your work and hence click through to visit your blog. Do not place links in the comments unless they are highly relevant to the discussion. If in doubt, leave it out. This is not the time to be labeled as a spammer. Once you are better known, people may give you the benefit of the doubt, but as a newcomer, people will be highly suspicious of your motives.

Link generously and in context to other blogs in your posts. On some blogs, if you link to them they will link back automatically using *Trackbacks*. What this does is leave a truncated summary of your blog post on their blog entry—it's sort of like your software telling someone else's blog that you wrote an article mentioning them. Trackbacks often appear like comments. Fewer bloggers support Trackbacks now due to the number of spammy Trackbacks being received.

Though linking out might not always earn you an automatic link back, it does often get the attention of the other bloggers. They will likely come and read your post, eager to see what you wrote about them. They may then become loyal readers of yours or at least monitor you. If you are lucky, some time down the road they may do a post linking to your blog, bringing in more new readers. Links from other bloggers are your very best source of new subscribers.

Encourage comments on your own blog as much as you can, especially in the early days when each comment is precious. One of the most powerful ways to convince someone to become a loyal reader is to show that there are other loyal readers already following your work. If they see people commenting intelligently and warmly on your blog, they infer that your content must be good because you have nice readers, so they should stick around and see what all the fuss is about. To encourage comments, simply pose a question in a blog post or ask friends to drop by and comment. But be sure to always respond to comments, to keep the conversation going.

EXERCISE

Do the blogs you frequent link often, or do they tend to hoard their audience? How often do you see familiar bloggers' names in blog comments? Make an effort to comment on a new blog every day and see if you notice any positive effects.

Network and Communicate

I have always said that "no blog is an island." As bloggers we *need* other people. It is other people who link to us, send us traffic, recommend us to friends, read our articles, and comment. Especially in the early days, you need to build a reputation as being friendly, useful, and approachable. Here are some pointers to help attract the people you want to follow your blog:

- **Network freely with your niche.** Networking is critical, so as well as being active in social media networking, join forums, e-mail lists, and newsgroups in your niche. Don't comment just for the sake of it; try to add value to conversations. When readers reach out to you with a comment, e-mail or link from their blog and follow up and interact with them. For starters, it's good manners, and it's also a good way to increase the chances that they'll return. Interact with those visitors who do try out your blog, and make it the best experience you can for them, and you'll find that they spread the word for you.

- **Encourage comments.** If you can make friends with fellow bloggers through commenting and participating in forums, you can occasionally ask for links. Do not be a pain; carefully consider the other bloggers' needs. Be smart, genuine, helpful, and polite. Rather than petitioning bloggers in a selfish way, put forward your link in a beneficial way that makes sense for them and their audience.

- **Join blog carnivals.** Sometimes blogs run projects or blog carnivals that can bring you some visibility. A *blog carnival* is a post in a blog that summarizes a collection of articles from many different blogs on a specific topic. The idea is to collect the best content on a topic in a given week. Often many other blogs link back to a carnival host, and as such, the people who have articles featured in the carnival often enjoy a spike in new readers.

- **Add a signature to your outgoing e-mail.** This is an oldie, but a goodie. Many bloggers do this. Simply add the domain name to your outgoing e-mail. If possible, add some kind of a benefit or "call to action" to encourage clicks; people need to know what's in it for them to check your blog out. Most e-mail programs allow you to do this automatically via a signature option. However, be careful with automatic signatures if you don't want your blog to be read by everyone that you e-mail.

- **Promote subscription options.** This encourages first-time visitors to come back; put it in the sight of your readers by placing your subscription options in the most prominent position you can. Your e-mail subscription or newsletter service will provide eye-catching sign-up forms for you to use in your blog, plus there are a variety of different buttons that you can make available to readers to help them to subscribe to your blog via their news aggregators. Many of the third-party plug-ins give you a feature to allow visitors to follow you in social media or sign up with one click, so they might also be worth investigating. At the very least, provide the option to subscribe via e-mail for those without RSS-reading accounts or software.

EXERCISE

If you are not a member of a blogging community, now is the time to get involved. Blogging forums are a source of a great deal of support and technical advice and are also excellent places to network.

Darren runs a professional blogger community at `http://problogger.com`.

Requesting Links from Bloggers

E-mailing bloggers for links can work if you do it delicately and respectfully. Get it wrong and, at best, your e-mail will be ignored.

Bloggers get hundreds of these types of e-mails; the more popular your blog is, the more of them you get. Sheer quantity and poor quality add up to such messages getting a poor reputation. Now I want make it clear that I respond to very few, and I rarely reply to them.

Never, ever have a link request e-mail as your first conversation with a blogger. Get to know them first. Do not be surprised, either, if a blogger that you think you know well ignores your link requests.

You have a much better chance of success if you follow this advice:

- **Be human**—Talk to bloggers as human beings; the more automated the e-mail feels, the more likely it is to be deleted.
- **Be truthful**—Don't lie and say you have loved a site for a long time that you only just discovered. If you do actually like it, tell them why. Even

better, tell them how you would improve it (without being insulting). I laugh every time people say they have been reading one of my brand-new blogs for years. Deceit, no matter how well intentioned, is a bad way to start a conversation.

- **Be specific**—The more vague you are, the more likely I am to not believe you. Do your research and stay away from generalities.
- **Be polite**—Demands do not wash. The other bloggers do not owe you anything. All the cost is theirs, and the majority of the gain is yours. You are sending a humble request; make it read that way.
- **Be interesting**—You have to sell your proposition. People are not going to link to you just because you ask. There is a high probability your e-mail will not be read past the first few lines, so make them count.
- **Be deserving**—Harsh but true. Would you write about something nobody will ever find interesting or useful just because someone begged you to? What about your article will the bloggers and their audience find interesting, useful, valuable, or entertaining?

The key point is to be interesting. What about this proposition ought the other blogger find interesting? "Because I asked" doesn't work. Picture what you are giving the other blogger to work with. You need to have an interesting story to write about and be able to spell out how that is the case.

Would you approach a potential date you just met by saying, "Let's go back for coffee"? You wouldn't pitch a story to a newspaper or magazine editor with, "Please write about me; I already wrote about you," would you?

Keep it real, be specific, keep it brief without being rude, and state the hook, idea, angle, or benefit. I guarantee you will get a much better reaction.

EXERCISE

Check out the downloads in the Problogger Book Member Download Area for more tips on generating traffic:

```
http://probloggerbook.com/bonus
```

If you have not already, sign up here (make sure you type the address exactly as shown):

```
http://probloggerbook.com/?/register/bonus.
```

E-mailing link requests and guest posting are not the only way to get links, fortunately; a popular technique is to write a link bait post, discussed in the next section.

Gaining Attention through "Link Baiting"

The term *link baiting* (also seen as one word, *linkbait*) is used by webmasters to describe a variety of practices, all of which seek to generate incoming links to a website or blog from other sites.

It is actually a difficult term to be definitive about because it covers a lot of different practices, ranging from running awards or competitions, writing snarky attack posts on high-profile bloggers in the hope of them biting back and linking to you, to providing other bloggers or site owners with useful tools.

In reality, the term link baiting is a new term for something old. On the web, links are currency; therefore, webmasters did all they could to get links from the earliest days of the web.

Is Link Baiting Ethical?

Link baiting is often written about in negative terms. I regularly see people writing off a post that others have written or a comment others have left as "just another link bait."

I personally don't like the term, on some levels, because of these negative connotations. *Baiting* gives a sense of trying to trick or trap unsuspecting people into doing something that they don't really want to do. Although this is accurate with some forms of link baiting, it is not true with others.

There is a lot of debate around both the term link baiting and some of the practices that people say it incorporates. Some argue strongly that it is just a by-product of quality content, others argue that many link-baiting strategies border on spam, and others seem to talk about link bait as being the answer to all web promotional problems (increasingly, SEO companies are offering link-baiting services).

So is link baiting good or bad? In my opinion it depends on the type of link baiting that you're talking about. I think some techniques that people use are good standard blogging techniques, whereas other things that people do in the pursuit of links are destructive to the blogging community, and I'd argue against them.

Like almost anything online, people use link-baiting strategies for good and useful purposes but also for dubious and unethical ones. I guess in part we each need to think about our priorities, values, and even intentions as we go about our blogging and explore this topic.

Successful Link-Bait Ideas

It is impossible to come up with a definitive list of what these practices are, because they are limited only by your imagination! In general, each tactic uses a *hook*—something in your piece that's unique or novel enough to stand out. Use the following list of ideas for inspiration:

- **Tools**—Create a useful, fun, newsworthy, or cool tool.
- **Quizzes**—Quizzes, surveys, and personality tests, such as "Which Star Wars character are you?" have long been popular with web users.
- **Competitions**—Organize a contest or drawing with a valuable prize.
- **Scoops**—Be first with the news or to try something new.
- **Awards**—Create an award for your niche.
- **Lists**—List the 10 best blogs in your niche, or the top products, and so on. Look to glossy magazines for inspiration; they are full of lists! Figure 7-2 shows how lists continue to work, despite some backlash.
- **Statistics**—Do a survey and release the results. One of my clients used to do a global survey relatively inexpensively that got them massive attention.
- **Freebies**—Give away something of value.
- **Interviews**—Interview a celebrity or someone popular in your niche.
- **Resources**—Create the ultimate resource or reference for a topic.

Why did I not list items that commonly appear in link-bait advice, such as "controversy" and "attack"? I have found that though you might garner some short-term attention using these methods, the long-term damage you would do to your reputation is simply not worth it.

The best link bait gathers links over time and grows with age. Next time you bookmark something, consider why you did so, and then use that knowledge to improve your next link bait.

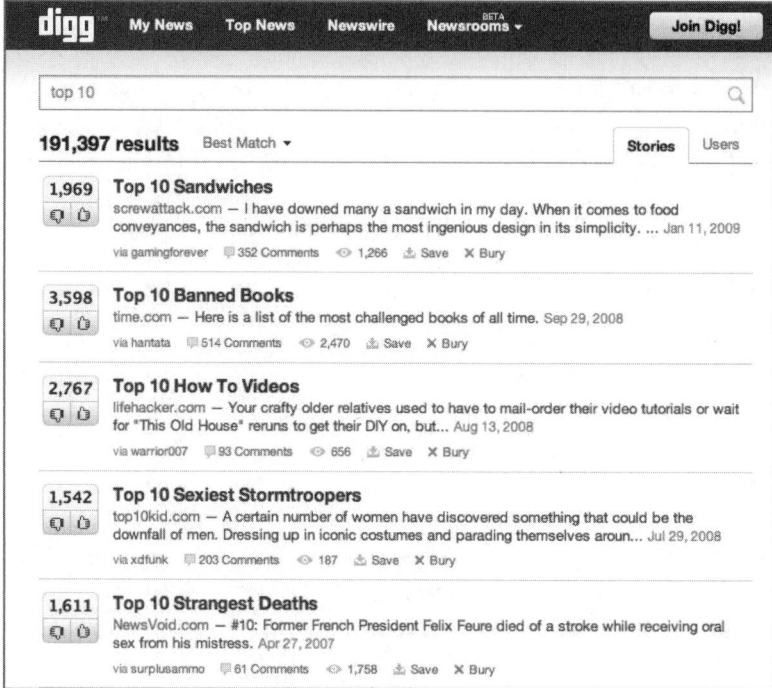

Figure 7-2: Lists vary in popularity but continue to do well.

Let's investigate one technique in depth: competitions.

Running Competitions

An increasing number of bloggers have been using competitions to create a buzz on their blogs. Figure 7-3 shows an example Digital Photography School competition.

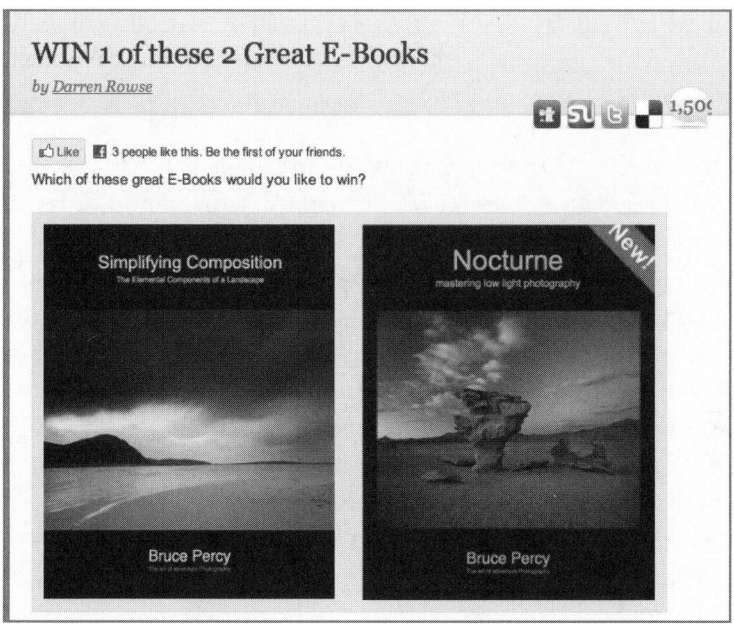

Figure 7-3: An example Digital Photography School competition.

Two benefits of running competitions on your blog are:

- **New readers**—Competitions are potentially good for drawing new readers to your blog if you have a way to get the message out.
- **Reader stickiness**—Knowing there is a competition result to come prevents people from leaving; otherwise they will not see if they won.

The risks with competitions are:

- **Distraction from usual content**—Your regular visitors do not come to see competition content, so they might become disenfranchised.
- **Few winners, many losers**—You cannot supply a prize for every participant, so many people will be disappointed.

My own experience with competitions is that if you design your competition well, you can get the benefits without the downsides hurting too much. Here are some tips:

- **Build an audience**—Although competitions can generate traffic, you need to have a critical mass of readers before launching in order to build participation.
- **Identify goals**—Before you design your competition you need to work out why you're having it. What is your aim? How will you measure the competition's success? Once you have your goals, you can then make better decisions about the competition format, prizes, promotion, and so on.
- **Offer prizes**—A number of thoughts come to mind when choosing prizes for a competition. Prizes should be:
  - **Relevant**—Match the prizes that you offer to your blog.
  - **Worthwhile**—The better your prizes are, the more buzz you will potentially create.
  - **Affordable**—Don't spend so much that you won't recoup the value.
- **Use sponsors**—One way to share the load with a competition is to have a sponsor for it. If you have a decent-size readership, you might be able to find a sponsor simply by asking.
- **Use affiliate links**—To help cover the cost of prizes, choose prizes that you can promote using affiliate programs.
- **Make requirements achievable for participants**—Don't make participants jump through too many hoops.
- **Make requirements achievable for you**—Competitions can be hard work, and people expect fair play. Don't make things more difficult than necessary.
- **Make just entering valuable**—An added incentive could be a free link to all participants, or could just be something from which they get enjoyment in addition to a chance at winning. For example, a caption competition can be fun to enter while reading other people's entries.
- **Set a reasonable competition length**—You don't want it to drag on for so long that your readers become sick of it, but on the other hand, you want it to be long enough for readers to enter, for the word to spread about it, and for sponsors to get their money's worth.

- **Promote your competition**—Unless you promote it, no one will know your competition is happening. Start your promotional efforts with your own readers via your blog, and also let your blogging friends know in advance. The best competitions have a mechanism for those participating to spread the word in some way; for example, if they refer a friend, they get additional entries in a draw.

Search Engine Optimization for Blogs

The web is full of great content that will never be seen outside of the author's screen. This is because the writer has failed to understand that just a few simple tweaks in the blogging process can increase search-engine visibility.

Many people try to paint search engine optimization as a nasty spammer tactic: "gaming" search-engine results for their own evil ends. This is simply not always the case. Like any powerful tool, you can use it for good or evil. Search engines are all about providing users with the most relevant results. Good SEO helps that; bad fills the engine with spam.

People often ask me how to get ranked number one for a particular search result. Unfortunately, the only people with definitive answers work for the search engines themselves, and they are not talking. Darren and I read a lot of the best search people's advice on the topic, but virtually every article is a "best guess" of some kind.

The best advice for people wanting to optimize their blogs for search engines is to start with quality content on a specific topic and then tweak it using the current best practice.

Though SEO can seem complicated and mysterious and can become something of an obsession for blog owners, you should know that, more often than not, blogs are not quite well set up for SEO right off the bat.

Search engine optimization techniques fall into two broad categories: off-site and on-site techniques, the discussion of this section.

Off-Site SEO

Off-site techniques are, as the name suggests, factors from outside the site that impact the blog's ranking in search engines. Many of these factors are outside the blogger's control; however, they are useful to know about. The most obvious and probably most powerful off-site factor is *inbound links*.

It is generally agreed that the links that point to a website are one of the most influential ways of climbing search-engine results. To put it most simply, every link to your site is seen by the search engines as a vote of confidence in your site.

The best inbound links:

- Are from highly ranked sites.
- Are relevant to your topic.
- Use relevant and searched-for keywords.

Of course, you do not always have control over who links to you, but when you do have an influence over how you are linked, these are the types of links that you should be aiming for.

How to Generate Quality Inbound Links

So how do you get such sought-after links? Now you know why we spent so much book space on discussing flagship content and link bait! Here are some more thoughts on how to attract quality links:

- **Offer valuable content**—The best way to get links to your blog is to write quality content that people want to read. You can solicit links with others, sign up for different link-building programs, or even buy text links on other sites, but the cheapest and probably safest approach is to build inbound links in a natural, organic way, as others link to your quality content.
- **Notify relevant bloggers of your content**—Though I don't advocate spamming other bloggers and asking for links, I do recommend that if you write a quality post on a topic that you know will interest another blogger, it might be worth shooting them a short and polite e-mail letting them know of your post (see the previous section, "Blog Relations").
- **Use directories**—An old way to generate inbound links was to submit your links to directories. I know of webmasters who still swear by the results of such a strategy, but I think the benefits are usually small at best.
- **Inter-link your blogs**—It is worth noting that you should be careful with this approach; if all your sites are hosted on one server, many think that search engines will work out what you're doing and the impact will be lessened.

- **Buy links**—Many professional webmasters have a budget to purchase links from other highly ranked and relevant sites. This is an expensive and high-risk strategy. In particular, Google has been a strong opponent of this approach and might slap you with penalties if you are caught selling links or are reported by a competitor.
- **Swap links**—An older technique is to exchange links in a "you link to me and I will link to you" way. Be careful with this; the technique has a poor reputation due to spammers mass-mailing link-begging messages and other bad practices.
- **Guest post**—The best way I have found to get quality links with good anchor text, while building relationships with fellow bloggers and their audiences, is by guest posting. Check out the section "Guest Posting for Links, Reputation, and Traffic" later in the chapter for how this works.

On-Site SEO Techniques

On-site techniques are things that you do on your own blog that help build a higher ranking. As with all SEO techniques, there are many tactics and a lot of speculation around each of them.

Identify a few keywords from your article that you want the search engines to find. What will visitors type into Google if they want information on the topic you're writing about? The answer to this question gives you a hint as to what keywords you need to repeat a number of times (or sprinkle) throughout your article.

You can feature keywords in the following ways with varying levels of influence on search results:

- In the URL
- In titles
- In links, both in and out
- Using bold text
- Using heading tags (H1, H2, and so on)
- In image alt tags
- Throughout the text of your post, especially early on, in the first few sentences

Of course, if you go over the top with keywords it will ruin your article. Don't sacrifice your readers' experience just for the sake of SEO. Yes, keywords can be important in improving search-engine rankings, but more important is to ensure that your content and design are user-friendly and helpful to readers. A site that is stuffed with keywords will appear spammy, so don't fall for the temptation.

Use internal linking to increase the visibility of other articles in your blog and use good keywords in the anchor text. Also make sure every page links back to your main page and any other important pages on your site. If you're writing on a topic you've previously written about, consider linking to what you've written before or use a "relevant posts" feature at the base of your article. You'll see that both Darren and I link key categories and articles from our sidebars and menus. One of the impacts of having them highlighted in this way is that because they are being linked from every page, they have become some of the most highly ranked articles.

In general, you want each article to be focused on one topic. The more tightly focused the theme of a page, the better, as far as search engines are concerned. Sometimes you might find yourself writing long posts that end up covering a number of different topics. They might relate loosely, but if search-engine ranking is what you're after it could be better to break up your post into smaller, more focused pieces.

Avoid duplicate content as much as possible. Google warns publishers in its guidelines about having the same content on more than one page. This goes for both multiple pages that you own and also pages outside your site. This is because a tactic of spammers is often to reproduce content on many pages or to steal content from other sites. There is some debate over what duplicate content does and doesn't include, but the best advice is to be very careful about how many places your content appears.

Bottom Line on SEO

SEO is important to bloggers but it is *not* the only game in town. Many bloggers have worried unnecessarily over their SEO at the expense of their human audiences, so we want to emphasize that your job is to serve people rather than robots!

Although the technical side of SEO is often emphasized, it is actually the human side that gets the best results. You want your content compelling enough to be shared and linked to by people so that the search engine software can detect the value in what you are offering.

The good news is that Google is completely in agreement. Its mission is to make its search engine deliver the best possible experience for its users, which means finding and serving up the best content for its readers. If you focus on giving your audience highly relevant, unique, and useful content, with one eye on the Google guidelines we outlined previously, then you'll give both your flesh-and-blood audience and Google what they need.

So, the bottom line is:

1. Make yourself aware of what your audience wants and needs, and in particular what they are looking for in search engines.
2. Create valuable content that has a positive impact on your audience so that it gets shared around and linked to.
3. Optimize your articles and your blog to encourage search engines to pick you up and rank you well.

PROBLOGGER BLOG TIP:
CHECK PROBLEMS WITH GOOGLE WEBMASTER TOOLS

Use the Google Webmaster Tools to check if there are any problems that are causing your site not to be indexed properly. You can also see the phrases for which you are currently ranked. The website is `www.google.com/webmasters` (shown in Figure 7-4).

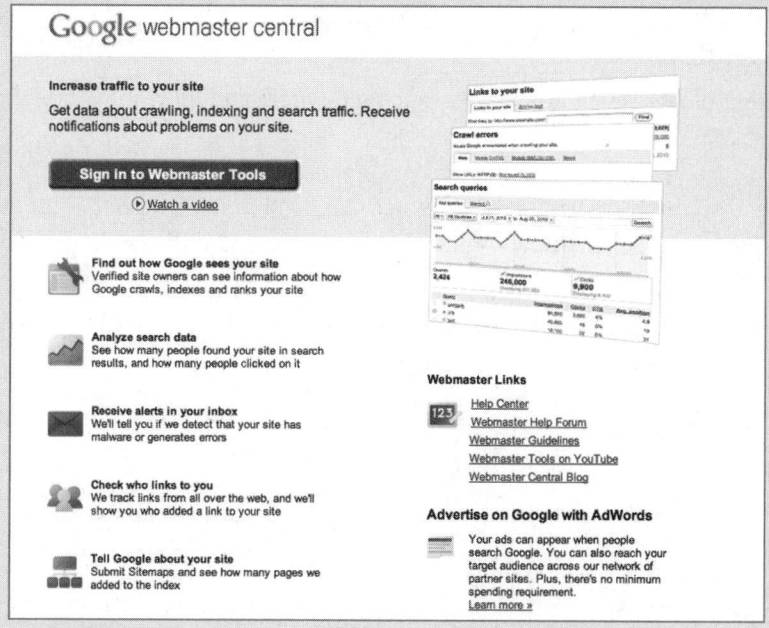

Figure 7-4: Google's Webmaster Tools.

Guest Posting for Links, Reputation, and Traffic

We have already covered how important it is to connect with other bloggers and to build quality SEO-boosting links. Now we should talk about a technique that can deliver both of these benefits and more.

This approach is one that I and many of the top bloggers use to get noticed and to build blogs. Of course we are talking here about guest posting, or if you prefer, guest blogging!

Guest posting is simply writing great content not for your own blog but for someone else's.

Why would you give away that wonderful article you spent so much time and energy creating? The reason is clear when you see the benefits you get back:

- The blog owner will be grateful for the unique and valuable content you are contributing to their site.
- The new blog audience will take notice of you.
- A portion of those new readers will follow your links back to check out your blog. Some of them may subscribe.
- Google will take notice of those links and improve your rankings in the search results.
- Other bloggers will notice you popping up more and more in your niche and remember you.

It's a real win-win-win. The blog owner gets to share additional content, their audience gets to consume that content, and you get additional visibility and a strong link.

So now that you know there are real benefits to guest posting, let's look at how you go about it.

Guest Posting in Practice

In most cases, it is not wise to write an article and then shop it around websites hoping that one of them will take it and use it. First of all, you run the risk of wasting your time because nobody wants it (although I guess you could then go ahead and use it on your own blog, if you think it is still a valuable article). More worrisome for your reputation is that more than one of them might accept it, making it content that's no longer exclusive, but rather duplicate material.

The best way forward is to write the most useful, exclusive, and relevant content for the most appropriate blogs. Of course, that is more work, but it does get the best results.

- **Research blogs**—Find the blogs in your niche (or related niches) that are influential with the kind of people you want to attract and accept guest posts.
- **Research topics**—Work up a list of what you might write for each. Pay particular attention to topics that their audience would find compelling and that would also form a bridge with the content on your own blog.
- **Submit your pitch**—Once you have done your research, you need to take action.

Your task starts with blog research. You want to avoid wasting your time here; only target the blogs with the best chance of a good result.

EXERCISE

Put some searches into Google for phrases that apply to your niche. Who comes out on top? Take a look at the pages listed in the results. Can you work out why they rank higher than the rest? Could you write a guest article for their audience?

Finding Good Guest-Posting Opportunities

You can search Google for blogs in your niche or you can look down the list of blogs you read, but the easiest opportunities for you are blogs:

- That are in your niche and clearly accept guest articles.
- That have an open guest article submission feature.
- On which you are already well known (or at least already read and commented on).

Look at it this way; if the blog doesn't show any evidence that it accepts guest posts, what are the chances you will be the first? I don't accept guest articles on chrisg.com and never have, but people still send me pitches at least once a week. On the other hand, you only have to look at ProBlogger to see that Darren does accept guest articles. Not only that, but he has a published guest article policy.

Don't overlook the third point, however. Your best chance of being published is on a blog where the owner and community are already well aware of you and your valuable contributions.

If your target blog meets the first two criteria but not the third, then work on getting better acquainted before making your pitch.

You might find the list grows to a large number, in which case you need to prioritize. Don't make the mistake of going only for the top-ranked blogs—those blogs get so many submissions that you might get lost in the pile. At the same time, at this stage you probably don't want to spend too much time on blogs with only three readers, two of which are the blog owners!

Once you have your short list of blogs, next you need to work out what you will write for them.

Researching Guest-Post Topics

Many guest-post pitches get rejected. It's a fact of life that your ideas will not always be automatically accepted for all number of reasons, not the least of which is because the blog owner is having a bad day!

There are, however, some ways to make sure you give yourself the best chances:

- **Research the blog audience and content**—Do a little homework on the blog that you'll be writing for. Your posts will be much better received both by the blogger you're helping out as well as the readers by answering some of the following questions before you start writing:

  - Who reads it?
  - What voice or style does the blogger write in?
  - What is the reach of the topic that is usually covered?
  - What posts get the most comments?
  - What level is the blog pitched at?
  - What are the unwritten rules of the blog?

- **Look for gaps in the blog**—Darren loves having guest writers that bring a different skill set and knowledge base to his blogs. In fact, he actively seeks out bloggers who add something unique and different to the topics he wants to cover while writing in a style that fits with his audience. As a guest blogger, you can really get on the radar of new readers by filling a need the target blog readers have and plugging a gap in the topic of the niche.

- **Seek inspiration**—My personal approach is to read the blog and note any time I am inspired. Where normally I would write a short comment, a lot of the time that comment idea could be expanded to a full article. This has the benefit of generating exclusive ideas that are guaranteed on-topic and that fit in well with existing topics. Bonus points if the articles that inspire you to follow up are also popular with the blog community.

Once you have some ideas, next you need to approach your target blogs with some headlines.

Approaching Blogs with Guest-Post Ideas

The easiest blogs to which you send your guest articles are the ones with guest-post submission policies or forms, so looking around a blog for those is the first task. Obviously, follow any published policies to the letter, and if there are no published policies or you have questions, follow up with the blog owner.

Some people advise submitting fully formed articles. I discourage that unless the blog you are writing for specifically asks that you do. My preferred approach is to give a couple of ideas of headlines for articles you might write, giving some indication of how those ideas would be valuable and relate to the topic of the blog and the audience's wants and needs. If the blog owner then asks you to go ahead, you know you are writing something that is more likely to be accepted, and you haven't wasted energy on a dud idea.

Maximizing Blog-Boosting Benefits

Obviously you are guest posting because you want to grow your own blog, but I would add a note of caution: In order to get the benefit, you really need to focus on providing value for the blog audience and blog owner. If they get value, you will get rewarded, but if your article just looks like a blatant grab for attention, you will neither get the benefits you are looking for, nor be asked back.

Don't view guest blogging as purely an opportunity for you to get new readers and promote yourself. Remember: The reason guest blogging is a good thing is that it's a win-win-win situation, where you as the guest blogger might raise your profile but where the blogger and their readers will come away from the interaction better off, too. Add genuine value to the blog you are writing on and you'll win yourself new fans with readers and the blogger, and could just find yourself with a regular guest-blogging spot. With that in mind, you might consider the following tips:

- **Request a byline.** As part of the agreement with the blog owner, negotiate a byline (or maybe a short paragraph) that enables you to sell yourself (within reason). Include a link back to your blog and subscription options as well as a brief biographical/descriptive sentence or two about who you are and what you do for your audience.
- **Link back with caution.** You can also sparingly link back to your own articles within your post if you have something already written that is useful and on-topic that could definitely add some value. Don't fill your posts with self-referential links—this looks cheap and nasty, and those links at best will get removed and at worst get your post rejected.
- **Share some of your story.** Although blog readers ultimately want great content on a blog, many also want to connect and relate to the person behind the content. This doesn't mean writing a biographical post, but it could mean sharing some of your experiences on the topic at hand.
- **Consider what is happening on your own blog during your guest-posting stint.** If you write for someone else's blog but let your own slip, you will lose your existing audience and you won't be providing much incentive to readers, who come over to check out more of your writing, to stick around. If anything, during the times that you guest post, make a concerted effort to improve your own blog because it's an opportunity to find new readers.

Being a good guest poster is like being a good guest in any situation. Do everything in your power to leave the place you are visiting in better shape than when you arrived, and you'll create a great impression.

Increasing Page Views on Your Blog

Keeping your readers engaged and coming back is just as important as finding new ones. Statistics have revealed that the average blog reader views around one and a half pages every time they visit a blog. The more pages a typical visitor reads, the better the job you are doing. What can you do to get readers to view more pages? Let's explore a few possibilities:

- **Highlight related posts**—One of the more common practices to encourage readers to read multiple pages on your blog is to highlight related posts at the end of your article.
- **Interlink within posts**—A similar but perhaps more effective technique is to highlight relevant posts within the content of your posts. If you're writing a post that mentions something similar to what you've written before, simply link to your previous post from within your article. For example, I've written about this technique previously in a post on increasing the longevity of key posts.
- **Highlight key posts and categories in your sidebar**—Highlighting your category pages is another useful technique to encourage your readers to find more posts on the same topic. To explicitly name what your category is can also be useful. That is, rather than just having the category name at the end of the post, try something like "read more posts like this in our XYZ category."
- **Create compilation pages**—Darren has a page at ProBlogger that lists his top 20 posts, and we have a "best of" list at Performancing (www .performancing.com) also. Many first-time readers use these pages to discover content to read. Every post a visitor reads increases the chances that they will become loyal readers.
- **Write a series**—You need to be careful when you write a series of posts over a period of time, but it's a great way to keep readers coming back, and—once the series is complete—to have readers surf through multiple pages on your blog. Don't create series just for the sake of increasing page views, of course—this can really frustrate readers—but use them on longer posts or when you genuinely want to cover a larger topic over time.
- **Use excerpts**—There is always debate over this topic. Should you show the full article on your homepage and feed or snippets? If you only have partial content visible, the reader *has* to click through to see the full thing. Though this is certainly a benefit of partial feeds, doing so will cause some readers to unsubscribe to your blog completely. This is a cost/benefit scenario that individual bloggers need to weigh.
- **Be interactive**—An effective way to get readers coming back to your blog many times over a day is to have a blog that people want to interact with.

Liz Strauss has "open mike" events in her comment area at Successful Blog (`www.successful-blog.com`), and this has made the blog less of a publication and more of a party!

Building Community and Getting More Comments

Jakob Nielsen's usability study found that 90 percent of online-community users are *lurkers* (those who read or observe without contributing), with only nine percent of users contributing "a little" and one percent actively contributing.

So one percent of your blog's users are actively engaging with your blog, and the rest are at best occasional contributors.

The study isn't just on blogging, so the actual numbers could be more or less than these and would no doubt vary from site to site anyway, but the principle holds true. The vast majority of readers leave a blog without leaving a comment or contributing to it in any way.

To some extent this is just the way it is, and we probably need to just get used to it; however, when it comes to comments there are some ways to encourage more interactivity on your blog:

- **Invite comments**—Regular readers of my blog will see I often invite people to comment, with a phrase such as, "What do you think? Please share your thoughts in the comments." When I specifically invite comments, people leave them in higher numbers than when I don't. Keep in mind that new readers who are unfamiliar with blogging don't always know about comments or how to use them, and sometimes people almost need to be given permission.

- **Ask questions**—Including specific questions in posts definitely helps get higher numbers of comments. I find that when I include questions in my headings, it is a particularly effective way of getting a response from readers because you set a question in their mind from the first moments of your post.

- **Be incomplete**—If you say everything there is to say on a topic, you're less likely to get others adding their opinions, because you'll have covered what they might have added. Though you don't want to purposely leave too many things unsaid, there is an art to writing open-ended posts that leave room for your readers to be experts also.

- **Be interactive**—If you're not willing to use your own comments section, why would your readers? If someone leaves a comment, then reply. This gets harder as your blog grows, but it's particularly important in the early days of your blog because it shows your readers that their comments are valued, it creates a culture of interactivity, and it gives the impression to other readers that your comments section is an active place that you as the blogger value. As the activity in your comments section grows, you may find you need to be slightly less active in it because readers will start to take over on answering questions and creating community; however, don't completely ignore your comment threads.

- **Be humble**—I find that readers respond very well to posts that show your own weaknesses, failings, and the gaps in your own knowledge rather than those posts where you come across as knowing everything there is to know on a topic. People are attracted to humility and are more likely to respond to it than to a post written in a tone of someone who might respond harshly to their comments.

- **Be gracious**—Related to humility is grace. There are times where you as the blogger will get something wrong in your posts. It might be spelling or grammar; it could be the crux of your argument or some other aspect of your blogging. When someone leaves a comment that shows your failing it's very easy to respond harshly in a defensive manner. We've all seen the flaming that can ensue. Though it's not easy, a graceful approach to comments, where you admit you are wrong, can bring out the lurkers and make them feel a little safer in leaving comments.

- **Reward comments**—There are many ways of acknowledging and "rewarding" good comments that range from "reader appreciation" posts through to highlighting particularly good comments in other posts that you write. Drawing attention to your readers who use comments well affirms them and also draws the attention of other readers to make good use of your comments section.

- **Make it easy to comment**—I leave a lot of comments on a lot of blogs each week, but there is one situation where I rarely leave a comment even if the post deserves it—blogs that require me to log in before making a comment. Maybe I'm lazy (actually, there's no maybe about it!), or maybe there's something inside me that worries about giving out my personal details, but when I see a comments section that requires registration I almost always (95 percent or more of the time) leave the blog without leaving the comment that I want to make. Though I totally understand the temptation to require registration for comments (combating spam in most cases), something inside me resists participating in such comments sections. Registration is a hurdle you put in front of your readers that some are willing to leap but at which others will balk (the same is often said about other comments-section requirements that go beyond the basics). Keep your comments section as simple and as easy to use as possible.

NOTE

As you will have gathered, growing your blog community can be vital if you want a successful blog. For more information on how to build a community, see Chapter 8.

PROBLOGGER BLOG TIP: IT'S ALL IN THE ENGAGEMENT

Page views are a consequence of reader engagement. How interested you keep your visitors over a period of time translates into repeat visits and increased page views. What factors keep you returning to a particular blog? When have you found yourself reading page after page and when have you taken one look and never returned?

Summary

Gaining and keeping readers comes down to having brilliant content and letting people know about it. This is a big job and should not be underestimated. Thankfully, although it is especially tough at the start, it gets easier as you build momentum.

8 Build a Sticky Blog Community

discovered the power of online community on the first day I went online. It was 1996, and I was a student wanting to get the Internet installed at home to help me research papers that I was writing for my degree.

I'd heard of people making friends online and saw reports in media of people even meeting partners on the Internet, but had always been very skeptical about the idea that anyone could build any kind of relationship through the web.

That skepticism was blown out of the water within hours of being online when I found myself in an IRC (Internet Relay Chat) room for Australians.

Within moments of entering the room I'd been noticed, welcomed, and drawn into the conversation.

Three hours later my view of how community could be developed online was completely changed. Three months later I'd spent an hour a day (minimum) in this room since that first day. Over the year or two that followed, I'd personally met 20 or so other members, had attended one wedding, had helped conduct an online memorial service for a member who'd passed away, and had become close friends with a number of others.

I had discovered the power for building community online—something that has shaped the way I've used the web ever since.

This chapter looks closely at the ways in which you can build a sticky blog community: a space in which readers eagerly engage with you and with one another in a way that sustains your blog as well as the community itself.

How Sticky Blogs Grow Your Audience

When I first came across blogging, I was immediately attracted to its potential for building community—between bloggers and their readers and between bloggers and other bloggers.

As I began to develop my own blogs, I experienced this community-building capability for myself. I discovered that one of the secrets behind growing the readership of a blog is to give people ways to participate in it, ways to belong to it, and ways to make it their own.

These are the things that make a blog truly "sticky" (meaning people want to "stick around" and not leave).

As I look back on the past decade of my own blogging, I've started 30+ blogs, but the only ones that remain today and had success were those that evolved into sticky communities, rather than just being information portals.

This section looks at the ways in which a sticky blog helps grow your audience.

Community Helps Make Your Blog More Useful

One of the best things about a blog with lots of reader engagement is that the blog becomes more useful for all concerned. Having a community of people sharing their ideas, rather than just one (that's you!), brings a diversity of ideas and experiences to every discussion. And that makes the experience of reading the blog all the richer.

Community Builds Social Proof

There's something very attractive to potential readers about a blog with lots of interaction and engagement. This is especially true in the age of the social web; users expect to be able to engage with others on a website. They also want to read blogs that they will want to share with their own friends, followers, and contacts.

So, build community on your blog, and you'll find it will grow much faster, because readers attract other readers.

Community Members Become Advocates

Readers who have a sense of belonging on your blog can become powerful advocates for you. As I mentioned previously, they will spread word of you to their own networks and help you to achieve your goals in surprising ways.

One quick example of this is when a group of my photography blog readers began a campaign to attract a large camera manufacturer as an advertiser for my blog. On other occasions, readers have landed me mainstream media attention. So advocacy doesn't stop at readers: your loyal community members can advocate for you in a range of different ways.

Communities Become Content Generators

One of the biggest challenges for many bloggers is coming up with regular, fresh content for their blogs on an ongoing basis. The exciting part about building a community feel into your blogging is that readers will often begin to start volunteering to create content.

Why Community Is Important for Monetization

Now you know why sticky communities help grow an audience. A bigger audience usually means the blog has a bigger potential for monetization. This section looks more closely at how audience growth can translate into profit potential.

Community Increases Page Views

When I analyze the traffic metrics on my blogs, page views are higher in those areas where more communal activity takes place.

For example, the forum sections on my photography blog (seen in Figure 8-1) receive up to ten page views per visit. That's a lot more than the less than two page views the blog area attracts per visit.

Having a dedicated community area within your blog can help you get the best of both worlds, especially if you can filter readers through to forum discussions from blog articles.

Page views are not the be-all and end-all of blogging, but if you're monetizing your blog with impression-based advertising they will make your blog more profitable.

Social Proof Makes Promotion Easy

In the previous section, you saw that readers like to visit and spend time around blogs that others are using and enjoying.

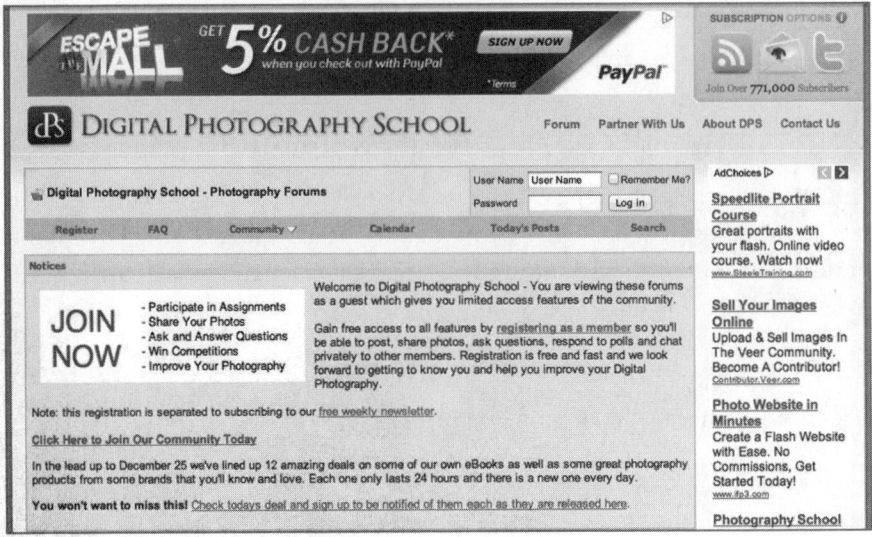

Figure 8-1: Digital Photography School forums.

The other benefit of that fact is that they like to share good content and resources with their followers. And that means that, as a blogger, you'll find promoting your blog easier:

- It's easier to gain subscribers if you can show readers how many people have already subscribed.
- It's easier to convince readers to share your content or promotions within their own networks if you can show them that others are already doing just that—perhaps through share buttons and social media share counters on your site.
- It's much easier to sell promotions to advertisers and sponsors if you can show them that your community is active in terms of sharing your blog with others.

Community Delivers Value to Advertisers

If you're selling sponsorship directly to advertisers on your blog, offering them some community interaction can make your blog a really attractive prospect.

Many advertisers want more than to just have their banner ad displayed on your pages—they want to really reach people with an experience. And they'll pay for the privilege.

Community Increases Blog Value

Over the years, I've had a number of companies approach me wanting to buy my blogs. One interesting feature of these conversations has centered around my blogs having such strong communities.

I find that when I share the fact that there's lots of community interaction on my blogs with prospective buyers, they become a lot more interested, and their offers increase significantly.

Though you may have no intention of ever selling your blog, knowing your niche community is such a drawcard for potential buyers and investors should give you some food for thought. In any case, as the previous points reveal, a sticky community is an essential element in a healthy, growing blog.

Key Steps to Growing a Sticky Community

Every blog needs a community, and the stickier that community is, the more strongly it supports the blog.

This is all very well for those who have an established readership. But what it you're just starting out? Good news: You can start to foster community at any stage in your blog's life.

I noticed that in the first six months of the growth of my photography site, most of my readers seemed to be in "consumption mode"—they were there just to consume content, not really to interact or participate.

However, in the next 6 to 12 months, a community began to emerge with readers interacting more with me, and with one another. Readers had really begun to take more ownership of the site, and were more regularly contributing not just in the post comments, but in terms of writing content, volunteering in the forums, and so on.

This seems to naturally happen over time. All the same, it was something that I had been quite intentional about fostering within the readership since the site began. You can see those first few months of your blog, when readers are in "consumption mode," as a time to set the foundations for the solid, close-knit community that's just around the corner.

This section walks through the key steps you can take to grow a sticky community throughout the life of your blog.

Start with Comments

Perhaps the most natural place to start to build a sticky community on a blog is within its comments section. This is a good place because most web users are hardwired to look for interactivity in post or article comments. The keys to building community in your comments section include:

- **Asking questions in posts.** This draws comments out of readers, and encourages them to express their ideas about your thoughts, and those of other commenters.
- **Interacting with readers.** If you're not willing to comment on your blog, why would others? Commenting gets the ball rolling, and paves the way for a richer exchange of ideas with your audience.
- **Modelling the types of comments and the tone you want your community to take.** If you want readers to feel safe and at home, you need to actively police and moderate the trolls and spammers who inevitably find your blog.
- **Following up on reader questions.** Answer all reader questions, whether they're asked in the comments section of your blog, or via e-mail.

Creating Reader-Centered Posts

Show readers that you value them by regularly publishing posts that are *all about them*. There are lots of ways you can do this:

- Answer reader questions in a post.
- Invite questions from readers either in posts, forums, or in post comments.
- Post a question for discussion. Dedicated "discussion" posts can be a good way to build community on fledgling blogs that are striving to create a sense of unity among readers, and those that don't have dedicated forums.
- Highlight a reader and his or her blog or comment in a blog post.

Focus on regularly building into the rhythm of your blog moments in which your readers take center stage. Create opportunities for your readers to contribute and be valued by their peers within your audience. This approach provides a strong foundation for a sticky community.

EXERCISE

I talked about social proof earlier (in the section "Community Builds Social Proof)," and reader-centered posts are a really valuable way to help build that sense of community—no matter how many (or few!) readers you have.

Write a reader-centered post for your blog and see what kind of response it gets from your audience. To get more insight, ask for feedback on the post through social media, as well as in the post's comments.

Using a Personal Tone and Personal Media

Rather than thinking of your audience as a crowd, it can be helpful to think of them as one person—just one individual that you need to reach. This philosophy can be important in having your work as a blogger really touch individuals:

- **It helps you develop a personal tone in your blog posts.** You'll feel more comfortable writing in a less formal style and using words like "you," "your," and "we" in both your blog posts and your interactions with community members and readers.
- **It makes you more inclined to see engagement with your readers as a personal activity.** This encourages you to try to reach readers using more personal media, like social networks, e-mail, comments, and so on.

Using a personal tone and communicating through personal media are important steps in making yourself genuinely accessible to your readers. I've found them really valuable as I've built communities around my own blogs.

Making Interactive Tools and Projects

Whether it be running weekly polls, using quizzes, running a competition in your comments section, or some other interactive tool or project, it's important to get readers involved.

The more you get your readers to do around your blog, the more ownership they'll feel over your site. The more opportunities you give them to interact, the more likely they'll be to feel aligned with your blog and readership, and to return to your blog in time.

I find that even the anonymous voting in a poll (see Figure 8-2) has the power to make a reader feel connected.

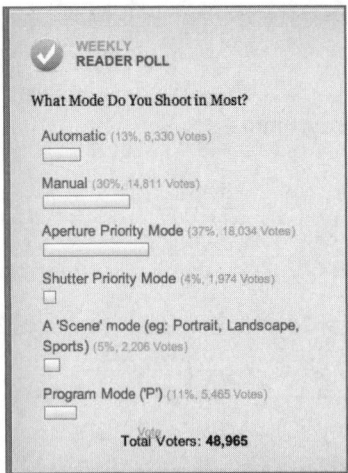

Figure 8-2: Polls encourage easy interaction.

Inviting Reader-Generated Content

Reader-generated content can be a big help in maintaining an ongoing schedule of fresh content on your blog. But another benefit is that it can help foster readers' connections to your blog.

The way I grew reader-generated content on my photography site was simply to start a photography tutorials area in the blog's forums. Within that area, I invited readers to submit their photography tips and advice.

Of course, in terms of the forums themselves, this added a new dimension to my community: It was a new way to help and interact with one another, and to make friends and learn new techniques.

But my other hope was that the area would help me to identify readers who had a talent and passion for teaching others. I've since used some of the best tutorials from that forum on the blog itself, and one or two of the authors have become regular writers for the blog.

PROBLOGGER BLOG TIP: ASK PERMISSION

Readers who make contributions to your community may not be comfortable with you highlighting those contributions for all to see. So if you want to point out an individual contribution, be sure to get in touch with that reader first—and, of course, let the person know when you intend to publish the post that was sparked by his or her contribution.

Becoming a Cheerleader

Look for any opportunity that you can to cheer your community along. I regularly attempt to give feedback to my photography blog readers on how well "we" are doing as a community.

When we hit a new milestone in terms of forum members or traffic numbers, I talk about it in our newsletter. When we're mentioned in a mainstream publication or other media, I let the community know.

My approach with this feedback to readers isn't to highlight how good *I* am as a blogger. It's to show the community what *we* have achieved together.

I find that each time I do this, the feedback is excellent and that it spurs readers on to help us grow and become an even better, stronger community.

Giving Readers Jobs

One of the best ways to build a sense of engagement and ownership for your readership is to give jobs to readers. You can't do this with every single one of your readers, but it's amazing how many people *don't* want to just read and consume—they want to be a part of building something that matters.

Jobs can be something like getting readers to help you moderate comments or making them full-blown forum moderators. You can ask readers to help you come up with poll topics, judge competitions, write guest posts, and more.

Giving the right readers jobs meets their desire to get involved and make a contribution, but it also engenders in those participants a real sense of pride and ownership around your blog—another foundation of a sticky community. Oh, and if you do it right, giving jobs to readers can also make your workload lighter!

PROBLOGGER BLOG TIP: MANAGE THOSE JOBS

If you give readers jobs to do, make sure you also provide the support they need to get the jobs done. And be sure to manage the tasks and your interaction with the readers you've chosen. The experience is meant to build trust and loyalty, not make the readers feel like they've been left alone with a task—or, worse, like you're not in control of the blog.

Assigning Reader Homework

Another great way to get a little more interactivity and buy-in from readers is to assign them homework in your posts. This is particularly effective if you have a tips or how-to blog where you're teaching people something. In those cases, it's fairly natural to finish a post by saying, "go and do this task, and let us know how you did."

Again, on my photography blog we have a photography assignment area in the forums (see Figure 8-3). There, we post a weekly assignment that readers go away and complete before reporting back with the image they've taken. Heaven forbid we should miss a weekly assignment—our readers would be up in arms!

The photography assignments aren't just about peer support—they also give readers a chance to show off their talents and what they're learning on your blog. They're a good way to promote peer approval and respect—two elements that are essential in a healthy, growing, and sticky community.

You don't need a dedicated forum area to assign homework. Just end a post with an invitation to readers to do something and to report back on how they did. You'll find that a percentage of your readers will complete the task, and in doing so—through putting your advice into action—they'll feel more loyalty to you and your blog.

Providing Multiple Avenues to Join or Become a Member

I've already mentioned the forums I've built on my photography blog. I can't express to you just how powerful that area of the site has become.

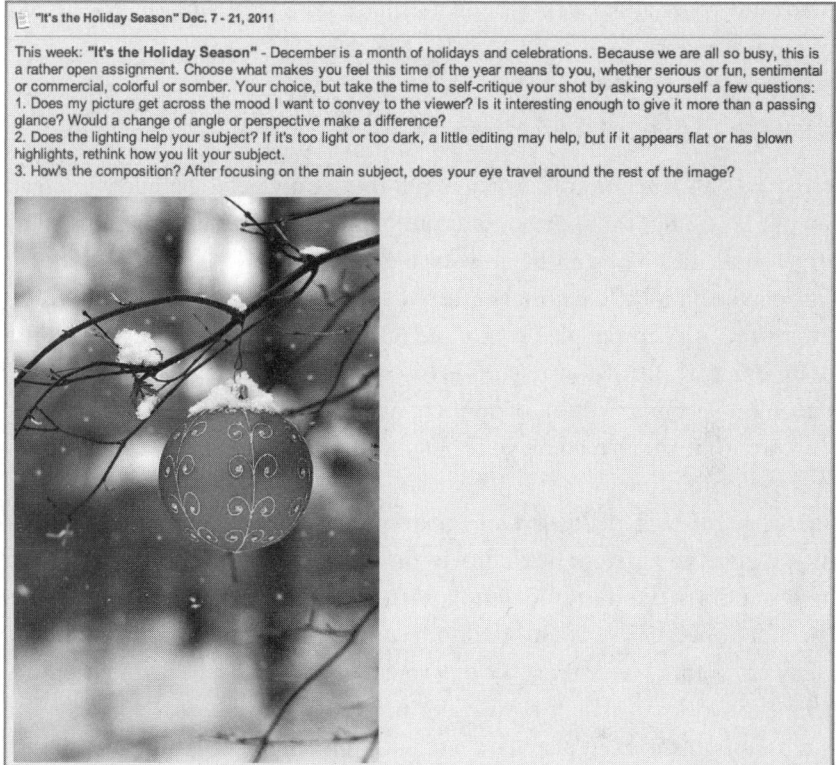

"It's the Holiday Season" Dec. 7 - 21, 2011

This week: **"It's the Holiday Season"** - December is a month of holidays and celebrations. Because we are all so busy, this is a rather open assignment. Choose what makes you feel this time of the year means to you, whether serious or fun, sentimental or commercial, colorful or somber. Your choice, but take the time to self-critique your shot by asking yourself a few questions:
1. Does my picture get across the mood I want to convey to the viewer? Is it interesting enough to give it more than a passing glance? Would a change of angle or perspective make a difference?
2. Does the lighting help your subject? If it's too light or too dark, a little editing may help, but if it appears flat or has blown highlights, rethink how you lit your subject.
3. How's the composition? After focusing on the main subject, does your eye travel around the rest of the image?

Figure 8-3: Example photography assignment.

Though the forum doesn't have as many unique visitors each month as the blog segment of the site, it is visited by a growing number of hard core fans. These readers visit on a daily basis and they've really created an amazing community around that blog.

Similarly, adding a weekly newsletter to the site has created another connecting point with readers. It also acts as a gentle weekly reminder to stop by and interact on the blog and in the forums.

I've found that having a blog, forum, and a newsletter is a lot of work, but a fantastic way to engage with different readers in formats that appeal to their learning styles.

Many readers have connected with the blog through two or even three of these avenues. Each time they access a new part of the site, they "buy in" just a little more. Over time, that buy-in adds up: Now the blog has some very loyal, devoted, and vocal advocates, who form the backbone of what has become a very sticky community.

Embracing Off-Site Media

When we talk about community, you might think only of blog readers interacting on our blogs. But these days, community engagement takes place in many locations, and they won't all be on your blog.

This can seem a little counter-intuitive for a web publisher. We often feel like we want to keep people on our site and get them interacting more and more on our turf. But what I've discovered over the years is that when you give people a secondary point of connection with one another, it deepens the connections that are formed on your blog. It's an invaluable step toward building a sticky community.

Having an off-blog, dedicated forum area is a great option for building community. It gives you greater flexibility in the way you interact with readers and strongly supports them in interacting positively among themselves.

The other obvious avenue for building community is through social media. You may not want to be active on every social network out there, but it's probably wise to work out which network or networks your readers are engaging with most often, and then provide them with the opportunity to interact with you (and other readers, with your help) there.

The ProBlogger Facebook page, shown in Figure 8-4, is an obvious example. There, I interact with readers, post articles, ask questions, and so on—and readers do the same.

Through our Twitter account, we hold conversations with readers who are Twitter users, and put them in touch with one another through hashtagged discussions and interactions. I'm also a big Google+ user, having found this network to be great for really rich, detailed engagements with my community.

Off-site media like these networks can provide new avenues for engagement that aren't possible on your blog itself. For example, forums and social media can give you great opportunities for "off topic" interactions that might not be particularly appropriate in your main blog. In effect, these sites can provide readers with a space to "play"—and to relate to you and each other on a broader level.

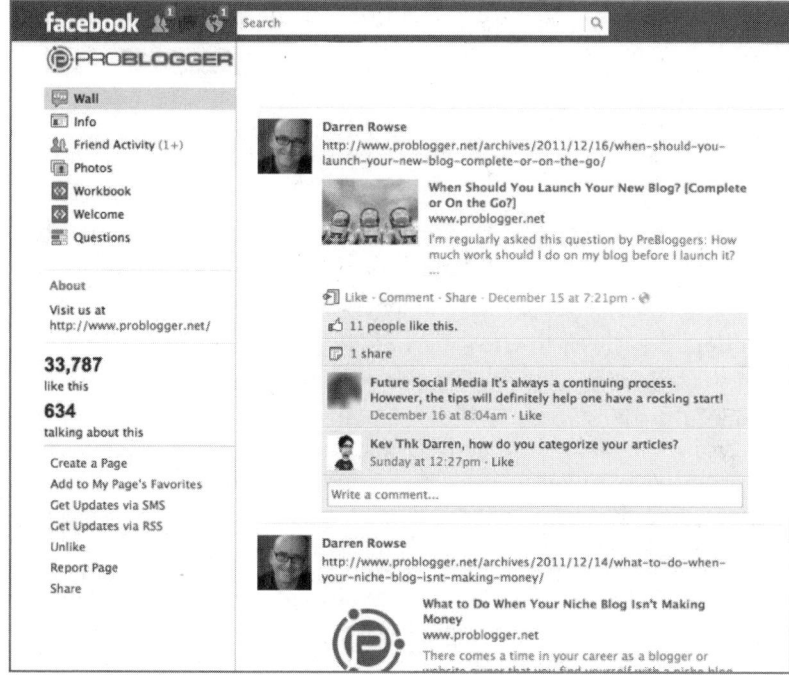

Figure 8-4: ProBlogger on Facebook.

Being the Community You Want to Form

Above all, the best way of building a community on your blog is to lead the way yourself: Start to *be* the community that you want to form.

This work is what will ultimately bring your community to life. And if you don't do it, you'll likely fail to build a community on your blog at all. Readers will take your lead but they're unlikely to want to join a community if you, as the leader, seem ambivalent about the whole idea.

Be the community you want to form from Day 1. Be passionate about engaging with readers and about building genuine relationships with them. As you've seen, a loyal community of fans can bring a lot to your blog, so why not let these people into your world? Invite their feedback on ideas, involve them in decisions, and let them know early on about any exciting changes you're making to your blog.

The more you respect their involvement in your blog's success, the more involved they'll become—and the stickier your community will be.

Engaging Your Audience

Building a sticky community takes energy and work. To make the community happen, the following sections talk more specifically about some of the key methods you can use to engage your audience, some of which were touched on in the section "Key Steps to Growing a Sticky Community."

In each of the following sections, I'll give you an example from my experience that hopefully gives you a few ideas about how you could apply these approaches to your blog and with your readers.

Setting Up Reader Homework

Assigning homework for readers has been a long-term engagement strategy on my photography blog, and I've been quite amazed by the results.

Firstly, here's how I usually do it:

- Each of my assignments is based on a tips post I've written on the blog.
- At the end of each tip I point to an assignment thread over at the DPS Flickr Group (www.flickr.com/groups/digitalps/). The assignment thread also links back to the tips post that contains the idea for the assignment.
- Assignments are simply an invitation for readers to take the concepts in the post and practice them, sharing the results of their photos in the Flickr group.

It's not rocket science, but this approach has helped my community members to get to know each other and to receive extra value out of the tips posts on the blog. In that way, it's a great tool for reinforcing my blog's brand.

These reader assignments offer a lot of benefits, though:

- **Reader technique improves**—I regularly get e-mails from readers thanking me for the assignment threads and asking for more. They tell me that having a practical space to do what I'm teaching—and to see how others are using the information provided—is helping them to improve their technique.

- **Participation levels rise**—The DPS Flickr group's membership is increasing, as is the participation rate of those members. The latest assignments have attracted hundreds of responses and users often start their own threads of discussion in the group, which is great to see. Of course, any time you get your readers to take a step toward doing something with what you write, you're a step closer to a loyal reader. A community of users is slowly developing around assignments.

- **Assignments drive traffic back to the blog**—I've started to notice that the discussion forum is actually starting to drive traffic back to the blog via the links in the introduction to each forum. Other Flickr forums are linking to our assignments, which draws new Flickr users to our forum and then to the blog and weekly newsletter. That's another one of the benefits of building an off-site community. Flickr is a natural gathering point for photographers, and the ease-of-use factor has come into play. As part of their normal Flickr rhythm, many are participating in the discussions and assignments.

- **Users create content**—Often, DPS Flickr Group members post content to the forums that would be suitable to use as blog posts. With their permission, I use this content on the main blog, once again interlinking the forum and the blog to drive traffic between the two.

Assignments do take a little work, because you need to:

- Write in a way that engages and motivates people to participate.
- Come up with quality assignments.
- Monitor or moderate the results and be prepared to engage with those who submit responses to your assignment.

Unless you're willing to take these tasks on, the results won't live up to their full potential.

I mentioned that there are benefits to be gained by creating a community around a site that's not your own. Initially, I set up the assignments on Flickr because it was easy and I had limited time to throw at it. My ideal at the time would have been to set up a forum using forum software, but Flickr was the next best option.

I've benefitted in a number of ways by doing this. But you'll always come up against limitations when you use third-party sites like this. Flickr groups give you little control over look and feel, or the format for discussions. It also restricts what you can and can't promote in the forums (you're not supposed to do anything for financial gain). So I decided that once I had a little more time and membership, I'd eventually transition to a forum over on my own domain.

Giving Readers a Job

Giving readers a job really does a lot to integrate them into your community.

I first learned this in my early days of being a church pastor. Many churches have a welcoming strategy for new people, which aims at serving them in any way possible. They go to extreme lengths to welcome people in ways that make them feel included, but that keep the new members passive.

I found in my early days of church work that we had a much higher success rate with integrating new people into our community if they were given a job right from the start. The jobs they were given were always small but they didn't allow new people to remain passive for long. Instead, the jobs encouraged them to belong by actively participating in the group.

By contributing in small but real ways, people almost immediately felt they'd invested something in the community, and they were more likely to continue to do so over the long term.

So from the beginning I was pretty sure that a similar thing would apply in building all kinds of communities—including blogging communities.

I tried a series of group writing projects on ProBlogger, and they proved to be a great example of this phenomenon. I'd estimate that between 30 and 40 percent of those who participated did so on their first visit to ProBlogger—and many of them stayed on to become regular commenters and even guest posters.

In a similar way, on my photography blog, I've run a number of threads in our discussion forum asking readers to submit photographs with tips on how they were taken. I then feature a selection of these on the main blog.

Both these ideas have the added benefit of creating user-generated content. But more importantly, the feedback that I've gotten from those whose work has been featured on the main blog indicates that they've been won over as loyal and active participants in the community.

Over time, I find these individuals are likely to contribute more content, that they become the blog's advocates, and that they actively support the blog's communities.

Answering Reader Questions

Readers ask questions in a variety of ways: through social networks, blog post comments, e-mail, in forums, and occasionally through posts on their own blogs.

You can answer those questions in situ—replying to that blog comment, or responding to that e-mail. And that's great. But another way to help build a strong community is to answer questions from readers in blog posts.

When a reader asks a question, I know that he or she is probably not the only person who needs more information or guidance on that point. So, to maximize the benefits across the full community, I try to take some questions and turn my responses into more public answers through a blog post. This way, I've answered the person who asked the question, but also hopefully shared some solutions with others who might have the same question.

The added bonus of this technique is that it lets you publicly highlight a reader's interaction. This achieves a few of the goals we've been discussing in this chapter. It makes a reader famous. It proves that you're accessible to your community. And it shows that while you might not respond to everyone who contacts you, interacting with your community and helping out wherever you can, is important to you.

Making Readers Famous

Responding to reader questions in a blog post is just one of the ways you can make a reader famous. There are plenty of others.

Although many blog tips focus on techniques to help make blogs (and their writers) more well-known, one of the paradoxical keys to blogging success is that many bloggers who build great blogs actually go out of their way to make their readers more famous and well-known.

When you create space on your blog to highlight readers in some way, the impact can be quite profound—particularly when you do it regularly. Two groups of people tend to be impacted:

1. **The group that you highlight.** This is the first, and most obvious group that benefits from your efforts. Having bloggers go out of their way to talk about you on their blog certainly makes an impression. It gives you a feeling of being valuable, promotes a sense of belonging and participation in the blog, and it can help you to achieve your blogging goals if the blogger sends other readers to learn more about you on your site.

2.   **The group that witnesses the highlight.** These are the readers who are also impacted when you make a reader famous. One of the lessons I learned very early in my blogging career is that when you publicly value one reader, others often feel valued too. It shows you have an interest in, and that you value, all of your readers—even though you can highlight only a few.

There are many ways to highlight your readers on your blog. Let me share a few that I've used:

- **Promote a comment to a post.** Readers often make insightful and wise observations in the comments of your blog. However, only a handful of people in the comment thread will read these comments. So why not pull those comments out and use them as the basis for one of your posts? This is a great way to highlight the shared wisdom as well as the person who made the comment.
- **Write a post about the reader's blog.** Visit the sites of those who are leaving comments on your blog and pick one that resonates with you to make a post about. One option is to write an unpaid review of the blog, highlighting the best posts and what you like about the blog.
- **Send your readers to comment on someone else's blog.** Write a post that links to someone else's great blog post, but instead of asking your readers what they think about it on your own blog, ask them to comment on the post on the author's blog. Shutting down the comments in your own post and saying that you've already left a comment on the other blog can help make this tactic more effective.
- **Give readers an opportunity to promote themselves.** Run a project or write a post that gives readers an opportunity to promote themselves in some way. For example, I've created a number of ways to give DPS readers a chance to show off their photography. In one post I asked readers if they had a photoblog and invited them to post a link to it if they did. Hundreds of readers left links to their blogs, and many e-mailed me later to thank me for sending them traffic.
- **Name a reader of the week.** I've seen a few blogs do this over the years. Simply choose one reader each week to highlight in a post.
- **Make a project, meme, or competition.** Long-term readers of ProBlogger will be familiar with the group writing projects that I used to run there. I would invite all readers to write posts on their blogs and then share the

links with each other—which always generated a lot of traffic between readers' blogs. Similarly, you can run competitions, blog carnivals, and memes, which all give readers an opportunity to highlight their own online presence, site, or blog. To find out more about what blog memes are and how they work, check out www.chrisg.com/what-is-a-blog-meme/.

- **Run a reader poll and highlight answers in a follow-up post.** One weekend, pose a question to your readers in a post. Then, in the week that follows, do a follow-up post where you explain your own thoughts on the question, and pull out some of the best comments left by readers. Alternatively, you could survey your social media followers on a topic that's relevant to your blog and then highlight their responses in a blog post.

- **Invite guest posts.** Often, a guest posting is thought of solely as a way to get free content for your blog. Though free content is nice, one of the things I love about guest posting is that it puts the microphone in the hand of someone else. It lets someone, who would normally be constrained by the comments section, have a little more power and influence on the direction of your community. This can have a real impact on the person writing the post, and on your readership as they see someone like themselves featured on your blog.

Of course, it's easy to make a reader famous if your blog has been around for a while and has developed a readership. Those who are just starting out will find it tougher.

If you're a new blogger, or you don't have any vocal readers leaving comments yet, try making another blogger famous by writing a post that links to his or her site and highlights that person to your readers. Remember: Other bloggers can be valuable contributors to your community, too.

Playing Matchmaker with Your Readers

We've talked about using off-site media to help your community members connect with one another, but you can go further than simply setting up a Facebook page or a Google group.

A quick example: On DPS, I once asked readers to add their Twitter accounts in the post comments. More than 630 readers listed their accounts. Many readers also went through the list and added other readers' accounts to their Twitter lists, so because of the DPS blog, we now had an offline community.

That was great, but the benefits of the Twitter connections went a lot further; in the weeks that followed my publishing the Twitter account request post, I noticed more and more of our readers getting to know each other on Twitter. Though it's difficult to measure, the anecdotal evidence that I saw suggested that this off-site connection improved the quality of comments people left on DPS.

I also had numerous thank you e-mails from readers who told me that they've met great new friends as a result of that post. There have even been a few readers who've started working together as a result of these connections.

As I say, it's difficult to measure the impact but from what I saw, the community on my site became stronger and deeper because I played matchmaker, and helped my readers get to know each other better.

I believe that the more connected people are with one another, the more likely they are to stay connected with the community.

Establishing an Intentional Engagement Plan

Another strategy that I find is a win/win for bloggers and readers is to set up specific times and places where your readers can interact with you in real time. Put aside an hour or half hour for this intentional community time, publicize it to your readers, and then make yourself available to interact.

One of the ways that I used to do this was by scheduling a live video session where I simply ran a Q&A with readers. I was always amazed at the response from readers who joined these chats. Though I felt a little odd talking to my laptop in order to answer basic questions about blogging, readers really did value the opportunity to engage and seemed to feel much more involved as a result.

Of course, now I can engage with readers through social media. Using Twitter hashtags or comment threads on Facebook and Google+, you can have a sort of public meeting with your community, and engage with them in real time.

This is a really friendly way to engage with readers and create buzz—and it's a great addition to your everyday usage of social networks for reader engagement.

Learning from Your Community

The way we've talked so far, you may be seeing your blog's community as being something like a party: You're setting up the venues and planning activities to catch readers' attention and then hooking them into coming back again and again.

This is one way to see your community, but it's not the whole picture. Think about your local community—I'll bet it's not a one-way street. There's an exchange, and you're among peers. Everyone has something slightly different to offer, and together, you're able to achieve more than you can on your own, as individuals.

It's the same with your blog community. If you tend to think of your blog's community as a group of people that you're giving something to, or providing something for—if you see yourself primarily as giving, and them as receiving—you're not going to get the most out of your community.

Not only that, but if you don't see your community members as your equals, your community won't be as sticky as it could be—no matter how many great competitions you run or how many readers you make famous.

In this section, it's time to step back from the "doing" work of community, and reflect upon the "thinking" work. If you take the philosophy that you're a part of your blog's community, and you can learn as much from your friends there as they can learn from each other, you'll open yourself and your blog up to a whole new world of possibility.

What kinds of possibilities? Here are just a few.

Content Ideas and Directions

Most established bloggers these days get some feedback if they tweet about their latest article. As your community grows, you'll be more likely to get feedback on posts through social networks, comments, or—if you have them—forums.

Reading this feedback is one thing, but the more involved bloggers will learn from it and really take it to heart. If you're not sure why readers feel the way they do about a post, ask them. And if you have a suspicion that a group of readers would like to see you publish on particular topics, ask them. This is, first and foremost, what I think community is all about: exchange.

Comments and feedback are always interesting because more subtle trends are usually lurking beneath the surface of many comments.

For example, readers might say they love a post you've written on headlines, because they're finding that their headlines are becoming stale and "sameish." This sentiment might prompt you to write a post that specifically targets longer-term bloggers, serving as a refresher on the basics of post title writing; you can then invite bloggers to rewrite a dull headline and submit it in the post comments.

Sifting content ideas from community discussions and feedback isn't difficult. And interpreting the subtleties of those comments for your readers' hidden desires is a skill that you can hone with time and experience.

Needs and Desires That Need Solving

Learning to identify readers' needs isn't just important for creating content that your community likes—it can also help direct your efforts to find sponsors, advertisers, and affiliate programs that your readers will respond to.

I always knew that my ProBlogger community was interested in writing—after all, producing good content on a regular basis is something all bloggers need to do. I also knew that a strong, unifying desire of my audience was to make money blogging.

The more time I spent talking with my readers, the more I learned about these desires. And I felt their frustration when they didn't see the earnings they wanted from their own blogs.

Eventually, while pondering this challenge, it dawned on me that one way to help solve this problem for my readers might be to provide them with other avenues to make money blogging—and so the ProBlogger Job Boards, shown in Figure 8-5, were born.

The job boards provide space for blog owners to advertise paid writing opportunities targeting bloggers who want to make money from their craft. From what I've observed, my readers see this as a good way to make some money blogging as well as to learn more and hone their writing skills. It also gives them extra motivation to keep working on their own blogs—something that's really satisfying for me to be part of.

The more involved you are with your community, the more involved your readers will become with you. And as that trust grows, the community will reveal desires, hopes, and dreams that you might have the ability to meet.

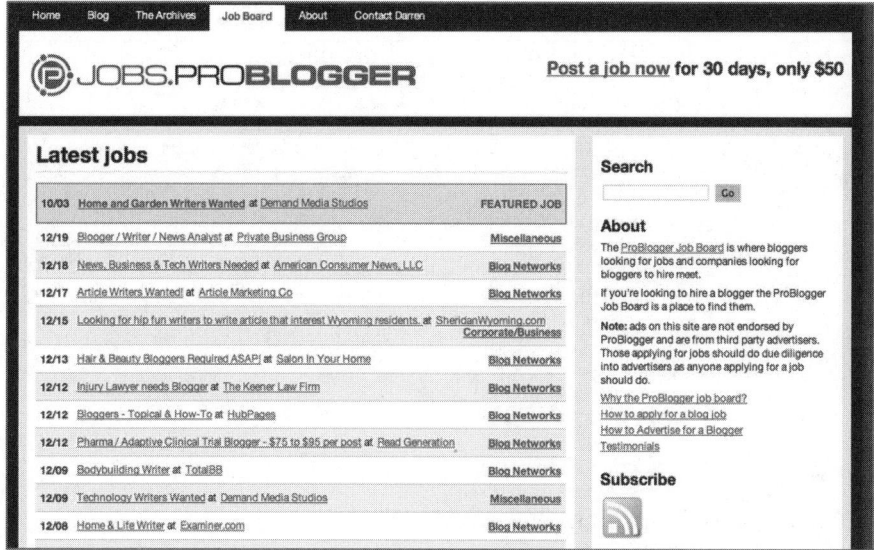

Figure 8-5: ProBlogger Job Board.

Likes and Dislikes That You Can Leverage

As with all aspects of community, trust isn't a one-way street. In a truly engaged, involved community, you, as the leader, will show that you trust your readers, too.

Evidence of that trust can come in many ways—giving readers jobs, which I talked about earlier, is one example. But it can go much further than that.

If you're willing to take them on board, you can learn a lot from the likes and dislikes of your community. If you're brave enough, you can use those preferences to help make decisions about your blog.

I love to ask my readers what they'd prefer. When I'm tossing around product ides, I'll often tweet to my followers to ask which idea they prefer, or which angle resonates better with them. Often, if my team is having trouble honing a sales page for a product, I'll call for some help from the community, and run the content past them to see what they think.

Having asked for that feedback, I *always* take it on board. Don't be tempted to just make a show of asking your readers for feedback—act on it. This is important in building a sense of ownership among readers, but it's also essential in making your work the best it can be.

I've changed everything from sales copy to designs to product plans on the basis of reader likes and dislikes. And my blogs are the better for their involvement.

> **EXERCISE**
>
> Take a look at your future plans for your blog; it could be something as simple as thinking about the next few posts you plan to write, or something as involved as a product launch you've scheduled. Choose an aspect of that task and put it to your readers to get their feedback. I guarantee the responses you get will surprise you—and make those plans more likely to succeed.

Product Ideas and Practicalities

If you've learned about your readers' needs, desires, likes, and dislikes, you'll find it much easier to develop ideas for products and services that will really resonate with those people.

After I published *31 Days to Build a Better Blog*, I found that while the book was relevant to a large portion of my blog's readers, there was a significant segment that needed help setting up their first blog in a way that would put them in a good position to become a problogger over time.

I learned about this segment through the responses I received to the *31 Days* product both during and after launch. I'd published the tasks from that book on my blog and when I updated these tasks, I saw a lot of engagement in the post comments and on social media from interested readers. Along with the enthusiastic responses, I could see that there was a segment of my community who didn't feel confident to tackle those tasks successfully.

The more I looked for information about this segment of readers, the more I found. By speaking to these people, reading their comments, and looking at what they were doing on their own blogs, I uncovered a strong need for practical guidance from the very beginning of the blogging journey. This was how the idea for *ProBlogger's Guide to Your First Week of Blogging* was born.

Most of the big-name bloggers have built products—and whole product lines—on the basis of their communities' needs. In a recent conversation, Copyblogger's (www.copyblogger.com) Brian Clark told me that when he started the site, he didn't know how it would make him a living. But he knew that if he built a strong community, those people would tell him what they wanted. They did, and today the company Brian built has a unique and successful product offering of software tools.

When you're open to learning what your community has to teach you, amazing things can evolve.

Potential Partnerships

The best bloggers value relationships, and a loyal blogging community can dramatically increase the number and reach of your online relationships. The potential of those connections is immeasurable. Although it's common to think of the people in your community in terms of what unifies them—what interests and needs put them into your target audience—don't forget that these are people with lives that are much broader than that.

Who knows what your readers know? Or *who* they know? The only way to find out is to ask—or to be transparent about what you're doing and what your needs are. That way, if they think they can help somehow, your loyal followers will get in touch.

Whether you need someone to lay out your next e-book or you're looking for post sponsors, your community is a great place to start the search. Your dedicated readers would love to help, so why not let them?

Through my community, I've found authors for posts and e-books, connected with advertisers, affiliates, and sponsors, and been put in touch with people I've ended up working with for years.

I've also had a lot of fun—meeting die-hard ProBlogger and DPS readers at festivals and events has been among the most rewarding and enjoyable aspects of my work.

PROBLOGGER BLOG TIP: DON'T BE SHY

Don't feel that asking your community for help will make you seem weak or lacking—it won't. Quite the opposite, in fact: Your readers will feel flattered that you asked, and eager to help. Showing that you're a normal human being, rather than an Internet rock star, is a great way to build real empathy and trust with your audience.

The Dark Side of Community

As you've seen, a sticky blog community is a great thing. It takes work, but the rewards are more than worth the effort you'll put in.

Of course, a blog community isn't all fun and games. Community management can be a time-drain, especially if you run your own forums, which I found to take a real time commitment. The number of places where your community is likely to hang out is always growing, too, which can mean engagement takes more time and can seem more disparate or disjointed.

But there's one key issue that any blogger with a community will face, and that's trolls—people who like to make trouble just for the sake of it. Let's look at the tactics you can use to minimize the impact of trolls on your blog's community.

What Are Trolls?

Trolls are negative types who take exception in some way to what you're doing, and decide to try to disrupt it in any way they can.

Some trolls start out on your blog as eager readers, commenting and engaging with passion. But then something goes wrong, and they become argumentative and disagreeable. They can try to derail conversations, start trouble with other community members, and usually end up creating big headaches for you.

If they're left to their own devices, trolls can form factions that seriously damage the community you've worked so hard to build. After all, no one wants to hang around a negative space where there's continuous sniping and mistrust.

Setting Up Preemptive Measures

With trolls, the saying, "an ounce of prevention is worth a pound of cure" rings especially true. As you begin to take community building more seriously, think about the kind of behavior you want your community to show toward one another and others online. Consider setting a few policies for community behavior so that you can spot undesirable behavior as soon as it arises.

Then, as you build your community, model the behavior you want to see your readers use. Be exemplary in the way you raise issues, discuss ideas, and treat the people within your community and beyond it. This gives your readers a strong lead to follow—it sets standards and reinforces the right kinds of expectations about how your community works.

Wherever you can, reward good behavior. Thanking a reader for giving good advice to someone else in your community—perhaps in a post's comments or on Twitter—is a simple example. But you'd be surprised at how big an impact this kind of action can have—especially if you make a habit of it. Also, don't overlook "reader of the week" posts and similar tactics for rewarding great contributors within your community.

> **NOTE**
>
> If and when you decide to make some of your community members moderators—perhaps for blog comments or on your blog's forums—take the time to outline their roles carefully. Talk with your moderators about your community's policies, values, and procedures, so that everyone's on the same page and knows what's expected. Putting these guidelines into a brief Google Doc that you can share with your community team might also be helpful.

These are all preemptive measures and if you put them in place, you'll likely have less trouble with trolls. But what happens when, despite your best efforts, some trolls pop up in your community?

Dealing with Trolls

My approach has always been to marginalize trolls. This doesn't mean you need to be rude, abrupt, or unkind—it just means that you need to take every episode of troll behavior and minimize it. As I mentioned, many trolls start out as ordinary community members, so if you can spot the odd occurrence of trolling before these people descend entirely into being full-blown trolls, you might just be able to turn the situation around.

Your best bet is always to be firm, polite, and calm with troublemakers. Acknowledge their arguments and explain reasonably and honestly why you disagree with them. This will give other community members a chance to chime in with their opinions in a respectful way—something they may not do if you don't make the first effort to get the situation back in hand.

If the troll persists without adding anything new to the discussion, you may decide to ignore them, but it's important not to do that rudely. Treating every community member's contributions with respect should be the first of your community policies. Guiding conversations is also your job as the community's leader.

Finally, as your community grows and develops a strong culture, you'll hopefully find that its members are more inclined to police the community in your absence. Through your example, they'll likely feel more able to handle much of the trollish behavior that crops up, and that's a huge bonus for you.

Group self-moderation reduces your workload but it's also an indicator that your blog community is becoming increasingly self-sustaining. It's taking on a life on its own as members help members and readers share with readers, all under the umbrella of your blog's brand. And that's the stickiest kind of blog community you can build.

Summary

Community is the lifeblood of blogging. The stickier your community, the stronger your blog.

Community was what inspired me to start my first-ever blog. Back in 2002, when I stumbled across the first blog I'd ever seen, I noticed two amazing things:

- Blogging gives the blogger a voice and amplifies that voice around the world.
- Blogging gives the blogger the ability to build a community around what he or she is exploring. It enables the blogger to have personal—yet public—interactions with many people to further explore topics.

The relational aspects of blogging were clear. I'd not seen anything on the web that allowed a person to grow a community around their own ideas before this. And I wanted to experience that for myself.

In this chapter, we've looked at the value that a strong, loyal, sticky community can bring to your blog. We've discussed the steps involved in establishing and nurturing that community, and we've discussed the kinds of lessons you can learn from your community. We've also discussed the dark side of community—and how you can brighten it up.

A sticky community is essential to a sustainable blog. Embrace the possibilities of community, and your blog will have a significant advantage over all those that don't.

9 Social Media and Your Blog

You cannot have missed the growing buzz around *social media* over recent years. It seems the television and newspaper media is obsessed with Twitter this and Facebook that. Perhaps this fixation is because the traditional media fear the new media as competition?

At its most general, social media encompasses every sort of social or community site, but each service or tool can be broadly categorized as *social bookmarking*, *social networking*, and *media sharing*.

This chapter shows you how you can use these various social media tools to your advantage.

Determining Which Social Media Sites to Use

Deciding which social media site to use depends largely on your goals and where your audience hangs out. Your most desired outcome determines which tools to use and how you interact with them. Social media services can deliver terrific benefits to you and your blog, and they are especially good for attracting attention and for encouraging engagement from your readers. With attention, you will potentially grow your links and subscribers, and with more engagement, you will deepen networking connections and retain more loyalty.

The confusion arises when trying to make distinctions, because all of these sites are blending features, with all social media sites allowing you to add friends, and most sites encouraging you to share or rate content.

In terms of promotion, the main draws are social bookmarking sites such as Reddit (www.reddit.com), StumbleUpon (www.stumbleupon.com), and the high-traffic media sharing sites, in particular YouTube (www.youtube.com). For networking you would look to Twitter (https://twitter.com) and Facebook (www.facebook.com), and for business networking or job-seeking, LinkedIn (www.linkedin.com).

Social Bookmarking

You know when you find a useful site that you expect to need in future, you bookmark the site in your browser so you have an easy way to refer to it. *Social bookmarking* started out as a way to share your bookmarks, so rather than sitting on your computer, you have them wherever you go and your friends can access them, too. The oldest and most famous of these sites is probably Delicious, but Delicious has faded in popularity and fame in favor of the new breed lead by Reddit.

Each of these bookmark sites has the potential to send you thousands of visitors, and they all work by members submitting content and allowing others to judge it or vote for it in some way. Getting popular on these services has turned into an obsession for many bloggers, which can be dangerous when it distracts you from looking after your regular readers.

Social Networking

On the other side are the *social networking* sites, such as LinkedIn and Facebook, which are all about creating connections between people and fostering communication.

In general, the features you expect to see on a social networking site or service are the ability to create a profile about yourself, to add people you know or discover to a list of friends, and to send messages to your contacts. Some services started out as glorified "address books," but once the members started interacting, the appeal quickly turned to having discussions and sharing links and content.

Media Sharing Services

This type of social media service blends many of the features of social bookmarking and social networking. *Media sharing services* started out as a way to store and share your own content, such as uploading your pictures to online photo albums so that your family overseas can see your wedding images.

Just like social networking sites you can befriend other users, and also much like social bookmarking sites there is often a way to rate or comment on content that other people share.

Every type of digital media has a popular service supporting it, from video (such as YouTube) through to PowerPoint presentations (slideshare, found at www.slideshare.net, for example)—if you have content, there will be a place to share it.

Implementing Social Media Promotion

Social networking sites can drive traffic, and some of the media sharing sites have terrific traffic potential, but for promotion, the biggest *traffic spikes* come from the social bookmarking services, so this section looks at those first.

To get traffic from a social bookmarking site your article must be submitted and get a lot of votes. This works differently with each service. Traffic from StumbleUpon comes via a special toolbar that you can download from its site. On the others you have to log in, find the appropriate article, and then hit the bookmark or vote button.

Because so many services are available, it is best to focus on just a few. I mainly focus on StumbleUpon because with just a few votes you can get a nice flow of traffic. I have friends who focus on Reddit because, although it is far harder to become visible, when your content does receive a lot of votes you get a huge traffic spike. Figure 9-1 shows an example of a traffic graph from one of my blogs.

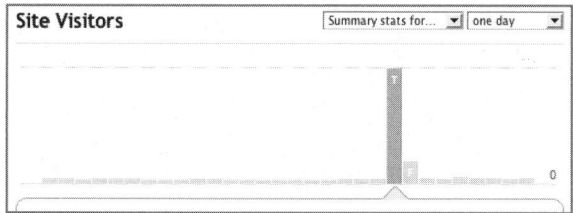

Figure 9-1: An example graph showing a traffic spike.

Writing for Social Bookmarking Success

In general, social media users are surfing. They are not keen on investing much time to discover if something is worthy of attention, so you have to pull out all the stops featured in Chapter 4:

- Write attention-grabbing headlines.

- Keep your paragraphs short and punchy.
- Use bullets, images, and subheads to aid skimming.
- Pull out interesting quotes and key points.
- Make content something people will want to talk about, share, or come back to.

In general, you'll find the content that does well in social bookmarking sites is very similar to the kind of content that bloggers are inclined to link to, so the tried and tested link-bait tactics shown in Chapter 7 work well. Just take care to monitor the target service to see what tends to be popular and what attracts few votes. Also make lots of friends; you will need their votes to get your content seen.

Social Bookmarking as a Popularity Contest

Most of these bookmarking sites allow you to send a link to your friends for their voting consideration. In addition, you can put buttons on the article itself, and, of course, e-mail your friends to get them to vote for it.

Becoming successful with social media is a lot like high school, really. Being "nice" is great, but being popular and having lots of friends is far more important. Obviously the quantity of friends is not the only criteria; there is no point in having 10,000 fans that ignore you, so you need a quantity of *engaged* contacts to make any kind of headway.

To even get a story seen in social bookmarking sites, you need votes. Hardly anyone looks in the dark and hidden corners of social bookmarking sites where new and unnoticed stories live. The popular pages get all the attention, followed by pages that are about to become popular with a little push.

You need a bunch of friends to give you a kick start. You can see how your friends are presented on StumbleUpon in Figure 9-2. Although the more the better, do not spam people, or you will suffer the consequences, which range from not gaining any benefits because your stories are automatically buried so your content is effectively invisible, through to, at worst, being banned.

Having some friends who are already popular will help you; it used to be that many sites, such as Digg (http://digg.com), would rank users based on usage history. If users had a pattern of supporting successful articles, their votes would gain more weight. This became distorted as members would game the system, so these kinds of factors have been downplayed in terms of technology; but in terms of social behavior, the "in-crowd" is still an influential force in any community.

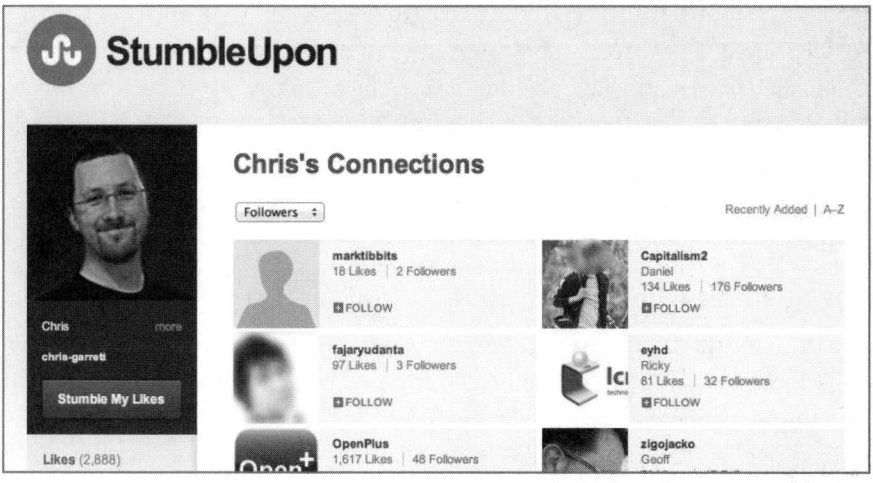

Figure 9-2 Friends in StumbleUpon.

Friends and adoring fans can help you get your stuff noticed. In that case, most of the work is done for you. In fact, being noticed may be all that is required. Sometimes, however, people see your content and "bury" it; and yes, you can get voted down.

You shouldn't be at all surprised at being voted down if your article doesn't have any substance. Unfortunately, just like high school, there is a ruling-class clique with their own likes, dislikes, and prejudices. So being popular is not enough if you break the unwritten rules. And being unwritten, rules can change without notice. I cannot list them here, but each community has developed a character and bias that becomes obvious from observing the popular content and comment areas. When you are using social media, hang out and observe. Look at what becomes popular, what stays popular long-term, and what gets to the front page and then disappears just as fast.

EXERCISE

Monitor Popurls (`http://popurls.com`) to see which types of stories are the most popular right now across social bookmarking sites. Pay particular attention to headline structure and the latest trends.

At one time, what traditionally was popular on Digg were the more geeky topics. Although this is still somewhat true, the demographics are changing to include more of the general population—people from all walks of life. Articles featuring Apple, Linux, Xbox, and so on still make a strong showing. Duplicated information and overly commercial or overly self-promotional content do not do as well. Unlike the way it was in high school, the young male geeks rule the roost. The same old advice applies here as much as anywhere else: Consider your audience. What will they enjoy and get value from? What is the best way to deliver it? What do you need to do to appeal to them?

Driving Traffic with YouTube

YouTube is the dominant video sharing service where you can find video clips about everything from people falling over to the latest music promos. If something has been captured on video, you can be sure someone has shared it on YouTube, legally or otherwise.

Thanks to YouTube's huge popularity and its near monopoly, YouTube videos can attract a tremendous amount of attention. Just one example of this high visibility is Susan Boyle's *Britain's Got Talent* audition video, which at the time of writing has received over 83 million views! To put that into perspective, the actual television show from which the clip was recorded was considered a hit with just 12 million viewers at broadcast.

Dwarfing even this amazing view count is Justin Bieber (Figure 9-3), who used YouTube popularity to burst onto the world music scene and who's video was the first to break the 500 million views mark.

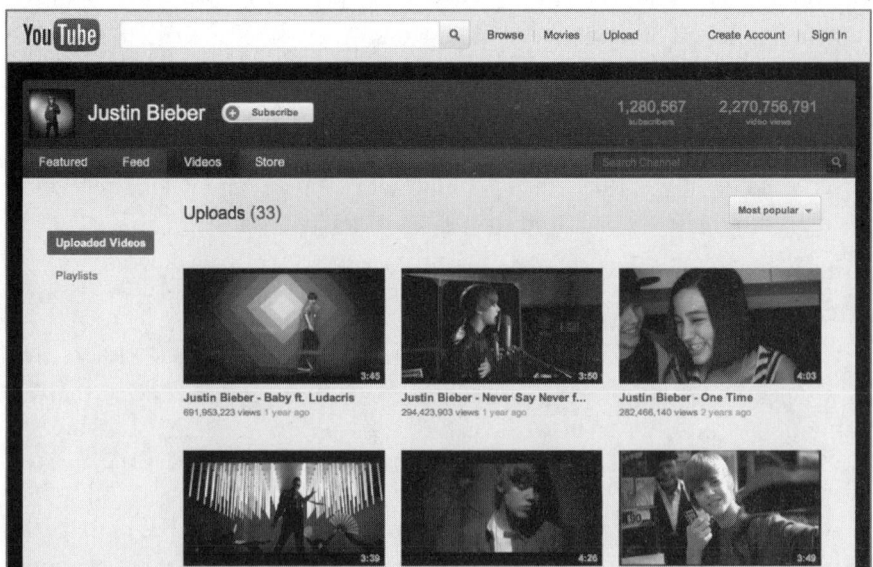

Figure 9-3: Justin Bieber on YouTube.

YouTube became such a dominant force that Google decided to stop trying to compete with it and bought it. Now YouTube is considered, by traffic, to be the Internet's second biggest search engine!

People search YouTube itself, but Google also gives YouTube content prominent placement in its search results. As you can see in Figure 9-4, if you search for **OK Go**, one of my favorite music video bands, Google places the Google News and YouTube results *above* the official OK Go website.

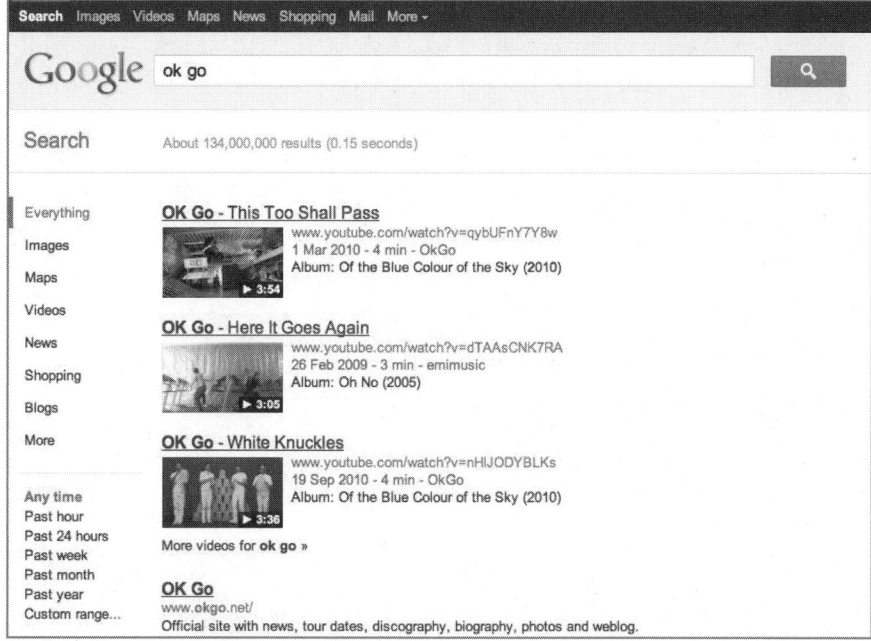

Figure 9-4: Google search results for OK Go.

This means that if you create a popular video with the name and description matching a sought-after search term, you are likely to attract a good portion of that traffic.

Another way to get more traffic through YouTube is to post your own video as a response to a popular video, as shown in Figure 9-5. It's also sometimes possible, with careful use of keywords in your video *meta data* (such as title, description, categories and tags), to have your video appear as a related video. The key difference between response and related videos are that *response videos* are recorded as a response to the original—kind of like a video comment. *Related videos* (shown in Figure 9-6) are other videos on similar topics or about the same subject matter. People checking out your video after they view the original video will drive up your traffic.

Figure 9-5: Posting a video response to attract attention.

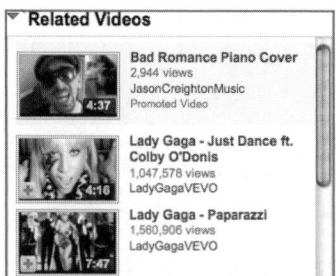

Figure 9-6: You can post a related video to grab some of the traffic a popular video is already attracting.

PROBLOGGER BLOG TIP: CREATE VIDEO EASILY

When most people think about creating video, they worry about needing technical expertise and expensive equipment. In fact, a YouTube video could easily be created with Camtasia (http://techsmith.com/camtasia.html) or other screen recording software, a cheap cell phone, or any other camera you happen to have available. Content is the important part; do not let a lack of Hollywood polish hold you back from creating.

Of course, so far all this traffic is taking place on YouTube and not benefiting your blog, so if you want to attract free traffic instead of spending money on YouTube advertising, you must ensure your video contains your blog web address. Include your address as a caption, watermark, or some kind of logo.

Be sure to place the link to your blog early in the YouTube description you write for your video (remember to include the prefix http://) so it does not get cut off after the More Info link.

Engaging Your Followers with Social Media

Social media is not just about generating traffic and getting attention. It can also be a key way to keep your audience interested and loyal, build your brand, and generate more networking opportunities.

Many people now look to Twitter and Facebook as not only places to keep track of their friends' latest activities, but also as a replacement for the traditional blog news feed. I am an example of this. At my peak, I subscribed to over 800 feeds in Google Reader, but now I check in on feeds only occasionally and rely on Twitter to deliver scoops in the niches I monitor.

LinkedIn is primarily designed for business networking, but LinkedIn groups also offer a chance to attract attention to your blog by connecting with others who share your interests. You could even create your own LinkedIn group to serve as an off-site discussion forum for your blog community.

No doubt many of your readers are using these social tools in a similar way, so having a presence and grabbing your brand names as Twitter account and Facebook vanity URLs is worthwhile.

In addition to sharing your latest headline, you need to interact with people and treat them as human beings rather than just a source of clicks. This means having conversations with them and sharing cool content no matter who created it or where you found it—it's not just about promoting your own articles.

Using Twitter

Twitter was originally a service that allowed you to provide *Status Updates* in the form of answering the question "What are you doing?" Although that was what it was originally intended for, it is now also used for the following:

- Chatting
- Getting help and answers
- Sharing links
- Getting news updates

- Making friends and networking
- Marketing
- Sending and receiving reminders
- Getting automated alerts
- Worshipping celebrities

Essentially it has become a combination of news feed, gossip hub, and catch-all text messaging system.

My own relationship with Twitter has mutated over time. At first I didn't get it; I thought it was a narcissistic waste of time. Then I gave it another chance, and fell in love with it. More important, though, I found it very useful.

Twitter is available from its website, via desktop software services that work with the system, and through a mobile web version for smart cell phones. You can connect your e-mail address, add your cell/mobile telephone number, and get text messages through the system.

The most popular Twitter client is currently TweetDeck (`www.tweetdeck.com`), which is available for Windows and Mac desktops, and also the iPhone.

About Twitter Messages ("Tweets")

Twitter messages are limited to 140 characters (a *character* is a press of the keyboard key—a letter of the alphabet, a space, a number, and so on). This keeps Twitter messages down to a size compatible with mobile networks.

You might think this size constraint is a bad thing, but once you get used to it, size is part of the appeal. Rather than pages of long, dreary monologues, you get a stream of snappy quips and informative nuggets. This shorter format of message style status updates and link sharing has led to this system being described as *micro-blogging*.

Whereas competitors allow you to share images and other media, Twitter messages are plain text, but you can share links just by typing them out in full. Long web addresses are automatically put through a web address shrinker, which conserves message space, but means you don't have the original web address as a clue as to where you'll land when you click them. If you are going to share a link, make sure you provide some descriptive context!

The service is still developing, both technologically (it is often down or unreliable) and in the way people use it.

The Three Great Non-Social Uses for Twitter

Twitter is not just for chatting with friends. It also provides real benefits for pro bloggers and businesses:

- **Inside scoop**—Follow the right industry insiders and you get the news before any other channel. I have gained access to information and beta accounts this way, and it can be very useful.
- **Traffic**—If you drop a link with a good intro, you can see click-throughs and comments as a result. You can track how many people clicked a certain link using a service such as bitly (`https://bitly.com`), which, in addition to shrinking the web address down to a more manageable size, also counts clicks, and identifies who shares the link. You get even more traffic and followers by being *retweeted*—a situation where other people share the message you posted—so encourage other people to share your links by retweeting theirs!
- **Networking**—I have stated many times how important networking is for bloggers. Twitter is a growing venue for this with fewer barriers and gatekeepers. Make sure you link to your Twitter account from your blog and from your e-mail signature to encourage people to follow you.

If you want more information about Twitter, check out Darren's Twitter blog, (`www.twitip.com`).

PROBLOGGER BLOG TIP:
USE TWITTER BUTTONS TO GET MORE TRAFFIC

Twitter users are always looking for cool content to share, so help them share your great stuff by using the official Twitter or TweetMeme (`http://tweetmeme.com`) button on your blog. You can either get code to copy and paste into your site, or use the WordPress plug-in, which does this for you automatically. Either method adds a button to your articles that counts how many times the post has been retweeted and allows visitors to click and retweet to their followers. Instant viral traffic opportunity! TweetMeme is only one option for adding a button, however; you can visit `http://wordpress.org/extend/plugins` to find some others.

EXERCISE

The best way to understand social networking is to get involved! Join the main social bookmarking sites and make some friends. Follow Chris and Darren on Twitter:

```
http://twitter.com/chrisgarrett
http://twitter.com/problogger
```

Using Facebook

Although Facebook started out as a very youthful environment, the demographic has widened now to include pretty much anyone. In fact, with a membership approaching a billion users, and millions of people logging in each day, Facebook now has a daily user base that dwarfs the combined population of entire *countries*.

Because you can find people with all kinds of interests and from all walks of life, it's certain that you can network your niche using Facebook. Search for the topic of interest and you are bound to find enough people who are interested in the same things as you to keep you busy for a long time.

Much like a blog, Facebook allows you to update your account with notes, videos, photographs, and links, plus, like Twitter, you can post short "status updates" to tell your friends what you are up to.

In addition to normal user profiles, anyone with a business or a huge fan base can also create Facebook Pages. With a normal user account, you are limited to 5,000 friends (unless you allow people to "subscribe" to your Facebook updates, in a similar way that people can subscribe to your blog), but with Facebook Pages there is no limit to the number of contacts you can gather to a page.

Darren's Digital Photography School uses Facebook pages to great effect (as shown in Figure 9-7), with upwards of 100,000 users and thousands of shares of stories.

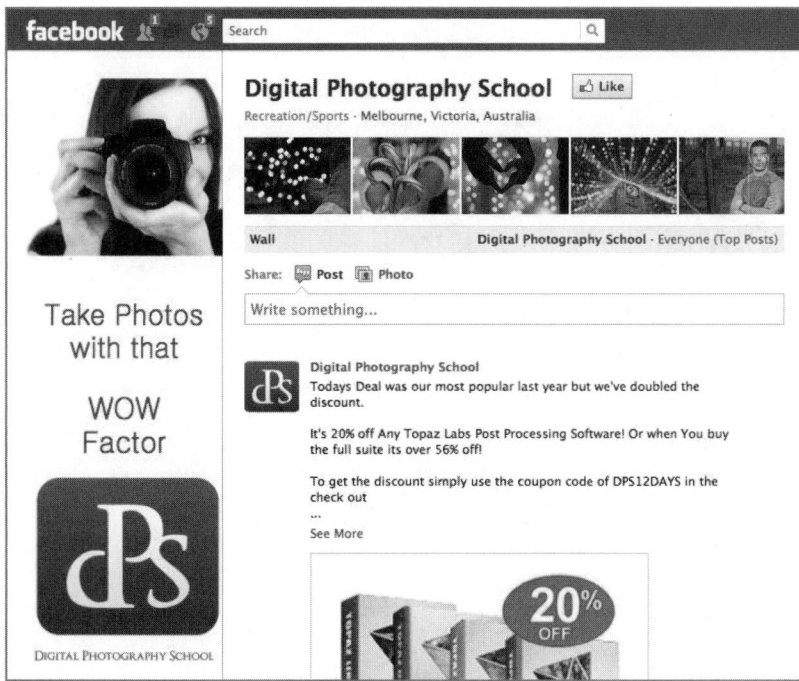

Figure 9-7: Digital Photography School on Facebook.

You can start a Facebook page by following these steps:

1. Scroll down to the bottom of the Facebook page and click Create a Page, the third link shown in Figure 9-8.

About · Advertising · Create a Page · Developers · Careers · Privacy · Terms · Help

                                 1● Chat (Offline)

Figure 9-8: Starting your Facebook page.

2. Select the type of page you want to create by clicking a category, shown in Figure 9-9. For example, as a test, I created a page for Apple gadget fans and called it "Apple Geeks" as shown in Figure 9-10. Because this page is about Apple-branded gadgets, I clicked it as a Brand or Product, and then selected Electronics from the drop-down menu on the next screen.

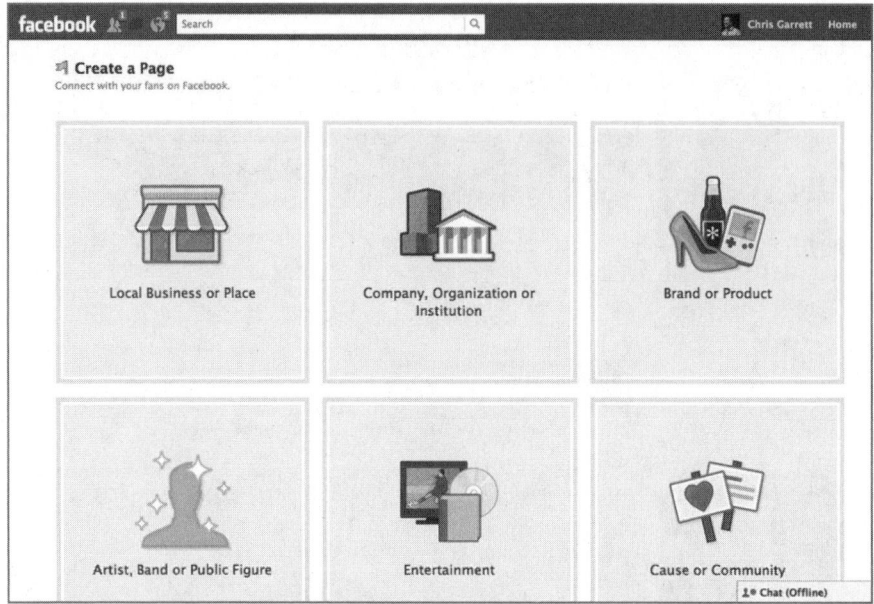

Figure 9-9: Selecting a category.

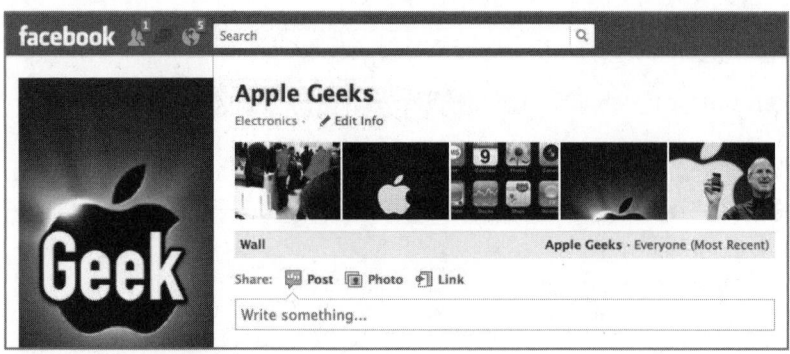

Figure 9-10: Apple Geeks—an example Facebook page.

3. Give your page a name, agree to the terms, and click the Get Started button (as shown in Figure 9-11).
4. Upload an image to represent the page.

Figure 9-11: Giving your page a name.

5. Invite contacts to the page.

6. Add some basic information (though you can click Skip and add these details later).

You can kick off your Facebook following by linking from your blog and from other social media accounts, such as your tweets.

Although you can use your connection to Facebook users to share offers, use affiliate links sparingly; the key to Facebook success is to share cool stuff and to encourage friends to share your stuff with their friends to get a viral effect going.

Using LinkedIn Groups

LinkedIn groups are a great place to find like-minded people and grow your network. They are also a great place to listen-in on discussions to find out what is important to the people who are active in your niche.

Just as you can use Facebook to grow a sense of community, you can create a LinkedIn group, if your audience is more likely to be engaged on LinkedIn. Who is more likely to connect using LinkedIn? Business people or people looking for professional or career progression would be good examples.

Why People Use LinkedIn

People are on LinkedIn to network and grow their connections, so they actively seek out people with whom they want to network via subject and industry. In addition, when people do connect, they often check out the groups to which their new contact belongs with the intent of following those links and becoming a member of those groups.

LinkedIn groups (see Figure 9-12) can help increase traffic to your blog; you attract people who want to discuss and network around your topic, and then you can lead them to your blog by doing the following:

- Putting your blog or website URL in the group profile.
- Adding your RSS feed to the News Section.
- Sending a weekly message to your group, much like a newsletter, and including related articles from your site.
- Adding a link to your site in the group welcome message.
- Creating a discussion that includes your link.

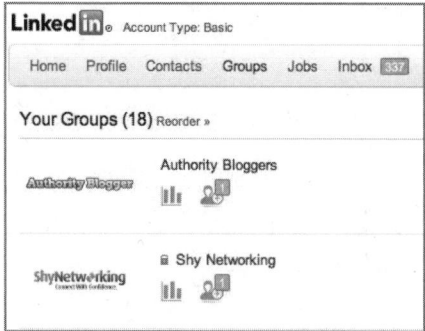

Figure 9-12: LinkedIn groups.

Joining LinkedIn

Joining LinkedIn is easy:

1. Go to the website (www.linkedin.com).
2. Add your first name, last name and e-mail address, and select a password. If you already have a Facebook account, click the Join Today link at the top navigation bar and then click the blue Sign up with Facebook button.
3. After setting up your password, you're taken to a page where you are asked where you live, and your employment information.
4. Before you can properly start using this new account you will need to click a confirmation link that will arrive via e-mail.

If you use a web based e-mail account such as Hotmail or Gmail, you're offered the opportunity to import your contacts to kick-start your LinkedIn connections. Of course, part of the power of LinkedIn is that you can manually search for contacts to whom you want to connect using the prominent search box. Some easy options to get started are to seek out past colleagues, classmates, and customers.

Creating a LinkedIn Group

My recommendation before starting your own group is to use the LinkedIn groups directory or look through your own contacts to see if they are members of any groups, then join a few groups, and learn how these groups operate as a member. This way you can work out if LinkedIn groups are for you and get a good idea of how they are used in your niche or industry.

To start a group, follow these steps:

1. In LinkedIn, click Groups ⇨ Create a Group. You'll be presented with the form in Figure 9-13, asking for group details as well as information, which LinkedIn uses to describe your group in the LinkedIn groups directory.

Figure 9-13: Creating LinkedIn groups.

2. You have several options to keep your management tasks down to a minimum, including keeping your group out of the public directory altogether and requiring your permission for anyone to join.

NOTE

Obviously these options should be weighed against the fact that you will restrict your membership growth if you make it too invisible or restrictive!

PROBLOGGER BLOG TIP:
OBSERVE AND GROW YOUR SOCIAL MEDIA ENGAGEMENT

Audience engagement is vital in social media just as it is with your blog. Having dozens of friends and fans is nice, but you need them to care about what you have to say in order to gain the real benefits. The first step is to *listen*. Observe how your favorite social media users behave to get ideas for what might work to increase and maintain social media engagement with your contacts.

Summary

Social media can be fun and can deliver enormous benefits to you and your blog, from increased traffic through to greater opportunities and income. But if you are not careful, it can soak up a great deal of your time, killing your productivity, especially if you get absorbed in Facebook, LinkedIn, and Twitter chit-chat or watch hour after hour of funny YouTube videos. If you work social media into your blogging schedule consciously, though, and learn what works for you, your blog and social media accounts can complement and expand each other in fantastic and unexpected ways.

10 Secrets of Successful Blogs

If you have read this far, it is safe to assume you would like to be successful in your blogging. In addition to reading and researching as much as you can about the techniques and tactics involved in creating a popular and profitable blog, a great way to do well in any endeavor is to learn from the best examples.

You have an advantage today that the pioneers did not. The bloggers who have come before you have made many of the mistakes and learned what works, saving you the trouble! This chapter takes a look at some example blogs and bloggers to see how they have achieved success in blogging in their own ways.

About Success in Blogging

What do we mean by "success"? For each blogger it's something different. It could be fame, income, sales, size of audience, and so on. Although Darren and I consider ourselves professional bloggers, we both arrived at it through our own routes and tactics. We earn money in different ways and have different goals. When you look at the other bloggers in this chapter, you can see how diverse professional blogging really is.

Before embarking on a blogging project, it is worth discovering what success would mean to you.

EXERCISE

Do you have a clear idea about what you want to achieve with your blogging? Take a moment to analyze your motivations; knowing what you hope to get out of blogging helps you focus your efforts on the things that will make it happen.

Analyzing Top Blogs

When we looked at the top blogs and bloggers around us, we found they had certain elements in common between them, regardless of niche, monetization method, and motivation. In particular, age, posting frequency, and social media all seem to focus heavily in their success.

What's the Average Blog Age?

Darren did some research a while back and discovered that the average age of most successful blogs was 33.8 months. The first lesson to take away is that blogging is a long-term thing, but it is possible to have success much faster—with luck and a lot of hard work.

What's the Posting Frequency?

In most analyses of top blogs, a noted trend is that many successful bloggers post more than the rest, especially when they are in the initial phases of their blog growth. Usually they post many short posts a day rather than attempt to create many in-depth articles. There seems a definite correlation between success and posting frequency.

It does make sense; the more posts you publish, the more chance for links and for readers to notice you. Search engines also like to see lots of fresh content, feeding as they do on text.

This can cause dismay for bloggers who struggle to keep pace. What you have to keep in mind is that most of the top blogs are written by multiple authors. Darren has this kind of output on ProBlogger—mixing in both guest content and content from Darren himself. Readers have come to expect this kind of author mix and schedule.

Team blogs can easily keep up a high post rate, and often need to if they are in rapidly changing news niches, such as TechCrunch (http://techcrunch.com).

Lately, though, there has been a backlash against too high a posting frequency, with bloggers and readers both expressing a preference for fewer, better-written, and well-thought-out articles. In many surveys, the answer to the question of why readers unsubscribe, "posting too often" usually ranks high. This was not so much a problem when the emphasis was on reading via Feedreader software, but when you are subscribing via e-mail, your tolerance level for how much content is sent to you can be very different.

Now, most bloggers take a middle-ground approach—maybe posting once a day, and supplementing their own output with guest writers. Copyblogger (`www.copyblogger.com`) is a good example; articles are written by a combination of in-house writers and regular guest writers almost daily, with the occasional one-off guest post.

On my blog, `chrisg.com`, I post when I have something useful to share, and aim for a "quality over quantity" approach. In fact, it might be weeks between postings (not that I would recommend this as a posting schedule!), especially when I am loaded up with coaching and consulting work. My readers are OK with this because they understand I am not producing a "magazine"-style blog and I do not post breaking news, so there is no pressure to maintain a frequent posting schedule.

EXERCISE

How often do your favorite blogs update? Are any of them updating a little too often? Do you find yourself skipping or missing posts? Do you look forward to the next post from a certain blog?

How Does Social Media Factor In?

A couple of years ago, Glen Allsopp worked out that the Top 100 blogs achieved front-page status on Digg (`http://digg.com`) 8,000 times between them. Most surprising was that the top five blogs did so 3,600 times between them—45 percent of the total for the whole list.

Clearly, this was back when Digg was at its peak of success and when visibility on Digg was a major source of traffic; still, this does show that the top blogs do well in social media. It's impossible without further analysis to know if this is correlation or causation, but it is an interesting statistic nevertheless.

The unfortunate consequence of this social media/blog connection is that many people observe the social media sharing and output on the big sites and think that to achieve a large blog audience, they must pound social media with their messages. In fact, it's better to contribute and join social media as a human being rather than use it as yet another place to push your links.

Personally, I think it works both ways; a social media sites' popularity is both a contributor and a consequence of blog success and is a tactic I encourage in all the blogs for which I write.

The aim is to maintain a good ratio between conversation, sharing good content from third parties (including links that you find and re-sharing what your network sends you), and posting your own links.

How Do Blogs Make Revenue?

The vast majority of successful blogs show some form of advertising, but with less than a quarter using Google AdSense. This trend continues—fewer and fewer of the top sites use AdSense apart from an "advertiser of last resort" type approach.

It is worth noting that when blogs get to this sort of scale, they have the traffic and audience to demand excellent deals, even from Google.

Many of the top blogs now hire ad salespeople, use the services of specialist ad companies—such as Federated Media Publishing (`www.federatedmedia.net`)—or are part of blog networks. At a certain size, a blog becomes a "media business" by any definition, so it tends to work that way, complete with chief executives, editors, and writers.

That said, a good many of the blogs that used to rely on advertising now increasingly use indirect methods, from affiliate partnerships through to launching their own products and services. For example, in my opinion, Copyblogger has transitioned from a blog to becoming a software and education company.

What's the Blog Language?

You might expect English to dominate blogging overall, but in terms of volume, Japanese takes the top spot with 37 percent, and English is second with 36 percent. When it comes to the Top 100, though, 80 percent are written in English.

> **PROBLOGGER BLOG TIP: NON-ENGLISH GROWTH**
>
> Expect to see a lot of growth of non-English blogs in coming years. Blogging is becoming increasingly popular around the world. If you can afford it or can find a linguist partner, it would be well worth having your articles translated.

Learning from Niche Blogs

We have already recommended in this book that you at least start out blogging in a niche. First off, a *niche blog* would be considered a blog that focuses on a specific topic that has appeal to a particular group of enthusiasts. Its traffic is generally smaller than a mainstream blog, but it's steady and can often grow a large following. If you have a lot of passion about a specific area, whether that be photography, gardening, farming, or spelunking, a niche blog may be the best starting point for you.

What Are Some Successful Niche Blogs?

The bloggers in the following list have made their blogs so highly focused and so identified with their topic that they are the leaders and standard-bearers for their chosen topic:

- **Strobist** (`http://strobist.blogspot.com`)—A photography blog that, rather than focus on the whole topic of photography, went super-niche and wrote about using small, inexpensive flashes. Now David Hobby has been able to take a leave of absence from his job as a photojournalist and is earning money by running workshops and developing his own range of training products.
- **Copyblogger** (`www.copyblogger.com`)—Lots of bloggers write about blogging; Brian Clark decided to start a blog about the art and techniques of writing, initially writing on his own and then bringing on guest writers (Chris included) and other partners. Copyblogger Media is now not only the most-popular blog on the subject, but also, through growth and merger, is a multimillion dollar enterprise with a whole suite of software, services, and products.
- **Lifehacker** (`http://lifehacker.com`)—Productivity is a massive subject online, and Lifehacker is probably the best known. Rather than just write about productivity in general, Lifehacker approaches the subject with a techie slant, which the audience really enjoys.
- **TheBudgetFashionista** (`www.thebudgetfashionista.com`)—Many bloggers have written about fashion. Kathryn Finney took the niche and decided to write a blog for real women with real incomes, in a warm and friendly style. It has really worked; the blog is successful, has spawned

a spin-off book, and has put Kathryn in the spotlight, with media and TV appearances on NBC, CNN, and Fox.

PROBLOGGER BLOG TIP: SPOT AND ANALYZE SUCCESS

Watching out for the lessons that are all around you is a great habit to get into. You can learn from the success of others in some surprising ways. It is not just about looking at fellow bloggers—read biographies or analyze your favorite celebrity or television show. Knowing how people got where they are helps you develop a "success" mindset.

Lessons from Niche Bloggers

So, what are the lessons that you should take away from studying successful niche blogs? They have to do with defining a clear identity, building towards a clear direction, and setting goals. The following steps walk you through how to start your own successful blog based on our experience:

1. **Identify an underserved niche.** It is very difficult to get a photography blog noticed in today's blogosphere. David Hobby chose a micro-niche, a niche of a niche, and served it comprehensively with his Strobist blog. Take it easy on yourself, and choose a niche where you can make a difference.

2. **Define your blog's mission and articulate it in a benefits-led way.** If a reader sees your blog's mission and thinks "so what?" you have failed. Be sure your blog's mission helps the reader. For chrisg.com, my mission is to "help people grow a profitable business by sharing their knowledge and experience with an audience of people who know, like and trust them."

3. **Decide if you want to be a media business or if your blog is for *marketing* your business.** This decision might not seem important, but it is best to know which type of business your blog is meant to support because it will define everything, from the monetization methods you employ to what your audience expects and requires from you in terms of content and frequency of output.

4. **Own your mission and stay focused.** It would be so easy for any of these blogs to see their growing audience as permission to cover anything they like. Once in a while they can get away with it—kind of like a pop star deciding to release a swing album. Too much, though, and the valuable and unique quality that attracted readers could go away.

5. **Make sure you stand out.** This is not about just being different, but being different in a way that speaks to your most-wanted target reader in a worthwhile and valuable tone.

EXERCISE

Out of all the blogs you have seen or read, which would you categorize as niche and which have more general appeal? Do these blogs change approach depending on their category?

Learning from Top Blogs

Although it's interesting to look at the Top 100 biggest blogs, few similarities actually exist between them once you get past the factors detailed in the previous section. To learn more, you need to look at some individual blogs.

ProBlogger

It's only appropriate to start with ProBlogger, seeing as pro blogging is what this book is all about!

ProBlogger's History and Mission

We have already covered the history of Darren's blog in this book—both in the book's introduction and, in part, throughout the rest of this book—so no need to repeat it here. Suffice to say that ProBlogger is the blog people think of when they think about making money from blogging.

Lessons from ProBlogger

How did Darren make his blog the first choice among bloggers? Of course, this didn't happen overnight, or easily for that matter. It was a long process of testing, tweaking, and hard work. We can benefit from what he learned during this hard-won experience, however!

Darren observed the following lessons:

- **Be first**—There was a time when it was easy to have first-mover advantage. Of course, that was when hardly anyone had the foresight to start anything other than a personal diary blog. There are thousands of blogs now on every subject—how can you be first? Be different. Find a gap and fill it. Demonstrate the benefit of your unique take.

- **Have staying power**—It's tempting to hear of six-figure incomes and become despondent at your own meager Google check. Darren didn't get there overnight either. Some of his biggest mistakes in blogging have been quitting, chopping, and changing. Don't make his mistakes; learn from Darren. Stick with it!
- **Show off your best stuff and follow through**—Put your popular stuff right up front where people can see it. When you visit ProBlogger, you are not lost for things to read. After people read your post, do they know where they can go next? Make it easy for people to take the next step with links and suggested next-actions.
- **Community counts**—Great content is important, but when it is combined with a vibrant community, that is when your blog will really take off. For more on building a community that sticks, see Chapter 8.
- **Test and research**—Blogging is a moving target. Determining what tactics work and what don't takes research, experimentation, testing, and discussion. Over the years, Darren experimented with new developments from MyBlogLog (now defunct) to Chitika (`http://chitika.com`). Make sure you keep up with the times. Obviously the best place to keep up-to-date with blogging news and developments is Problogger, but you should also make sure you follow the social media accounts of well-connected industry figures and subscribe to the news blogs that cover your own niche.
- **Privacy**—Don't reveal too much personal information. You will need to draw your own lines for what you will and will not make public, but remember once that information is revealed there is no way to remove it completely from the Internet. For example, Darren does not use his children's first names in articles. Decide what you are going to keep private, and make it stay that way.
- **Stay positive**—I don't think I have ever seen Darren go off on a rant. This builds up a tremendous amount of goodwill. You will never hear a bad word said about him. Blogging success is as much about networking as it is good writing. What are people thinking and saying about you?
- **Get help**—Darren has a whole team of paid and volunteer helpers, and partners on various projects. One person cannot keep such a business empire humming while maintaining a comfortable level of family sanity; delegating allows Darren to fill in the blanks of his expertise and experience.

EXERCISE

Log in to the Problogger Book Member Download Area to catch up with more case studies and interviews with successful bloggers:

```
http://probloggerbook.com/bonus/
```

If you have not already, sign up here (make sure you type the address exactly as shown):

```
http://probloggerbook.com/?/register/bonus
```

TechCrunch

TechCrunch (Figure 10-1) is the most popular tech news site. Mike Arrington took the blog from nowhere to a site that can make or break tech startups. He built up a staff of writers spread around the globe, so there is almost 24-hour coverage. Recently, the site was acquired by AOL, and Mike moved on to new pastures.

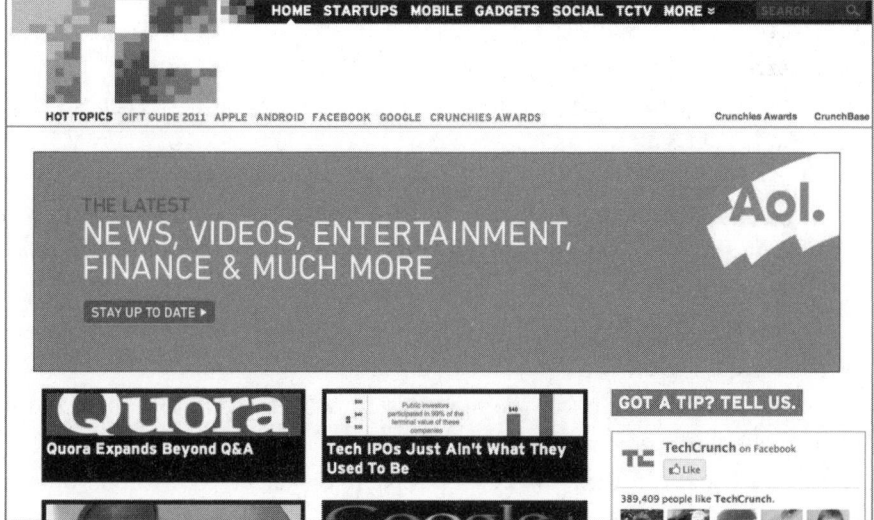

Figure 10-1: TechCrunch.

TechCrunch's History and Mission

According to Wikipedia, TechCrunch was launched in 2005, at which point it made a total of $200,000 a month in revenue. Now with over three million regular readers and a new owner, I am sure that has increased despite the global advertising downturn. Advertisers benefit from both the massive amount of traffic the blog generates and awareness from the specific target audience.

Scoops made TechCrunch the draw that it is now. Having a direct line to insider gossip means TechCrunch breaks the news and everyone else has to follow. This is vital for a news site in terms of building authority and credibility. Opinions and editorials are great, but people universally sit up and take notice of big news along with a description of how that news affects their industry. Combining both is a magic formula.

You could say TechCrunch can base its success on getting to the news first, but it also benefits from a self-fulfilling cycle; everyone reads TechCrunch, so people now come to TechCrunch first with stories, which get lots of coverage, which means everyone reads TechCrunch!

In addition to the blogs, TechCrunch also launched TechCrunch20, a conference that showcases startups and their products and services—yet another way they build awareness, credibility, and revenue.

Lessons from TechCrunch

With its knack of getting the story first and its vast following, the lessons you can learn from TechCrunch are:

- **Break news**—Get news early, and post it fast.
- **Build a network**—Get to know all the movers and shakers in your niche.
- **Get big**—Scale matters in news; the more people with their ears to the ground, the more news you can dish out.
- **Know your worth**—As you grow, do not be too shy to ask for more money from advertisers.
- **Don't just report; analyze**—News gets recycled, even when you are the one to break it (and being the one to break news gets harder and harder), so provide value above and beyond the headline—supply context and insight.

Scobleizer

Robert Scoble is one of the most well-known veteran bloggers and probably the best example I can give of an employee blogger. Although he has his own popular Scobleizer blog (http://scobleizer.com, shown in Figure 10-2), his earnings mainly come from the people who employ him as a blogging personality.

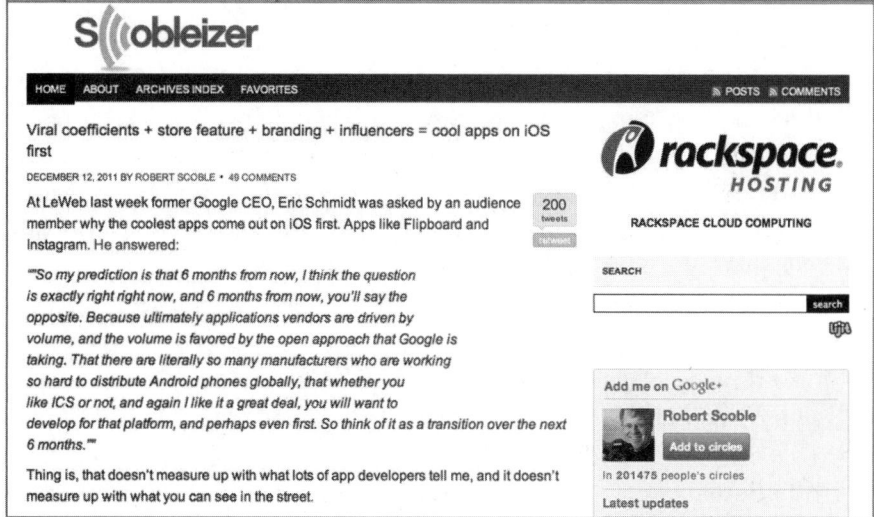

Figure 10-2: Scobleizer.

Scobleizer's History and Mission

Most people first heard of Robert when he worked for Microsoft as an evangelist. His most recent gig is working with the web hosting company, Rackspace (www.rackspace.com).

His claim to fame is his connections; he seems to know all the big names personally. This powerful address book has been at the core of his blogging career, especially with his videos, in which he goes out and interviews interesting people from the industry.

Though he obviously makes good use of his high-profile connections, he is a massive networker online, too, having a massive following on Twitter and a huge number of Facebook friends.

Lessons from Robert Scoble

Obviously, Robert's secret stems from his efficient use of contacts and quick reactions. With his knack of getting the inside scoop first and his vast following, the lessons you can learn from Robert are:

- **Network**—Be a hub and a connector. Robert seems to spend as much time having lunches with movers and shakers as he does blogging and speaking. Blogging is as much about relationships as it is writing. To succeed, you need great content, of course, but it also helps to be well connected.

- **Links should be unique and interesting**—Link to great stuff that others haven't noticed. One of the great things about Robert's sharing is that it doesn't just replicate the popular social media stories—he has his own sources. If you are linking out to the same old stuff, people won't need your feed cluttering up their stream. Find fresh and exciting new stuff, though, and your readers will reward you.

- **Nobody is perfect**—Many bloggers try to project an image of perfection. Admit when you are wrong; there is no harm in it. In fact, it could do you a world of good. I believe part of Robert's success in helping Microsoft repair its relationship with the public was Robert's willingness to admit when mistakes had been made, personally or by the company. This builds trust.

- **Little and often**—Some days Scoble posts a lot. Darren has commented a couple of times about the dangers of misjudging posting frequency. Some readers are put off by too much content too fast. I believe it works for Robert because he posts little and often. Small, bite-sized, 15-second posts work well.

- **Adopt early**—Robert is the ultimate early adopter, which can cause its own problems and sometimes wasted effort (especially when the next-big-thing turns out to be a dud), but he is always in the know and always there in the right place and at the right time as far as the growth of social Internet services is concerned.

EXERCISE

Robert Scoble owes a large part of his success to his networking skills and huge network of contacts. To Robert, it's not just about how his network is valuable but also how these contacts value Robert as part of their own networks. Identify what you can offer the contacts you make then plan how you're going to grow your network starting today.

The 4-Hour Workweek

Timothy Ferriss was nominated as one of Fast Company's "Most Innovative Business People of 2007." He's the author of the #1 *New York Times*, *Wall Street Journal*, and *BusinessWeek* bestseller, *The 4-Hour Workweek*, which has been translated into 33 languages.

Tim Ferriss exploded onto the scene in 2007, seemingly from nowhere. His impact was due to a killer blog (Figure 10-3) and book-launch combination. Both the blog and book mutually fueled the buzz, meaning at the time there were few bloggers who hadn't at least heard about him.

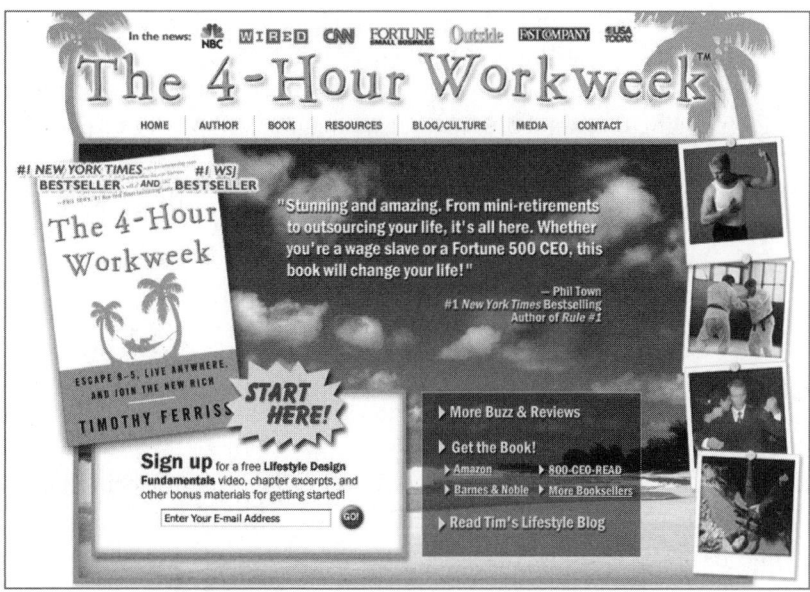

Figure 10-3: The 4-Hour Work Week blog.

The 4-Hour Workweek's History and Mission

Tim's book aims to show readers how to have the life they want while making the money they need to sustain their lifestyle. From his website, www.fourhourworkweek.com, his mission is to:

> Forget the old concept of retirement and the rest of the deferred-life plan—there is no need to wait and every reason not to. Whether your dream is escaping the rat race, high-end world travel, monthly five-figure income with zero management, or just living more and working less, this book is the blueprint.

Lessons from Tim Ferriss

Tim Ferriss' success comes from the powerful combination blog and book, as well as the eternally interesting story of obtaining sought-after life goals, freedom and wealth. From Tim's work we learn the following:

- **Craft your posts**—Tim does not post several times a day and, in fact, there can be several days between posts. He explained in a ProBlogger interview that this allows him to more carefully craft his articles and tweak his headlines; it also allows time for comments to accumulate.
- **Say what you mean**—Some of his posts are intentionally controversial. He says top stories almost always polarize people, so he tries to take a strong stand on one side or the other of an issue.
- **Cover topics that anyone can comment on**—Tim suggests that you consider blogging on subjects that you can imagine allowing your parents, siblings, or friends to share.
- **Focus on a beneficial outcome**—"4-hour workweek" and "4-hour body" have explicit benefits that capture attention. It is obvious what you are going to get and why you would care.

PopCrunch

No relation to TechCrunch, PopCrunch (www.popcrunch.com, shown in Figure 10-4) is a blog in the super-competitive celebrity niche, bringing all the celebrity gossip together in an online version of the celebrity magazines you see in the supermarket newsstands.

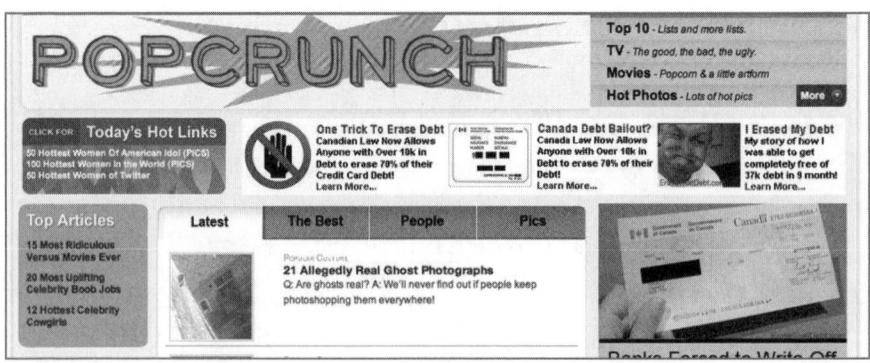

Figure 10-4: PopCrunch.

PopCrunch's Mission

The key to PopCrunch, just like TechCrunch, is getting the story out first. Revenue for the blog all comes from leveraging its traffic with advertising. Whereas other blogs use traffic as a draw for advertisers along with branding and reputation benefits, PopCrunch, in the main, sells impression-based CPM ads, meaning the more page views it gets, the more money it makes. This pays off because PopCrunch clears a good five-figure income each and every month—and much more when it manages to scoop a big story.

As you can imagine, PopCrunch uses every traffic trick in the book, from SEO to really working the social media sites.

Learning the scale lessons of TechCrunch, Ryan Caldwell, PopCrunch's founder, prides himself on putting every cent of revenue back into the blog—from hiring help through to technology—in order to grow.

Lessons from PopCrunch

PopCrunch is full of clickable lists that immediately catch your attention, most of them of the "Top 10" nature. A visit to his full-of-eye-candy blog can satisfy even the most ardent of celeb junkies. What can you learn from this?

- **Learn and implement**—Do your research; find out what works; use what you learn from other niches in your own.
- **Use mix media**—Try video, try audio; see what your audience reacts to.
- **Promote**—Yes, content is king, but who will notice anything without the traffic? Push the traffic any way you can. Only when you really reach the top can you stop promoting completely.
- **Reinvest**—If you want to grow and keep growing, eventually you are going to reach the limits of what one person can do. There will be work you can't do because of time or ability, or repetitive work that you would rather not have to do or *should* not do. This means, like Ryan has done, reinvesting the income from your blog back into your business to attract helping hands, and building systems to automate the rest.
- **Diversify**—Although PopCrunch is very much single-minded, to the point of being dangerously dependent on one form of monetization and only a couple of traffic methods, Ryan's company is well diversified across niches and business models.

> **EXERCISE**
>
> Look around your niche and your favorite blogs. Look closely to see how they operate their business. How big is their team? Where does their content, revenue and traffic come from? Are they experimenting or doing anything out of the norm? What can you learn from each of the blogs you find?

The Key to Blogging Success: Bloggers Tell Us Their Success Secrets

In the previous section, we analyzed some of the top money-making blogs in depth, but we felt this chapter wouldn't be complete without getting some outside insights and observations. For this new edition of the book, I thought I would ask some successful blogging friends what they thought was the secret to blogging success. The following list contains their answers.

- **Chris Brogan** (www.chrisbrogan.com)—"It's simple to me. Be helpful. This is what set me apart from everyone else. . .I believe more bloggers have to go beyond writing their opinion and follow that opinion up with something actionable."

- **Daniel Scocco** (www.dailyblogtips.com)—"First of all, you need to pick your niche/topic wisely. Sure, it must be something you are interested in ([or] else you would burn out rather quickly), but it must be something that a significant number of people will find interesting as well. If you decide to blog about the qualities of the Sri Lanka mango tree, for instance, it will be very hard to find readers for your blog. In other words, find a compromise between your interests and topics that are somewhat popular.

  "Second, make sure your content will add value to the life of your readers, [or] else they will have no reason to visit your blog (let alone to return frequently, which is your goal). By value I mean entertaining them if you have a humor blog, helping them save money if you have a personal finance one, informing them about the latest and best mobile phones if you have a gadget blog and so on.

"Third, you need to be persistent and promote your blog. Ever heard the motto 'if you build it they will come'? Well, it doesn't work like this with blogs and websites—at least not initially. In the beginning, you'll hardly have any readers, so whenever you publish a great post, you'll need to work your arse off promoting it around the web (e.g. Facebook, Twitter, other blogs, etc.)."

- **Lewis Howes** (www.lewishowes.com)—"I think you need to stand for something and have a clear focus. If it's an average blog with no stance, you won't go far and your readers will be average as well. Figure out a niche early on, and dominate that niche...then you can expand and grow from there."

- **Mary Jaksch** (http://alistbloggingbootcamps.com)—"To be successful, a blog needs to be created around the needs of the readers. This means that the blog topic is attractive to readers, and that the design reflects the blog's core message.

  "If you want your blog to be successful, each blog post needs to be insanely useful. The whole reader experience needs to be user-friendly. This means that posts are scannable, that it's easy to find your way around the blog, and that the blogger is a real person with a real presence.

  "Blogs that go nowhere generally revolve around the ME-tape in the blogger's head: 'I, me, mine, myself.'"

Summary

Looking at the various writing styles, promotion tactics, and ways people approach earning from their blogging, you can tell there is an approach out there to suit anybody. You have seen a famous employee blogger, bloggers who write books, people who earn from advertising, and those who make money from courses. It is clear there is no single "right way"; success is limited only by your imagination.

Though you can derive a great deal of pleasure from the activity of blogging, for most people blogging is a means to an end. As you have seen in this chapter, how you approach it can be as diverse as the people who take part. We hope you can find some ideas and inspiration from these successful bloggers' stories.

11 Creating Something Worthwhile

So you have started a blog. You might want to make money from it, or you might have some other goal in mind. You are in it for your own goals or you want to spread your ideas. This is all well and good, but to actually achieve those goals, you have to network, gather readers, build traffic, and build links. Basically, to achieve your goals you have to serve an audience.

What does "serve an audience" mean? Rather than prioritize your advertising, affiliates, and sales, you have to give readers what they want or need. It means making something useful, something that people will want to talk about (favorably).

This is the real trick, the difference between winning and losing, and the subject of this chapter.

Knowing Your Audience

Before you can serve an audience, you need to know who they are! You need to really understand your readers, both through research and planning before you launch, and through talking to them after you launch.

If you are already a member of the community in which you are working, you will have an advantage here; however, you still need to consider who your target readers will be and what they would like to see. Consider the following:

- What are they called?
- Who do they think they are?
- Who are they really?
- Who do they want to be?
- Who do they like?

- Who don't they like?
- Who is their peer group?
- Who do they not identify with?
- What are their beliefs?
- Where do they live?
- Where do they work?
- Where do they learn?
- Where do they want to be?
- What are their needs?
- How old are they?
- How youthful do they act?
- How conservative are they?
- What are their driving ambitions?
- What are their wants and needs?
- What are their pleasures?
- What are their pains?
- What do they love?
- What do they hate?

To really appeal to an audience, you have to go beyond "nice," "ok," and "good enough." Ask yourself how you can take your blog to the next level, to be not just merely adequate, but must-have. Not just interesting, but *compelling*.

EXERCISE

Create *pen portraits* for your reader group. This means writing down everything you know about them, and describing them as well as you can so you have a fully formed impression of what they are like and what will please them. Once you have a good idea of who you are targeting, try to brainstorm content ideas that they would absolutely *love*.

Being Remarkable

Thanks to Seth Godin and his books, in particular *Purple Cow*, many bloggers know and understand the need to be "remarkable." Remarkable is what makes ideas spread. Essentially, you need your content to be good enough that people "remark" on it to others. The problem is that being aware of the need is not the same as putting it into practice. Take these points, for example:

- **Attention is not compelling**—Stripping naked or shouting "fire" gets you noticed, but is not valuable. Forget attention seeking and create value.
- **Be radical**—Half-measures won't do. People only remember the biggest, fastest, richest, easiest, hardest, most expensive, cheapest, and whatever superlative you can think of.
- **It's not fashion**—Fashion is fleeting. It is following a bandwagon; if it is already being talked about, you are already too late.
- **People should care**—If people do not love it or hate it, then you need to push harder. "Like" is not remarkable; it should cause passion.

NOTE

This is not about *you*. This is about your reader; leave your ego out of it. One of the biggest mistakes bloggers make is being all me-me-me.

If you manage to make something remarkable, your task of spreading your message and promoting your blog will be so much easier. A successful blog is all about having your brand spread far and wide.

EXERCISE

Seth Godin tells us to look out for *purple cows*. Think of things in your life that are remarkable. What lifts them above being "average," "normal," or "nice"? When was the last time you told someone else about a blog or article you happened across?

What Causes Ideas to Spread?

If you think about the last time you told someone something you heard, it will likely have been the following:

- **Different/New**—People do not talk about things that are usual and ordinary. People take notice of things that are new or different. English

Cut (www.englishcut.com) was the first blog about men's suits that anyone had heard of; start a similar blog like that today, and nobody will take notice.

- **Newsworthy**—News is probably the biggest type of information to spread, but that doesn't always mean it is new or different. In some cases it is the nature of the story that helps it spread. Sometimes ordinary things can become news if they happen to someone important.

- **Easy to understand**—If you have to puzzle over something before you get it, it will in most cases seem like too much effort, even if you think it is important in some way. Simplify your message, and it will spread more effectively.

- **Easy to remember**—How will people spread your ideas if they can't remember them? It's just like jokes; some of us have a talent for remembering and telling them, but even though I love to listen to comedians tell complex stories, I can recall and retell only the most basic.

- **Easy to communicate**—Politicians use sound bites for good reason; they are easy to remember and communicate. Make it easy to get the point across. Provide "send to friend" and bookmarking features.

- **Beneficial**—Will your story help someone? Will it make them laugh? What will the sender and recipient gain? The more beneficial, the more it will spread; self-interest almost always comes into play.

- **Emotion**—There is a good reason why human-interest stories do well. We are hard-wired to be interested in people, and in particular, the underlying emotion behind a story. The more touched or emotionally impacted they are, the more likely people are to respond, remember, and share (Figure 11-1).

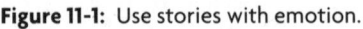

Moving the Fear Line

Imagine being under water, upside down, trapped in your Kayak.

You can feel your lungs burning because you didn't have time to grab a full breath ... though you are surprising yourself how long you are managing to force yourself from gasping down a lung full of water ...

All you can hear is your heart pounding.

Scary?

I don't need to imagine what that would be like because I can remember in vivid detail. In fact I have had nightmares about it.

My overriding thought was drowning myself was a heck of a way to celebrate my birthday!

Figure 11-1: Use stories with emotion.

EXERCISE

For a week, make a mental note of every piece of news and gossip you come across. Try to determine how the piece of information was transmitted to you, and which ones you take note of or share and which ones "wither on the vine."

Making Your Blog Useful

Useful blogs can be difficult to define, but we can all spot one. Spend any meaningful time in the company of a blog-reading tool, and we become masters at it. We decide the fate of a feed in an instant sometimes, like cruel judges on some reality-TV talent contest. But the question is: What defines those blogs that make it? Why are some blogs useful and others a waste of time?

Ask yourself what your favorite blogs have in common. Think of your absolute, number-one, favorite blog in the world. For Darren it is Lifehacker. For me, it is Scott Adams' Dilbert blog (www.dilbert.com/blog).

Why do you like the blog that you've identified? What keeps you going back so often?

Scott Adams is an incredibly witty guy, but he also makes me think. I go to his blog to escape, to think about something other than work. With Lifehacker there are a few things Darren enjoys, but the main factor is that it's a blog that regularly provides life-enhancing tips.

In general, your audience wants to move toward or away from something. They may want to escape a situation or pain, avoid future problems, or bring something pleasurable or beneficial into their lives.

The most popular topics often come down to relationships (dating, family, parenting), health (diet, fitness), and money (business, investing). Your challenge is presenting the required information in a useful way that also makes your content stand out from the crowd. Take a look at how you can do that in the next few sections.

Useful-Blog Properties

We'll all have different answers to what makes a blog useful, but if we gathered the properties of those favorite blogs together, I expect we could group the answers into one or more of the following categories:

- **Entertaining**—Blogs are increasingly being used as entertainment. People are going to them for laughs, gossip, and fun conversation. You can turn an ordinarily dry topic into a more uniquely entertaining experience by bringing out some of your own personality and sharing humorous anecdotes from your own experience.
- **Educational**—Some blog readers are primarily interested in learning something new about a given topic.
- **Informative**—Many successful blogs are built on the thirst that some people have to be informed on an issue, product, or topic.
- **Thoughtful**—Some blog readers want a place where they can open their minds to new viewpoints, and have a good, old-fashioned dialogue, debate, or even a fight over an issue.
- **Breaking news**—Many blog readers just want to be kept up-to-date in a field.
- **Community**—Some very successful blogs tap into the need that people have to connect and belong. Quite often the topic is secondary to these connections.

Each blog has the potential to be "useful," and each successful blog will approach it in its own way, perhaps using a combination of the preceding factors.

When you know your readers, you can really help them solve their problems and achieve their goals. Your content should get your readers one step closer to where they want to be.

Now think about your current or planned blog; which of the preceding properties can you provide?

PROBLOGGER BLOG TIP: THE ULTIMATE GOAL

Creating a blog that people absolutely cannot live without is a rare thing indeed, but should be your goal. If you do not strive to make your blog the best it can be, it will be easy to slip into "good enough" and then on toward mediocrity. Always be thinking, "How can I make this better?"

Creating Useful Content Today

Whether you have an existing blog or want to get started today, read through the following tips and implement them right away.

Add Value

Don't just report the same news that everyone else is reporting; add value to it by expressing your opinion, analyzing it, helping readers interpret it, and so on. If your blog is a "newsy"-type blog, the next time you write a post, take a moment before hitting Publish to ask yourself if you've added anything to the story. Tell your readers what you think, make a comment about how it applies to you (or might apply to others), look back and identify patterns in the story, or look forward and make a prediction about where things might be headed. Though some people do want to hear the latest news, they'll become loyal to you as a news source if you help them make sense of it.

Ask Questions

Asking questions brings you closer to your readers and gives you insight into how they think. This works better on some blogs than others (the topic and reader numbers come into play), but a real question for readers is a great starting place for useful content. I love to ask questions on my blog, and I try to do it regularly.

When I launched Social Media for Business Workbook (http://socialmediaworkbook.com), I put a survey form right on the homepage to capture my readers' questions. Make note of the question "How difficult has it been to find info or help with this" (see Figure 11-2), which is almost as important as the question the user types above it. I don't *just* want to know what is on my audience's minds; I want to share solutions for which my audience has been looking but which they have not been able to easily find. You are not going to stand out when you only share easily found content that your reader can get elsewhere.

Figure 11-2: Social Media for Business Workbook research phase.

Mine Your Feedback

Your comments and inbox are rich sources of relevant material and burning questions. If readers take time to ask you a question, you know it matters to them—and more than likely to many of your other readers as well.

PROBLOGGER BLOG TIP: STEAL FEEDBACK

Read blog comments and forum messages in your niche (see Figure 11-3) and take a note of good questions and suggestions! Using feedback doesn't have to be restricted to messages sent to you directly.

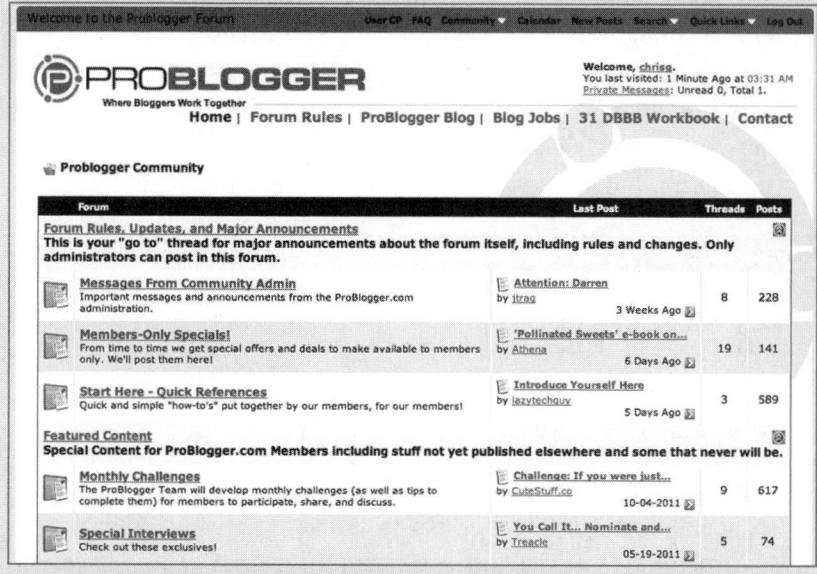

Figure 11-3: Monitor niche forums to find audience questions.

Tell Your Story

Telling *your* stories can be very powerful. Put yourself into your posts; talk about how you learned what you are talking about. Give examples, be humorous, and express emotion. Readers want to connect with you, and telling a story rather than "just the facts" helps bring the topic to life. Whatever your topic, keep the following in mind:

EXERCISE

What stories do you have to tell? What are the lessons you learned? Next time you are relating a story that you think is interesting, make a note of it for use in your blog.

- **Be entertaining**—Be humorous, intriguing, irreverent, fun, push boundaries, surprise your readers, include a little spice. Use entertaining pictures, video, audio, and so on. Be playful.
- **Be informing**—Produce "how to" or "tips" posts. You might also want to do "introduction to..."-type posts. Ask readers what they want to learn about and then answer their questions.
- **Build a community**—Write inspirational posts with heart. Pay a lot of attention to the readers you have, ask lots of questions, answer their questions; empower people to contribute as much as they can. Include everyone; do not fall into the trap of "in" jokes and shorthand. Warmth, welcoming, and discussion are the keys to a great community.

EXERCISE

When was the last time you felt welcomed into a community? When did you feel unwelcome or even hostility? What did the community members do differently in each case? Can you implement any of those positive factors into your blog?

Each blog will have a different mix of goals and objectives. You might want to attempt to achieve more than one goal, but the key is to know what exactly you're aiming for!

Summary

The most critical aspect of this chapter is to put your audience first and do it in a new and original way. As time goes on, standing out among the crowd is going to get harder and harder. You need to find a way to better serve readers while covering new ground.

Aim to be unique, remarkable, compelling, and, most of all, useful, and you will have success long after many other bloggers have given up.

12

Taking Your Blog to the Next Level: A Case Study

Much of what we've covered so far focuses on the introductory stages of blogging, but what happens when your blog has been around for a while and you want to take it to the next level? How do you expand it from being just another blog that has a few readers and that makes a part-time income to becoming a profitable business in and of itself?

In this chapter, I walk you through the way that I've grown my Digital Photography School (DPS) blog into a blog that is read by more than 5 million visitors a month, and which has sent blog buyers my way with seven-figure offers.

The Launch of DPS—Years 1–2

On a rainy afternoon in April 2006, I received another e-mail from a reader of my existing camera review blog asking for advice on how to use his camera in low-light situations.

I'd been developing a small blog that aggregated camera reviews from around the web for a couple of years now, and e-mails asking for advice on how to use cameras was a pretty regular thing to hit my inbox. I'd only ever written camera review posts, and avoided "how to" content on my existing photography blog. I usually replied to these requests for help with a "sorry but I don't write that type of post" e-mail.

On this day, I was about to send this type of reply when, on a whim, I decided to write a short tutorial on how to use a camera in low-light situations. After completing the post, I was about to publish it on my review blog when an idea struck me: What if I started a new "how to" photography blog?

Without a lot of thought, I registered www.digital-photography-school .com (something I wish I'd put a little more thought into as it is quite a mouthful), found a free template, added the first post, and launched the blog (see Figure 12-1).

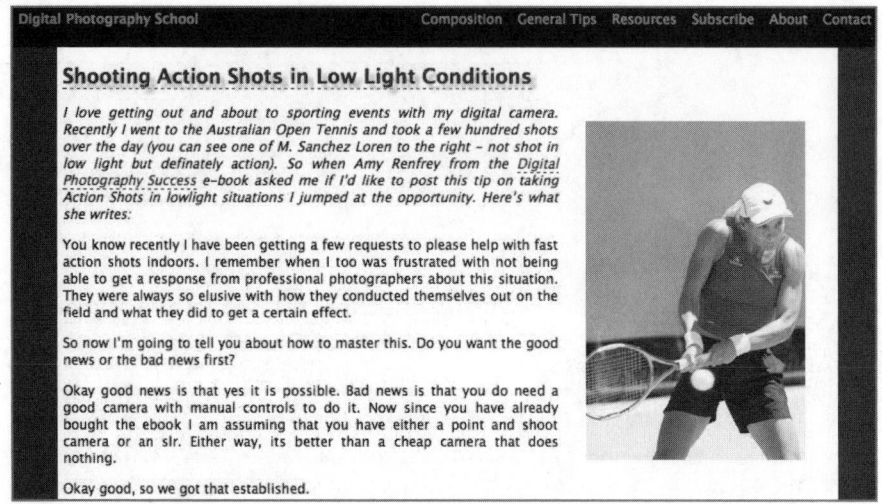

Figure 12-1: Digital Photography School's first blog posting.

Over the next few days, and before promoting the new blog anywhere, I wrote more posts so that the blog would have a few articles to read. I then linked to it from my existing review blog and it was launched.

That first week or so the blog had around 200 visitors and made less than a dollar via AdSense.

Building Foundations

My strategy with DPS was always to approach the first two years of the blog as a *launch phase*. My hope was to spend these initial years focusing on a number of foundational activities that I believed would ensure that blog reached its potential later on. The following sections outline where I spent most of my time in the first year.

Foundation 1: Content

Given that this book is about making money from blogs, we've spent a lot of time on the topic of "content." The reason for this is that both Chris and I firmly believe that for a blog to be successful, it must be useful to readers by providing content that solves their problems and meets their needs.

As a result, the first year of DPS was all about identifying the types of problems that beginner photographers have and writing posts that provided them with solutions. These days the blog covers a wider array of topics and levels.

During the first two years of DPS I wrote 95 percent of the content on the site. I did occasionally attract guest posts from photographers from other sites, but the bulk of it was an in-house activity. This was partly because I am a bit of a control freak and wanted to ensure that the quality was high, but it was also something I did while the income of the site grew to the point where we could hire staff writers.

Foundation 2: Promotion

I utilized many of the techniques covered in Chapter 7 of this book in building my readership. Networking with other bloggers, optimizing the blog for search engines, and writing content for social media sites like Digg (http:// digg.com) and StumbleUpon (www.stumbleupon.com) were all very important in the early days.

In addition to this, I also asked myself two important questions:

- Who do I want to read my blog?
- Where do these people already gather online?

These are crucial questions for any blogger to ask—if you can identify who your potential readers are and then find where they're gathering in numbers online, you have some great places to start when promoting your blog.

For me the answer to the first question was simply "beginner photographers."

Knowing this helped me to identify their gathering points, which included the following:

- **Photosharing sites**—Mainly this was Flickr, where I hung out more and started a *group* to attract readers (see Figure 12-2).
- **Other photography blogs and sites**—At these sites, I began to write a few guest posts and to network with site owners.
- **Photography forums**—Where I became more active.
- **Blogs on related topics**—For example, I began to submit stories to Lifehacker, a blog with a broader topic than DPS but that linked to DPS numerous times.

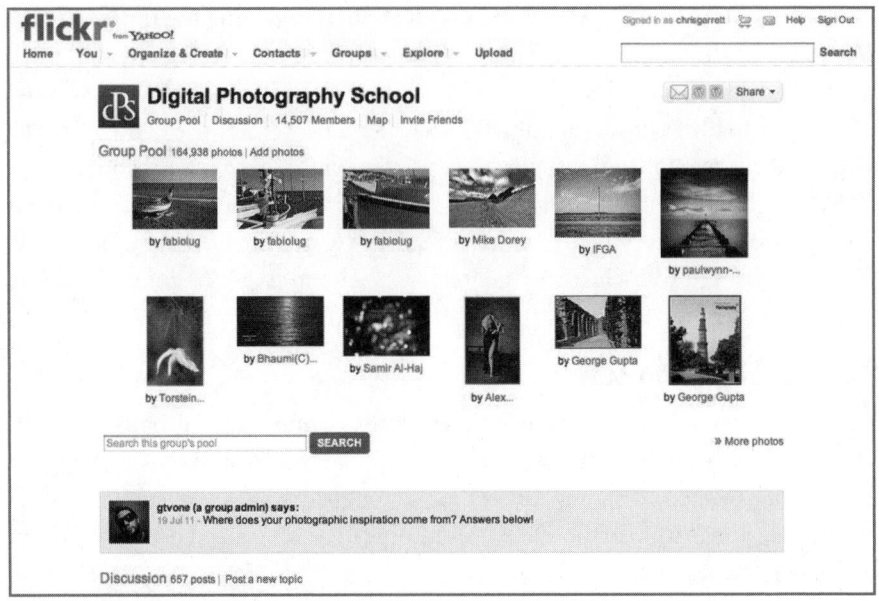

Figure 12-2: Digital Photography School on Flickr.

After I identified several gathering points for potential readers, I worked hard on being a genuine and useful member and contributor of these sites. This, in time, drew people to check out who I was and what my site was about.

Foundation 3: Community

When I started DPS, it didn't have any kind of community at all. In fact, it wasn't even set up to enable readers to leave comments (a bit of an experiment to see how it would go).

Although I did leave comments switched off for a few months, I did move toward adding several community elements to the site in the first year, including a Flickr Group that enabled readers to interact and share photos. I also ran some competitions.

When I did switch on comments, I also began to regularly ask questions, run polls, have debates, and give readers opportunities to share photos.

Also after around six months, I added a new forum area to the site. I used vBulletin (www.vbulletin.com) as the forum platform and started it with a small number of discussion areas. I quickly found a number of forum members to help me moderate the forum on a voluntary basis. This forum area has grown to well over 200,000 members and is a thriving part of DPS today.

Foundation 4: Capturing Contacts

Perhaps the most important thing I did from the very first month of DPS was to being sending a weekly e-mail newsletter. This started after family members asked how they could find out about new articles on the site. I explained that they could subscribe to my RSS feed; their blank face made me realize that many people have no idea what RSS is or how to use it.

E-mail is a far more familiar technology for most people, so I started a newsletter and invited readers to subscribe (see Figure 12-3) and give me permission to e-mail them once a week with the site's latest tips, tutorials, reviews, and offers. To this day more than half a million subscribers are newsletter subscribers.

Figure 12-3: Digital Photography School's e-mail subscription page.

I describe how I used these e-mails to drive traffic, build community, and make money in the section "Getting the Readers to Subscribe," later in this chapter.

Monetization

In the first two years, my primary focus was on creating quality content, promoting my blog, building a community, and capturing contacts with my newsletter.

Making money from the site was not my primary concern in this phase; however, I didn't ignore it completely. From day one the site was monetized through two primary means:

- **Advertising**—I've always run AdSense and Chitika ad network (`http://chitika.com`) ads on this site. Although these networks don't convert brilliantly in some niches, they outperformed other monetization strategies in the early days of the site as I built a readership. In time, and as reader numbers grew, the site also began to attract more direct advertisers and sponsors. This is slowly starting to replace the ad network ads, which now fill in remnant and unsold ad units.
- **Affiliate promotions**—As a secondary income stream, I've done some affiliate marketing. Initially I restricted marketing to promotions of cameras, other photography products, and books on Amazon, but toward the end of the second year, DPS started to promote other people's photography training courses.

Consolidation and Expansion—Years 3–5

During the first two years of DPS, readership grew considerably. My focus on providing useful content, heavily promoting it, and then capturing those new readers with the newsletter and forum worked well, and the site grew to around 25,000 visitors a day. It finally began making enough money for me to consider expanding the site.

Over the course of the next couple of years, I added staff writers, expanded topics, updated the site design, expanded the use of social media, and more.

Staff Writers

After the site became profitable, I began to advertise for paid contributors to the site. I did this with a simple ad on the ProBlogger job boards (http://jobs .problogger.net) and quickly had more qualified applicants than I could use. I settled on five weekly contributors to supplement my own articles.

Over the last year, I grew this writing team from 5 to 10; when some moved on, I hired others. I also formed a secondary group of guest writers who occasionally submit content on a voluntary basis. These guests were either readers who want to help the community or were photographers from other sites who want to grow their profile.

Expansion of Topics

Initially, DPS unashamedly was all about beginner photographers and focused solely on writing tips dealing with how to use cameras. After we grew our readership to a point where things were very solid, I made the decision to expand the site to include two new areas: post production (how to use Photoshop and other software), and camera reviews.

This expansion grew largely out of readers asking questions about these topics in the forum as well as my suspicion that they would be profitable areas. The camera review area is particularly profitable due to affiliate promotion on Amazon, and the fact that cameras are a bigger ticket item and lead to healthy commissions.

As part of this expansion (and the hiring of extra writers), I've now increased the posting frequency on DPS from once per day to two articles per day (which also helped grow traffic to the site).

New Design

DPS has had three designs since its launch. When I started it, I launched with a free template that I tweaked to make it a little more unique. Twelve months in, I hired a designer to come up with a more professional site design, but the site quickly outgrew that look and layout.

Late in 2008, I hired Matt Brett (http://mattbrett.com) to give DPS a complete overhaul. This design made way for the expansion in topics, integrated the forum and blog a little better, and promoted multiple page views for first-time visitors to the site, which led to the better capturing of new readers to our newsletter.

Such custom designs are certainly not cheap, but often lead to a noticeable increase in page views. The designs also give first-time visitors, potential advertisers, and other key influencers in the niche a good first impression of your blog.

Social Media

I have always been intentional about developing a social media presence with DPS since its launch. However, there has been a real shift in how I've done this in the past two years.

Early on, the focus was much more about writing content for social bookmarking sites like Digg, Delicious, and StumbleUpon. Though DPS still receives decent traffic from social bookmarking sites, I focus less upon targeting these sites today.

Instead, I am much happier to let our community submit content to these sites as it wishes and focus more on building a presence on social networking sites like Twitter (http://twitter.com), Facebook (www.Facebook.com), and Google+ (https://plus.google.com), which have DPS-specific accounts and pages. Facebook has particularly become important for what DPS does because it is used by so many people for photo sharing.

Increased Focus on Affiliate Marketing

During the third year of DPS the global financial crisis began. As I began to see the economy failing, I realized that relying so heavily on advertising as a revenue stream was not a good move. I decided to diversify my income.

One diversification strategy was to focus more on promoting products with affiliate marketing. I began to seek out existing affiliate programs in the photography space to promote. At that time, not many existed, although I did find a couple of e-books and training courses that I promoted heavily with good results.

The problem I faced was that after I'd promoted these resources to readers once or twice, conversions dropped drastically because readers would either buy the product or decide not to. I needed more products to promote.

I had exhausted existing quality products to promote, so I began to approach others who were selling photography products without having affiliate programs to see if they'd be interested in starting affiliate programs for DPS. I was surprised to find that almost everyone I approached said yes and started up affiliate programs for DPS to use.

As a result, the affiliate marketing grew from about 10 percent of revenue to around 35 percent of it in a year, more than making up for the slump in advertising revenue (which turned out to be not as bad as I'd anticipated).

DPS E-books

The other diversification strategy that I worked on in the fourth year was to begin developing our very own product—an e-book on portrait photography entitled "The Essential Guide to Portrait Photography." You can learn more about it at www.digital-photography-school.com/portraits.

The e-book was a collection of edited and updated posts from the DPS blog on the topic of portraits. It also was bundled with a series of interviews from professional photographers sharing their tips on portraiture.

The e-book, which launched in November 2009, was around 80 pages long and packed full of information. It was professionally designed and proofread, but 70 percent of the content was previously published on the blog. I added some new content and updated the older content, but still wondered whether people would be willing to pay for something that they could find in the archives.

It sold at $19.95 USD (discounted by 25 percent in launch week) and during its first week of sales generated more than $70,000 USD in income. Sales continue at a rate of 10–30 copies per day, and so this first e-book continues to be a worthwhile revenue stream even months after its initial release.

After the success of this first resource I decided that e-books and other photography resources would be a continued focus for DPS moving forward. Since that first portrait e-book, I have released a further seven e-books on topics ranging from travel photography, to photographing children, to basic technical information on how to use cameras to their potential. You can see the full range of eight photographic e-books at www.digital-photography-school .com/learn. Worth noting here is that, whereas the first e-book was largely previously published content from the blog, the next seven e-books were almost completely new and unique content—not previously published.

Though DPS continues to sell advertising and promote affiliate products in year 5, the main source of revenue has become the e-books that it sells.

DPS resources have become so successful that I have developed a small team of experts in producing, designing, and editing e-books to help increase the quality and quantity of what we can produce.

Although having a team might sound beyond where you are currently at, do remember that it all started with a blog and that the first e-book I released was a relatively short one that was largely based on content already published on the blog.

The key is to produce a product of your own. Though selling advertising space and promoting affiliate products are legitimate ways to monetize a blog, you are ultimately sending people away from your blog by promoting them. Develop your own product and you not only retain your readers, but you keep the money that they spend on your products too.

DPS Today

Digital Photography School is certainly not the largest or most profitable blog in the blogosphere today. In many ways I look at it and see a relatively young blog that can be expanded in numerous ways. However, it has grown from a blog making less than a dollar a week with a handful of weekly readers into one that is read by more than 5 million readers a month, and that generates hundreds of thousand dollars in revenue a year.

It has also overtaken ProBlogger as my largest blog.

The following sections describe two key aspects of how I manage the DPS blog today.

Using E-mail to Drive Traffic and Make Money

E-mail newsletters are a central strategy in the development of DPS. Ever since launch, I've offered readers the option of subscribing to receive updates from the site via a simple weekly newsletter that gives them links to new content on the site and hot discussions in the forum.

The benefits of this newsletter to DPS are numerous:

- **It drives significant traffic each week to the site**. Newsletter days are always DPS's biggest days.
- **It makes money**. I sell advertising space to advertisers, launch our own products, and run affiliate promotions through the newsletters I send.

- **It builds community**. Newsletters can be used to build community morale, launch competitions, and direct people to interactive areas on the site.
- **It's great for branding**. Having a weekly point of contact with readers reinforces the DPS brand and builds reader loyalty.
- **It is central in the promotion of DPS e-books**. Every time I launch a new product, I see by far the most sales come when it's promoted via e-mails.

First a word about technology: I use Aweber (`www.aweber.com`) to deliver my e-mails. However, many e-mail newsletter services are available, and you can use any one that allows you to set up an auto-responder or sequence of e-mails. Others that I have used include MailChimp (`http://mailchimp.com`) and Campaign Moniter (`www.campaignmonitor.com`).

> **NOTE**
>
> The process I'm about to share started out very, very simple and has slowly developed with time. In fact, it continues to develop as I learn more, and by no means is where I want to take it…yet.

Let's start with a visual on how my process looks before I explain the elements, shown in Figure 12-4.

If you'd like to subscribe to the newsletter to experience it firsthand, you can do so at `http://bit.ly/subscribeDPS`.

Getting the Readers to Subscribe

Because e-mail newsletters are such an important part of my site, I put a lot of emphasis on getting this conversion moment with those who visit. I attempt to get readers to sign up at a variety of places around the blog. Some are subtle (including in sidebars), and others are not (including a pop-up signup box that readers see 20–30 seconds after they arrive on the blog).

The pop-up is set to show only once per visitor (unless they're blocking cookies), and although it is intrusive and I was very hesitant about adding it, it has been incredibly effective at getting readers to sign up. Before I started using pop-ups I averaged 40 confirmed subscribers a day. After adding the pop-up, I averaged 350 per day. (This is now well over 700 subscribers a day.)

The pop-up does annoy a handful of readers. (I get an e-mail or two per month with a complaint about it.) However, because of the payoff, it's something I've decided to continue.

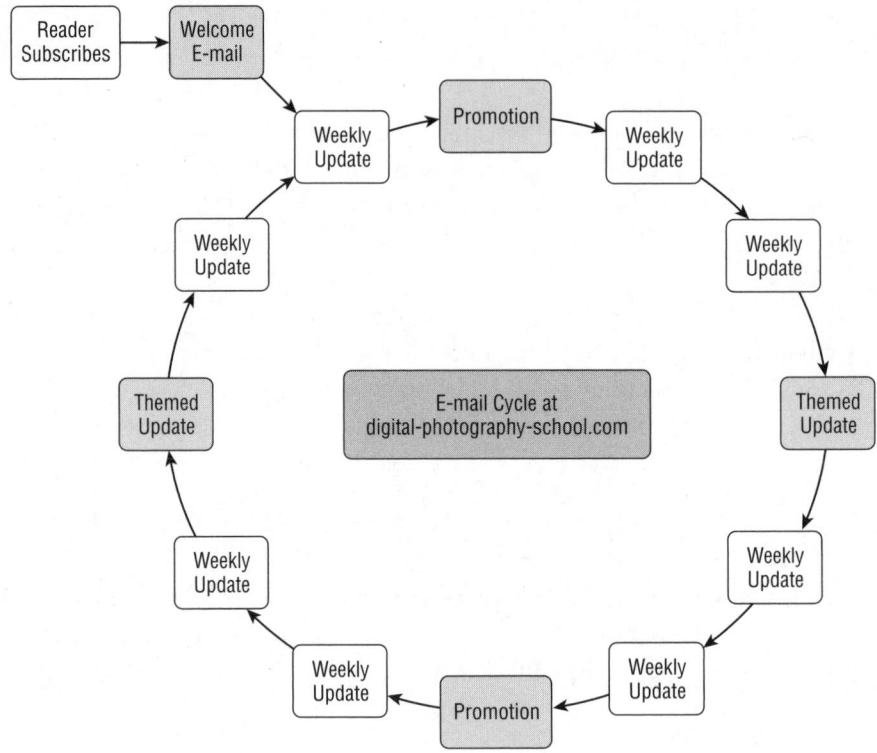

Figure 12-4: How to drive traffic to your blog using e-mail.

Sending a Welcome E-mail

When new subscribers sign up and confirm their subscription (via e-mail), a welcome e-mail goes out immediately. This e-mail is all about making them feel good about subscribing and giving them a quick introduction to the site.

I'm presuming that most people who sign up for the newsletter are new to the site, so it's a great opportunity to introduce myself, show them around, and help get their expectations right about the site.

This welcome e-mail has a site logo, my picture, some links to key parts of the site like the forum, some suggested reading for catching up on key posts in the archives, and some information about what the subscriber will receive in the coming weeks in terms of future e-mails.

The e-mail also asks people to add the address from which the e-mails are sent to their white list/contact list to help ensure e-mails are delivered to their Inbox, not trapped in a spam filter.

This welcome e-mail is written in a personal and friendly style, and seems to resonant with readers because I get a lot of replies from new subscribers thanking me for the personal welcome.

Providing Weekly Updates

Weekly updates are what readers get the most. They're largely updates on what has happened on the blog/forums in the past week. They are delivered every Thursday and readers come to expect them at that time—in fact if I miss one I soon hear about it from disappointed subscribers.

I usually have the following sections in these weekly updates:

- **Welcome**—Usually, this is just a sentence that introduces the week. If there's something important in the newsletter, I highlight it here. Sometimes I also offer a quick update on something cool that happened on the site during the week (record day of traffic, milestone in terms of subscribers, a mention in the press). This kind of update seems to build morale/momentum among readers.
- **Quick Links**—Here I share the weekly assignment, any discussion-oriented posts/polls, any competition announcements, and occasionally a "featured post" that I want to push traffic to.
- **Tips, Tutorials, and Techniques**—This includes new blog posts of a more general nature.
- **Recommended Resource**—Most often this is an affiliate promotion (a great product), but occasionally this section functions as a message from our sponsors, which is a sold-ad position.
- **Post Production Tips**—Here I include updates from this section of the blog.
- **New Gear, Tips, and Reviews**—Again, I offer updates from this section of the blog.
- **Hot Forum Threads**—This consists of a bit of a summary of key threads happening in the forum.

Although the preceding list provides a basic newsletter template, I do mix things up a bit. Some weeks I run a little promotion of our Twitter or Facebook accounts. Other weeks, I might throw in some older posts from the archives, and sometimes I run a promotion encouraging readers to forward the e-mail to a friend. Really, anything can go in these e-mails as long as they're on topic and useful.

Keep in mind the main goals of these weekly updates:

- To drive traffic to the site.
- To build community, and reinforce your brand with readers.
- To make money through the promotions.

Readers love these newsletters because, although they're largely links to the site, the links are all content rich and useful resources. I title these e-mails "Photography Tips for Your Weekend" and that's how many of our readers use them—as a springboard into their weekend with their cameras.

> **NOTE**
>
> I put together these e-mails manually. They take me an hour or two a week to do. You can use tools that send out automated update e-mails (Aweber has one), but I prefer to do it manually to ensure that the Weekly Update e-mails are tailored for maximum impact and usefulness.

Providing Themed Updates

Themed updates are all about sending readers back to old but useful content around a single theme. The idea came about when I realized that new readers of my blog were not seeing the majority of my blog's thousands of pages of content. Although I occasionally link back to key posts, most of my archives don't get a lot of traffic.

Here's how my themed updates work.

I use the auto-responder or follow up feature of Aweber to set up these e-mails. This means that they go out at predetermined intervals to readers a certain number of days after their last scheduled e-mail.

1. The first e-mail in the sequence is the previously mentioned welcome e-mail.
2. Thirty days after the welcome e-mail, the subscriber receives the first *themed e-mail*. The topic is "Exposure" and is a newsletter that contains a short intro to the topic of how to get good exposure in photography and then includes some links back to some of the blog's most useful tutorials on that topic. This e-mail also recommends some good books on exposure (with affiliate links).

3. Thirty days after the Exposure e-mail, subscribers get another themed e-mail about composition that contains links to some of our best posts on that topic. (Remember, they're getting weekly updates in between.) It also recommends good books on the topic (with affiliate links to Amazon).

4. Thirty days later subscribers get an e-mail on portraiture (same format as the previous one with links to archive posts and books).

5. Thirty days later they get another themed e-mail (and so on).

The main goals of these themed updates are as follows:

- To drive traffic to the site, particularly older posts.
- To make money through the affiliate links. Although they're not big-ticket items, they do convert.

These e-mails do take some time to set up, but once they are set up, they become automated and go without me ever having to think about them. With 500+ people signing up for my newsletter every day, I know that 500 people are getting each of these e-mails on a daily basis. I have six of these e-mails set up in a sequence at present and add more to the list every now and again, so I know 3000 people in total get one of my themed e-mails each day—forever. This is a set-and-forget traffic generator!

Sending Promotional E-mails

This is the most recent addition to my sequence of e-mails and I'm still perfecting their use, but the signs are very promising already.

I use the auto-responder sequence mentioned previously to deliver these. (They're going to go out every month or two.) The content of these e-mails highlights a resource or product that I recommend to readers.

The products are either my own products or affiliate products from which I take a commission on any sale. DPS discloses that relationship in the e-mail and gets a lot of positive feedback from readers on the disclosure.

The key to these *promotional e-mails* is to choose products that you genuinely recommend (or to develop your own great product). The reason for this is that at any point subscribers can leave your list. And they will. If you push too hard or recommend dodgy products, they can leave (with a bad taste in their mouth).

The first of these promotional e-mails in the sequence goes out eight days after someone signs up for the newsletter. (This ensures that they get at least one of the weekly updates first.) The e-mail simply reinforces my previous welcome to the list and offers the reader a 25 percent discount on our Portraits e-book, letting them know that DPS has previously offered all readers the chance at this discount and wants to extend it to them also for a limited time.

This is a low-pressure sell and a short e-mail. It simply makes the offer and then backs off to let the person make a decision.

The second promotional e-mail goes out a couple of months later and is for a high-quality photography training course. Again, it's a low-pressure sell— no hype, no obligations. We simply make a genuine recommendation and let people make up their minds.

Promotional e-mails are a new addition to my e-mail sequence, but I'm already seeing great conversions.

The main goal of these promotional updates is to make money through sales and affiliate promotions. The money these e-mails earn starts with a bang when you send it out to the bulk of your list on the first day, but after that it becomes a steady trickle. Keep in mind that once you have a number of these e-mails set up in your sequence, you can have a number of promotions paying off each day.

Concluding Thoughts on the DPS E-mail Sequence

This mix of e-mails gets very positive results. I work hard to keep them a win-win for our readers and blog by providing useful and relevant information and generating income. So far I think I've got the balance right. I regularly get e-mails from readers saying thanks for the newsletter, and if I'm even an hour or two late sending it, I get e-mails asking where it is. On a revenue front, it's increasingly profitable; between the sales of products and the ad revenue increases from the increased traffic, it certainly has become a central part of my income stream to have this e-mail list.

With the cycle as it is, readers do occasionally get two e-mails in a week. However, it's never more than that, and on most weeks, it is just the one weekly e-mail. I make it clear when they sign up that it's at least weekly, to get this expectation right, because I don't want them feeling duped into signing up.

I also use Aweber's scheduling feature for the auto-responder e-mails, which allows me to specify what days of the week they can go out. I schedule the sequenced e-mails (the themed and promotional ones) so that they never go out on a Thursday or Friday (the same day as the weekly ones).

Holiday Promotion

In December 2010, I decided to test an idea that I'd seen on a number of other sites in the lead-up to Christmas—a *holiday-themed promotion*.

I called it DPS's 12 Deals of Christmas. Over the 12 days leading up to December 25, I e-mailed my newsletter list with 11 deals on photographic products. Each deal was a discounted offer on either one of my own e-books or an affiliate product that I earned a commission on. Each deal lasted for only 48 hours. On the 12th day I re-opened all previous 11 deals for one last time until New Year's Day.

I was terribly nervous about e-mailing our list 12 times in 12 days and didn't know how the promotion would go—but I was surprised at how positive the feedback from readers was.

December 2010 also turned out to be the most profitable month ever—to that point.

In December 2011 I repeated the promotion, but took it to the next level by hiring a campaign manager, creating a dedicated landing page for all the deals to be listed, increasing the discounts we offered to our readers, and shortening deals to just 24 hours only.

The result was fantastic—we almost tripled the previous monthly revenue record and again received a lot of positive feedback from readers who enjoyed the event.

Summary

It can be easy to make the mistake of coming across an established blog and thinking that it has always been the way that you see it today. My hope is that this case study will not only illustrate some of the techniques and strategies for building successful blogs that Chris and I have spoken about in this book, but that it will also illustrate how blogs evolve and grow over time.

13 Going Beyond Your Blog

In this book, we set out to give you the best possible introduction to all the varied options available to you as a professional blogger. These approaches will ensure that your blogging is both effective and profitable. With that in mind, we would be remiss to leave out the less well-known options that have been growing in popularity over the past couple of years. We are seeing more and more bloggers who have no interest at all in earning advertising income, but who have seen how having a popular blog can help them achieve their big personal, career, or business goals.

This chapter looks at a type of blogging where growing a compelling blog is an effective asset that works toward reaching important end goals, and what those goals might be.

What It Means to Go Beyond Your Blog

In the early days when we talked about blogging there were two main categories:

- **The "blog for non-commercial reasons" group**. These were people who would blog for pleasure, for social reasons, as a journal or diary, or as a creative outlet.
- **The "blog for profit" group**. These are the people who had profit as a motive, expressed either as the priority driver, or as a secondary consideration.

Both Darren and I started out in the first group and ended up in the second, as you have seen in our blogging stories.

Mingled somewhere between the two tribes is a third category which, until recently, went largely overlooked. Now it is possible that the third group is as popular an approach as the former two.

Why are the people in this third group blogging? Well, let us, for a moment, look at what a blog can do for you. It can let you:

- Regularly and easily add and update content.
- Build attention and retain that attention with a list of subscribers.
- Interact with an audience, answer questions, and take feedback.

Outside of direct monetization through advertising or even selling digital products such as e-books, a whole universe of benefits rolls out of these abilities. Just a few examples would be:

- Growing your visibility and building an audience of people who want to hear from you.
- Spreading your ideas.
- Tracking your learning and growth.
- Increasing your credibility and spreading a positive reputation.
- Showcasing your skills, knowledge, and experience.
- Demonstrating your successes and results.
- Connecting with like-minded people.

Essentially, a blog can be an effective resume, brochure, business card, advertisement, portfolio, manifesto, networking profile...and much more.

The Blogging Goal Triangle

I imagine blogging goals as a triangle (see Figure 13-1):

Figure 13-1: Where do your blogging goals fit?

If a blog can bring you a greater or lesser mix of these returns—providing immediate revenue, a creative outlet, and building a community—what goal might you have for your blogging?

The following examples illustrate some of the goals you might have for your blog:

- **A book deal**—Goal: *Audience*—Publishers are now noticing many bloggers because of their blogs (the authors of this book, for example). Some bloggers are even writing their books, one blog post at a time! If you want to be traditionally published, having an interested and sizable audience is a great advantage.

- **Charity, non-profits, and causes**—Goal: *Community*—A charity can tell the world all the good deeds they are performing, bring in volunteer help, and get donations. Causes and non-profits can spread the word about their campaigns and ideas. This is all possible when you use blogging for your publicity and news delivery vehicle. Pulling together a community can definitely help reach these goals.

- **Professional and personal networking**—Goal: *Audience and ideas*—If you want to grow your professional or personal network, blogging is a great way to get noticed and to build long-term relationships. Building a solid network requires attracting an audience and offering something of value to your network connections, which often means sharing interesting ideas or the value of your experience.

- **Speaking and performing**—Goal: *Audience*—If you want to attract more attention and opportunities in professional speaking and public appearances, blogs are an excellent way to showcase your ideas, promote upcoming appearances, get new gigs, and keep in touch with past audiences.

- **Startup funding**—Goal: *Ideas*—If you have a startup idea but no access to funding, blogs can help you build buzz and attract interest.

- **Recruitment**—Goal: *Audience*—For any organization struggling to attract the right people, a blog can help showcase openings and provide information about processes and culture while being a magnet for the right people.

- **Career advancement**—Goal: *Audience and ideas*—On the other side of the interview table, a blog can help you further your career and open doors to advancement. Again, it is about sharing your experience and ideas with the correct audience.

- **Freelance business**—Goal: *Business, expertise, and marketing*—Rather than finding a traditional full-time job, you can build your own freelancing business by attracting work from your target market via blogging about your experience and expertise.
- **Share and sell your craft**—Goal: *Creative outlet*—For artists crafters, blogs are a growing channel for attracting awareness or even buyers for your creative work.
- **Build your fan club**—Goal: *Audience*—Musicians, stand-up comedians, and even politicians are building a fan-base via blogging.
- **Customer service and loyalty**—Goal: *Community and marketing*—Companies don't look to blogs now as just a form of advertising their products and services but are also using the communication and interactive nature of blogs to keep their community of existing customers informed and happy.
- **Coaching and training programs**—Goal: *Education and marketing*—As well as being an excellent way to sell your coaching and training, blogs are an effective way to deliver education. Blogs are increasingly penetrating traditional education and entering the classroom, but are also allowing more and more teaching to be delivered via virtual classrooms.
- **Community and membership sites**—Goal: *Community*—Rather than a fixed-term interaction, blogs can be a way to foster community and membership over the long term.

Of course, there is no reason to pigeonhole yourself into a restrictive category. I share this to illustrate that there is a whole world of opportunity and your blogging can achieve many things for you, your business, or your community outside of how people see "professional blogging," such as more visitors and advertising revenue!

To further develop these ideas with you, I will draw from my own experience of being an "accidental entrepreneur," getting magazine and print book deals, speaking gigs, freelance work, training and coaching clients, and all the stages my blogging went through to where I am today.

Community Interaction Leads to Attention

Some benefits that you get from blogging, and in fact are the whole point for a lot of people, made me run and hide in the early days. As a shy introvert, getting noticed was *not* high on my priority list initially, but it happened anyway!

During the early 1990s I cut my "web developer" teeth with obscure personal hobby websites, developing sites for small businesses, and developing public web and intranet sites for the local college. Through these projects I learned a few things—with the help of the computer programming bulletin boards, news groups, and e-mail discussion lists—and I wanted to share these ideas and solutions with the communities that had helped me.

Of course, my solution was to write blog-style articles. In the beginning it was more to save time than anything; rather than duplicate brief responses to questions I could just point people at a detailed "how-to" resource article. It didn't feel like work; in fact, I found I enjoyed writing, and even better, discovered that people enjoyed what I wrote. Despite not having any writing or journalism qualifications, I even got published in magazines (Figure 13-2).

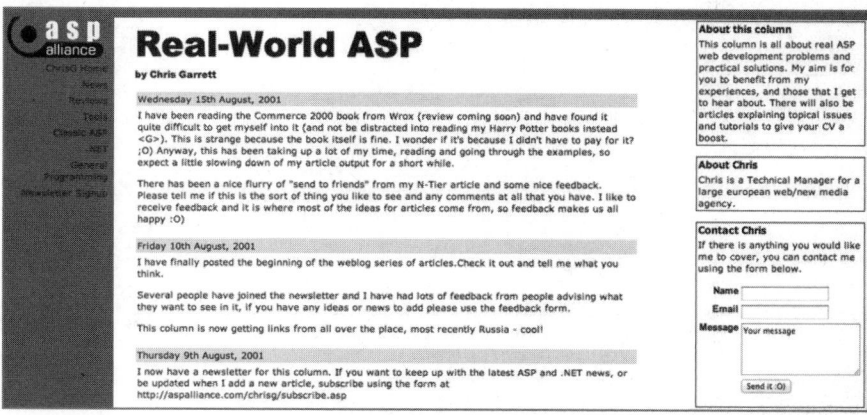

Figure 13-2: My ASP programming column in 2001.

By the early 2000's, my articles attracted a lot of attention. As I became more deeply involved in these communities, lots of great opportunities started opening up. I was invited to mastermind groups and asked to speak at conferences; before long I had publishers approaching me to get involved with books they wanted to release.

This attention also had a dark side—people resented the visibility I was gaining and questioned my motives, calling me "self-aggrandizing." If it wasn't for the support of my wife and the positive feedback I was getting from people who were grateful for the solutions I shared, I might have quit there and then.

Rather than quit, I decided to fill the requests for more hands-on help that I was getting weekly. Many companies reached out and asked me to assist their teams with technical challenges, training, and coaching.

In the beginning, I politely turned these queries away; I had a full-time job, and besides, I was giving away everything I knew (or so I thought). As time went on I could see I was closing myself off from something that could be both rewarding for me and useful to other people.

So that was how I got into *indirect monetization* completely accidentally (see Chapter 1 for a description of direct and indirect monetization). Rather than setting up shop and promoting my business, I had attracted an audience that was telling me they wanted to purchase my services, and exactly what those services were! Figure 13-3 shows a web page announcing what training I had to offer.

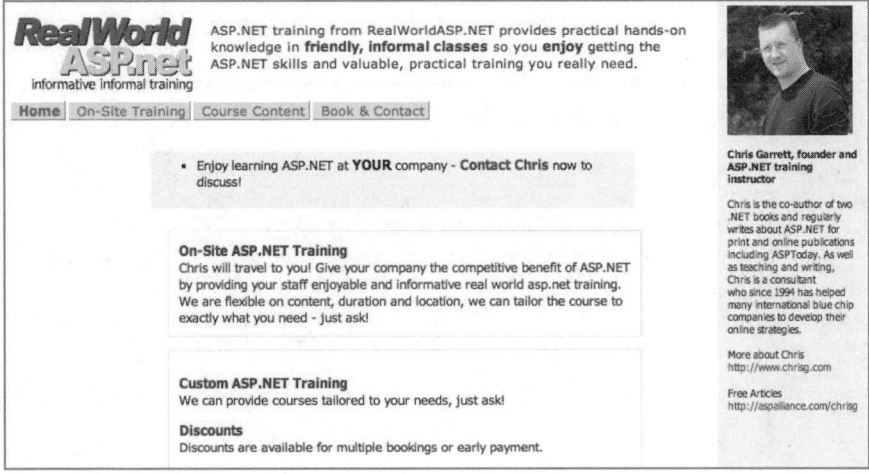

Figure 13-3: From articles to offering training.

Now that you know a bit more of my story and how it relates to the subject of this chapter, we need to dig out what you can learn and the specific processes you can work through toward gaining some of those rewards for yourself.

Getting Known, Spreading Your Ideas, and Attracting Visibility

More and more people are starting blogs because, for professional or personal reasons, they want to become more visible and get their ideas "out there." This is not necessarily because they want to be a celebrity or become world famous. It could be that they want to attract more customers to their business, to change the world, or to attract opportunities.

The following sections investigate some of the ways that you can use your blog to gain the next level of visibility or to further compound this visibility—whether that's getting published in traditional media or starting a public-speaking venture.

Going from Blog to Print

Once you have attracted a growing audience, you will be in a great position to get published in "traditional media."

Writing for print is a great way to build your authority; many people are willing to believe you are an expert just because your words have appeared in print. There is some truth to that, of course; outside of self-publishing, getting published in a magazine or book often means that you have overcome certain obstacles and that your work has been checked over by editors.

Print is also a great way to market your services to less technical or more traditional audiences. You would think putting information into articles and books would remove the need for your consulting or service work, but in actual fact it works as proof of your expertise and capabilities; people see you as *the* person to turn to and it increases your sales potential.

This kind of writing can pay quite well; marketing yourself this way could earn you a tidy side income!

How Print Writing Sells You

When someone picks up a book, they think, "this person knows their stuff." Next they either think, "I can do this myself now" or they think they need an expert. Who is the likely expert going to be? There is a reason why "they wrote the book on it" is a phrase associated with someone being the recognized authority on a subject.

The same goes for articles in magazines and journals. In fact, when constructed correctly those articles can give clarity to a problem readers were previously willing to let go unresolved.

When you write your brief biography for your book or article, include the URL to your website. This allows people to contact you and it works as a great introduction to you and your services.

While you might feel this is stepping too far into self-promotion, don't hold back from supplying a website. A link to a resource that gives readers even more useful information or your e-mail address with an invitation to send you questions is seen as a helpful and friendly bonus rather than a potential sales pitch.

How Your Blog Can Help You Get into Magazines and Trade Journals

So, you've seen the benefits of appearing in print, but how exactly do you achieve that? Of course, the answer is that having a popular and expert blog on a topic opens doors!

Once your blog builds up a big enough audience and profile in your niche, you could well have editors approach you to write for them. This is obviously the best outcome because there is no pitching involved.

As you are networking, you might cross paths with magazine editors in your target subject area. After breaking the ice and having a conversation, you could ask them if they are open to you sending along ideas and ask what kinds of articles they are looking for. You might already be on their radar, but they won't necessarily be aware you are open and willing to write. Also, look out for any time a publication that might be a good fit for you makes broad invitations for submissions.

Unless you are approached to write a piece, you'll have to go through the article-pitching process. In this case, your blog can serve as evidence, by providing writing samples and your portfolio, and can also help build your credibility.

Your first task is to work out what your target audience reads—there is no point in doing all this work if nobody in your market is going to notice. The best way to find out is to ask; failing that, look at circulation information from likely periodicals.

- **Research the magazines**—What kind of content do they publish? Do they take freelance submissions or do they restrict outside input to their letters pages?
- **Read several issues**—You need to get familiar with the publication, and you can't do that with one copy. If you need to, order back issues.
- **Find out about upcoming stories**—Some topics will be obviously seasonal, but a good tip is to ask for their editorial calendar. Some freelancers have told me they pose as potential advertisers to get publications to give up their editorial calendar, but I recommend honesty!
- **Talk to the right person**—Look for the people who handle submissions and see if they publish their policies before approaching them.

- **When you make your approach, be nice**—Don't come across as arrogant, pushy, or demanding. It is not a good idea to hassle someone who is obviously busy and who holds your submission's fate in their hands!

Editors will have their own preferences for whether you should e-mail, phone, or write a letter, but if you provide something useful and interesting—in a polite way—most won't object regardless.

Don't send the full written piece. Instead, send a message with your idea, along with an outline. A query to the appropriate editor who handles the type of article you have in mind will have much more success than a 2,000-word article printed and put in the post addressed to "Editor" at the publication name.

Once your idea is accepted, you will need to find out the desired length (word count) of your article and what deadlines you will have to meet. If in doubt, write too much rather than not enough, because editors can cut, but they will struggle to add.

What often happens is they will tell you that your writing is nearly there but it is not quite right. Be flexible. If you do get rejected outright, move on to the next publication. It probably won't hurt to ask why you got rejected, but don't expect a response.

Book Writing

The first major challenge that faces you is, obviously, the writing challenge. A book is a major undertaking, as anyone who has attempted to sit down and write one will tell you. The more comprehensive the book, the more of a long haul it will be.

I should tell you now, don't write a print book for the money alone. It's not worth it. In fact, I have consistently received a better income from print magazine writing than from the four books I have co-authored. Figure 13-4 shows my author biography for one of my books on Amazon.

The problem is that thousands of new books are published every week of every year. It's a never-ending treadmill, and really, unless you are J.K. Rowling, you are going to have an uphill battle to get your book noticed. In fact, even she had her book turned down by nearly every major publishing house!

There is an opportunity hidden in there though: That treadmill needs to be fed with new material, so publishers do need to find a constant stream of new authors. If you ignore the purely monetary aspects and focus on the authority and marketing benefits, the potential is pretty bright.

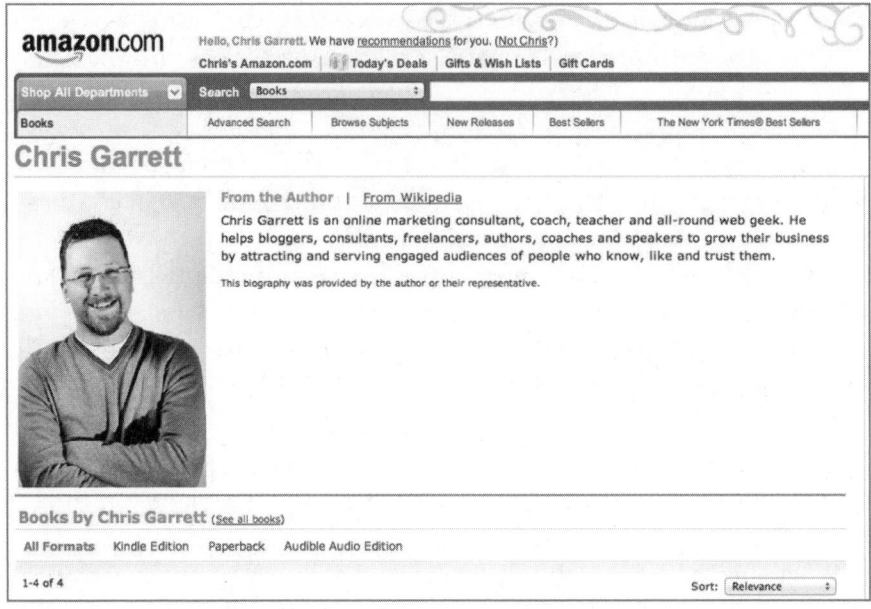

Figure 13-4: Chris' author page at Amazon.

Publishers need authors as much as authors need publishers. Publishers need access to markets, too. A blogger brings both. Believe me, once you have a popular blog on a subject, publishers will be much more open to publishing your book.

I know whenever I mention "you should write a book" there will be an inevitable "who, me?" reaction. Yes, of course you. If I can do it, you definitely can. Everyone really does have a book in them. Nobody else has had the experience, life, knowledge, personality, delivery, and point of view that you have.

Why You Should Write a Book

So if there is no money in it, why write a book?

Well, I wouldn't say there is no money; in fact, a popular self-published book can and will make money, but here are other compelling reasons to write a book:

- **It solidifies your expertise**—By writing a book on your subject, you really do become an expert. I am not kidding! While writing, your thoughts are organized into a logical step-by-step sequence; your knowledge is filed into nice tidy boxes when you block out chapters;

explaining concepts clarifies them in your own mind; plus you are forced to do additional research or back up your claims to avoid leaving gaping holes.

- **It establishes visible expertise**—Nothing says "expert" like "wrote the book."
- **A book is just the start**—Use your book as the foundation for seminars, courses, workshops, and so on.
- **Books recruit customers**—There is nothing like writing a book to make customers believe in you. Plus, they will read the book intending to do things, and then call you for help when they get into a muddle. You can even give copies of your book to potential clients—much better than a business card!
- **It generates speaking opportunities**—Blogs and media will want to interview you. Conferences love to introduce people using their credentials. Which is better: "works for SomeCo" or "is the author of…"? The subject of your book also is an obvious topic for people to invite you to talk about.

To Submit or Self-Publish

The decision of how to publish comes down to finances and goals.

Niche self-published and electronic books have more profit potential overall than niche publisher books. However, more mainstream books from major publishers have more profit potential due to distribution and reach advantages.

Electronic books are pure profit, pretty much, but it depends on how well you can market them. Still, even with affiliate commissions, an electronic book will usually pay better per copy and have lower overheads than a print one.

Perhaps unfairly, perhaps not, self-published and electronic books have lower credibility and status than a traditionally published book. It is easy to understand why; anyone with a big enough checkbook can self-publish and making electronic books does not need even that. That said, your readers will not necessarily know your book is self-published, especially if they bought it from Amazon, and holding a book in your hands always feels more substantial and impressive than bits and bytes on a screen.

People are therefore most impressed by authors who are published by major publishing houses, but do not let that hold you back from self-publishing if you cannot, or will not, go with a major publisher. Although a big publisher is where the biggest authority gains are to be made, if you can write a super popular e-book that dominates its niche, it does not matter how your book is sold. I am thinking here of examples like Aaron Wall's *SEOBook*, which ruled the SEO niche for years until he pulled it from the market in favor of an online member site (www.seobook.com).

A choice you can make as a compromise is to start with a blog, move to e-book, and then self-publish or find a publisher. This approach will help you move into publishing with confidence, a ready market, and a manuscript. Of course, the publisher will demand changes, but you will at least have a head start.

Getting Your Book Published

Selling your book to a major publishing house is either a dream or a nightmare for most people. It's a dream because it is a wonderful feeling to walk into a bookstore and see your book on the shelf. It's a nightmare because of the challenge and hard work involved.

Some of us are lucky enough to be approached by publishers, mainly people with a large audience and a well-defined niche. Most books, though, are pitched to publishers, sometimes more than one. If you are pitching, make sure you do one publisher at a time; if publishers find out you are hawking the same book to multiple publishers simultaneously, that could sink you before you start.

Doing Your Homework

Before you even approach a publishing house, you need to have your ideas nailed down and have thought through all the questions you will need to answer:

- Are there enough people willing to buy a book on this subject?
- Could you write 50,000–100,000 words on this subject?
- Can you convince a publisher that you are the right person for the job?

The surprising answer to #1 is often "yes—other publishers have books on the same topic." If those other books sell, then yours (assuming you have an interesting, beneficial, and unique approach to the subject) ought to have as good a chance as any. Check bookstores and libraries for competing books; have a look through them to see what you need to present, but also what fresh view you have to offer. A good tip is to read detailed reviews of each to see the good and bad points of other books.

You need to start an outline for the book early on. Although dealing with a publisher means your book will change, you need as much structure and planning at the start as you can manage; most people overlook how much work is involved.

Aim for ten solid, detailed chapters with compelling headlines, estimated page counts, and any suggested illustrations. Subhead and bullet-out the points you will cover and what the reader will gain. The more details, the better.

Approaching Publishers

Once you have an outline you need to prepare to approach publishers with:

- An overview of your idea, including major reader benefits. (Save time? Make money? Find a partner?)
- How your book is better than the competition.
- Why you? How are you uniquely qualified to write this particular book? Editors understand you can research a topic you need to know more about and they don't require you to know everything, but you must have a good answer to this!

Remember the publisher *wants* to recruit authors, but only if their books will sell. They have bosses to convince just like you have a publisher to convince. Make their job easy and everything will go smoothly.

If you are asked for a sample chapter, give them Chapter 1, because that introduces the reader to the subject matter and gives the editor and publisher a good idea of how you will approach the whole book. Alternatively, for computer programming or other highly technical books, you might be asked to provide a particularly "meaty" chapter that demonstrates examples of key features that you wish to deliver.

Should You Get an Agent?

Although I haven't always had particularly good experiences with agents, I am told by other authors that you should get an agent, especially if this will be your first book.

The myth is that an agent will get you more money and a better contract, even taking into account their cut. In reality, an honest publisher will give you a good deal anyway and most published authors can give you almost the same advice for free.

In general, an agent should look after your interests in return for a healthy commission. That's the idea; it doesn't always work out that way, so good references (and preferably a personal recommendation) are absolutely essential.

You don't *have* to have an agent in most non-fiction negotiations. I have worked both with and without, but a publisher may take you more seriously if you do have one.

Tracking Down Your Target Publisher

Most publishers now have websites listing their submission guidelines, but finding the right one for you might not be so simple. If you prefer the personal touch, the best way to find a publisher is to ask for recommendations from people who have had their books published. After that, look at books on similar topics to see who published them. You can usually find the names of the editors in the front of a book; see if you can find them on the publisher's site or elsewhere online and drop them a courteous note.

Another great way to increase your visibility and get your message out there is public speaking. Much like writing a book or having your articles published in magazines, public speaking is also a way to spread your message while potentially earning a great income. If you can combine blogging, a popular print book, *and* lots of paid public speaking, you could do very well financially indeed.

Speaking from Blogging

Speaking to an audience is a wonderful way to make a connection, teach, get a point across, and demonstrate your knowledge. It builds your reputation and allows you to test your ideas and anecdotes live.

Having a popular blog can make you a draw on the speaking circuit. There is a definite attraction, not just because you have information to share, but also because people want to meet their blog "celebrities" and hear them speak in person.

When I talk about "public speaking" here, I know there will be a good number of readers who gulp with terror. After all, it is one of humanity's most common fears. That said, it can be very beneficial, and for some, extremely profitable.

Though you might think of speaking as something very formal, in fact, the speaking opportunities you can gain from your blog could be anything from a small, local social group, all the way up to international conferences. Every step on the speaking ladder has advantages and benefits, so public speaking is well worth looking into and trying out as your confidence grows.

Getting Speaking Opportunities

Events large and small need to recruit speakers. It doesn't matter if it is a local breakfast meetup or a huge trade show; any event requires content and the right people to deliver that content if they are going to sell tickets. Many of these speaking slots are filled by people pitching ideas to the organizers.

You might ask yourself "why me?" but realize the better question would be "why not?" You have content to share; otherwise you would not be able to blog for very long.

As well as content you need experience, but unless you want to join a speaker's club, such as Toastmasters (www.toastmasters.org), you'll need speaking gigs in order to gain that experience. While you're starting out, take any opportunity that comes your way just to get out there so you can learn and develop your speaking style. Attend presentations to get a feel for the kind of talks and presentation styles that work in your niche and start volunteering for small spots.

It could be that once you share enough content and build enough of a profile in your niche that conference organizers will approach you. That is how I got started, and how most of my speaking engagements come to me even now. In the beginning it was very nice to get that kind of validation and encouragement, because I am certainly too shy and introverted to have pitched for those gigs.

After filling their crowd-pleasing keynotes and attracting industry celebrity (or actual celebrity) speakers, organizers will give preference to the best, most relevant ideas, and also to the people who they think can sell the most tickets. If you can demonstrate that you have compelling content and can gather an audience, you will have more success than having great ideas alone.

Using Your Blog to Promote Your Speaking

The key to getting more and better speaking opportunities is marketing your speaking "product":

- Write articles that would work well as presentation topics.
- Have a page on your blog about your availability as a speaker (see Figure 13-5).

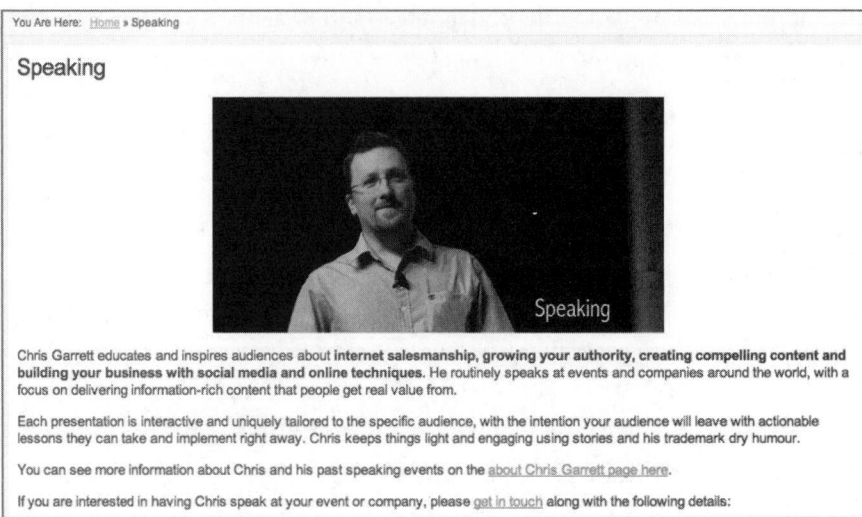

Figure 13-5: Chris' speaking page.

- Tell people about upcoming talks you will be giving.
- Provide audio and video of you presenting.
- Make it easy to get in touch with you!

If you want to get invited to speak then you need a page on your site all about your speaking availability. On your speaking page, you'll need to provide all the information an event organizer requires to make a decision about booking you for their event. This includes:

- Your target audience.
- Topics you speak about.
- Any experience you have.
- Testimonials.
- Contact information for making bookings.

Speaking Compensation

There are big benefits to just being up on stage and delivering your presentation. Each and every time I give a talk, my subscriber base grows, I get more social media contacts, and a lot of the time even more customers. Over and above these benefits you can also get compensated for speaking. The following are things to remember—tips and pointers regarding compensation:

- **Start by speaking for free and work yourself up**—To begin with, you might have to accept lots of speaking opportunities without any pay just to gain the experience and exposure. As your experience grows and as you become more in demand, you will be offered more compensation or can start negotiating compensation.

- **Your event admittance should be free**—Even the smallest events should give you free entry to the event. It is very rare that you would be expected to buy a ticket to the event you are speaking at, though it does unfortunately still happen.

- **Ask for travel compensation**—Next to being paid to speak, the best outcome is getting your travel and/or accommodations paid for. Once you are established, unless you are speaking for a charity event, this should be the minimum requirement. Getting compensated for attending an event you would have attended anyway is a very attractive prospect, especially when you take into account the networking and visibility benefits.

- **What to expect for compensation**—Finally, being paid to attend is where things get very interesting and also very complicated. How much you get paid varies depending on your experience, reputation, your subject, and the type of event (private company training day, national association, trade show—the types and categories are too numerous to list). It's possible to be paid a few hundred dollars when you start out and up to tens of thousands of dollars if you are a big-name celebrity or best-selling author. If this is a route you would like to seriously pursue, you might consider getting a speaking agent to handle opportunities for you.

As well as being a great way to attract contacts, networking often generates the best speaking gigs. Networking is crucial to enhancing your visibility and reputation, and, in fact, your business success; your networking can be very much enhanced through blogging. The next section explores networking in detail.

Networking, Making Contacts, and Building Partnerships

To network effectively, you must have the correct approach and mindset:

- **Generosity**—The best networkers are out to help. They know that the key is to be valuable, not seek where they can extract value.
- **Approachability**—People should feel they can talk to you, that they are safe talking to you, and should expect to get an answer.
- **Humanity**—You are *you*, an authentic and true representation, a fully formed three-dimensional person, with interests, passion, family, friends, and a life outside of your niche.
- **Fun factor**—A sense of humor is always attractive, providing you find humor in appropriate places and never at someone else's expense. Nobody likes to surround themselves with people who are serious all the time, nor do they like someone who uses humor to bully. Where possible, emphasize the positive. Be an uplifting presence in your network's life.
- **Humility**—Accept praise with humility. Say thank you. Admit when you make a mistake or do not have the answer.

Networking Confidence and Self Esteem

When I coach people in networking I often sense a lot of fear and resistance, and this fear might be something that is holding you back now. I know I struggled, and some days continue to struggle, with the same self-limiting thoughts:

- What will people think of me?
- It is OK for them, but it is different for me.
- I don't want to feel rejected.
- One day I will finally stop caring about what other people think.

Any of those thoughts resonate with you?

Some people are naturally bubbly and outgoing. My brother got those genes; I was left with the dorky ones. The rest of us have to make a conscious effort to approach others and we have the fear that we might interrupt, not be accepted, give a bad impression, say something stupid, or not be good company.

Networking face-to-face does not come naturally to me because I do not like introducing myself. It feels awkward, and the more I focus on this discomfort the bigger hash I make of it. The approach that I am sharing with you in this section helps me get around the nerves to a great extent but, being a natural introvert, those nerves will always be there, so it becomes a case of learning strategies to manage the best I can.

The good news, though, is that even I have managed to benefit in some really cool ways. If I can do this, you certainly can!

Know Yourself

Understanding who you are is vital. You need to fix in your mind your personality, your own values, and what you have to offer. Otherwise you let others choose that for you.

Even more important at this level of the game is for you to grow to like yourself. If you doubt your own worth, you give people the impression that you are not worthy of their attention.

We attract who we attract. By being aware of our own "polarity" we will understand better when someone is or is not a good match for us and we will not try to win losing battles. Don't be distracted by lost causes while ignoring your ideal communities that would really connect with what you have to say if you only let them.

This leads me to the next important point…

Not Everyone Is Going to Love You

Sorry, but it is a fact of life that you will meet people who just do not connect with you. And that is fine.

Think about it…do you like everyone you meet? Of course not! OK, you might not take an instant dislike to folks, but then again, I expect the majority of people you bump into are not exactly your choice of BFF either.

It is perfectly acceptable to not create a connection with someone else, and it is perfectly OK for you to decide you are not keen on other folks too.

You might have heard me say that I am constantly being given negative feedback. Some people just do not recognize how awesome I am. It's true! But at the same time, I get people who love what I do.

It would be unhealthy to fixate on either of those extremes; you have to remember that your best efforts will not just miss a part of humanity, but that there are people out there who feel bad when they see someone good or successful. By seeing a happy person, somehow some people feel diminished.

I met a wonderful singer and songwriter, Christine Kane (http:// christinekane.com), at a conference. As a performer, she had her fair share of both fans and critics. She taught me a phrase that applies very well here:

SWSWSWSW
Some will.
Some won't.
So what?
Someone's waiting.

Don't sweat the wrong folks; their loss. Put your energy into finding the good ones. For everyone out there who is a bad match, there will be many out there who think you are brilliant.

EXERCISE

Networking can be time-intensive, so while it is great to get contacts through serendipity, it is also good to prioritize your efforts. Take a look at your niche and make a list of the top 20 people you would most like to be connected with. Add notes for what you know about them already, such as what they are interested in, where they hang out, and what you might be able to help them with. Make a point to have some sort of small contact with one person on your list every day. Perhaps answer a question that they ask in social media, recommend an article that matches their interests, comment on one of their articles, reply to a Facebook message, or share one of their links in Twitter.

Meeting Your Heroes

Besides our normal day-to-day networking connections, sometimes we set a goal to make a connection with big stars, heroes, celebrities, and leaders. This can be both daunting before, and an ego risk when, we do achieve it.

A journalist friend once said:

"Never meet your heroes, they are always a disappointment."

I thought it was just this friend being a negative sort; she was often one to find the cloud around every silver lining. But then I mentioned it to another friend a few years later and she said, "Well, actually, she has a point."

Shocking, to say the least.

When you finally meet someone who has been a dream connection for you, there is the risk of getting burned in two ways:

- They reject you, brush you off, or humiliate you.
- They let you down, offend you, or do not live up to their reputation.

The fact is that both of these are rarely their fault. You create a larger-than-life image of them that reality can never match.

There are also the people you meet that you would never expect to give you the time of day, but in fact exceed all expectations and turn out to be wonderful—much better than you gave them credit for.

Rather than feel disappointed or risk rejection in meeting heroes and celebrities, my friend had the approach of lowering her expectations to a realistic level, always remembering their humanity first and fame second, and never putting these people on pedestals. She met rock stars, politicians, and TV and film personalities. Once she recognized they were flesh-and-blood human beings like the rest of us, she had a much richer experience.

As my dad often says, "they put their trousers on one leg at a time just like the rest of us."

Keep in mind that the people you meet are human beings and their press rarely matches who they really are. Accept them for what they are, and take the good away from any contacts you do make, while letting go of any negatives from such a meeting.

Once you have visibility and a strong network, you will be well-placed to start offering your own premium products and services, as illustrated in the next section.

Selling Coaching Programs and Consulting

First, we need to agree on what we mean by coach or consultant. Essentially, a coach or consultant gives guidance and advice to customers who need it. A key difference is: While a consultant is essentially being paid to give answers and advice, a coach might not always provide direct answers, but instead prod the client into taking action and ask questions that help the customer come up with their own answers.

I didn't set out to be a consultant. When I got started as a coach and as a consultant, it was through customer demand. People wanted answers about how to do certain things, or help with their problems, and they were willing to pay for the service. Eventually though I put together a step-by-step system that became my coaching program.

What do you need to be a coach or a consultant? The bare minimum you need is some knowledge or experience that customers might benefit from. We all know how to do things or have experience that we can teach other people, providing we can see the true value in it. Obviously, if you want to sell your consulting or coaching service from your blog, you will need a specific page on your site that describes the service offer and how to get it too!

What You Need to Get Started

After you have worked out the knowledge or experience you are going to share in your service, and put up a page offering this service, I would advise you consider some things of a more technical nature.

At the most basic, you just need an e-mail account. You can do quite a lot over e-mail, with the advantage that the client gets detailed notes and can scroll back through previous conversations. I use Skype (www.skype.com/intl/en-us/home) and recording software to capture our calls in case the client wants them to reduce the need for detailed notes. You absolutely *must* build an e-mail list. I use AWeber (www.aweber.com/) and recommend it to anyone.

If you are doing group coaching, you need to build a membership site. You must share previous calls and notes. Avoid all the complicated software out there; you don't need it, and I would be wary of paying a monthly subscription for something you don't own and that could be taken away from you without notice. I use Wishlist (http://wishlistproducts.com), which is a WordPress plug-in. It's robust and industrial strength, but very easy to use. I use it for all my courses and membership sites now. There is a less capable but free alternative called S2Member (www.s2member.com/), which is available from the WordPress plug-in directory and also from S2Member directly.

Getting Customers

People will want to know what is inside your head in a way that is tailored to their particular situation. The more in demand that advice is, and the more people who know you offer help, the more customers you will get.

However, the mistake most people make is that they expect people to buy on their first visit. That is unlikely to happen.

This, of course, is where blogging and content marketing come in.

Use your content to draw people to you, and then introduce them to your offer. You need to talk about the challenges your customers are facing in a way that allows you to impart ideas and experience, while getting people to want to hear more. This builds your subscriber list and allows you to get in front of your prospect multiple times.

So, at the very least, build an e-mail list, build a page where you discuss your offer, and take their money—use PayPal (www.paypal.com) to begin with. Easy! Well, OK, "simple" might be a better word.

Most of my customers come from three different places:

- **Referrals**—Do a great job of wowing your existing clients and they will bring friends. Again, it is about results mostly, but also their relationship with you. When they praise you, ask for referrals.
- **Networking**—If you are looking for business people, use LinkedIn (www.linkedin.com). Life coaches can find many people on Facebook. Live events and workshops (see the section "Speaking from Blogging") can be very effective for attracting customers too—developing a relationship is so important that seeing you face-to-face makes a huge difference.

NOTE

For more on social networking, see Chapter 9.

- **Forums**—By answering questions and showing you "have the right stuff," you will build a reputation, and again, allow people to get to know you.

In all cases, prospective clients will check you out, because they are doing due diligence on something that requires commitment. Make sure your blog has these vital elements:

- A great first impression that presents you in a positive light.
- Content that speaks to their challenges.
- An effective subscription-capture mechanism.

PROBLOGGER BLOG TIP: MAKING FRIENDLY OFFERS

Though a lot of bloggers are daunted by the thought of selling, you can take the pressure off yourself by thinking about it instead as putting your products and services out there for people to buy. Your offer simply has to provide the information they need in order to make an informed decision:

- What are you providing? (Clearly, honestly, and simply tell people what it is that you are offering.)
- What will you or your services do for the person reading? (List the benefits to show what your product or service achieves, solves, or changes.)
- What should they do next? (For example, "Hit the 'Buy' button.")

Five Lessons from My Journey

Although I have discussed the great opportunities and benefits that came my way from blogging about my computer programming solutions and experiences, eventually I grew tired of trying to keep up with the ever-changing world of web development and I wanted to focus on the online business aspect of my career. This meant taking a step back and analyzing how I had arrived where I was, pulling out the key factors that helped me rather than held me back, and working out what I needed to do to get known in this new space.

Some of the broad lessons can be summarized as:

- **Be a part of your niche community**—Rather than "talking at my audience," I was working *with* a community (not even "my" community initially). Getting involved in your niche as a participant means that rather than advertising and promoting you are instead interacting and understanding. I was getting as many answers back as I was offering in the early days, and nobody had their guard up because I had nothing to sell. It was only after offering valuable contributions to existing communities and sites and having people pointing to me as a helpful resource that I earned any kind of an audience of my own.

- **Offer what your audience wants, not what you want**—Another vital ingredient that many people miss is that the most important factor is not what *you* want, but what your *target audience* wants. It's a lot harder creating something and then trying to drive attention to it than finding what people are looking for and supplying it. Plus, once you get started serving a real need, it actually gets easier! People start coming to you with their problems, questions, challenges, and frustrations. Essentially, people bring content ideas to you. Once you have attracted an audience, you can develop what you think is important or give people what they need; usually people are more attracted by what they want and will actively look for someone who can supply that.

- **Make friends and solid networking contacts**—I often say "no blog is an island" but still people try very hard to do everything and get by on their own solo efforts. Of course, it is not impossible to succeed without any external help, but it is so much more difficult and frustrating to try to do it that way. We need other people to supply traffic, links, support, help, answers, and opportunities. Plus, making friends is so much more fun than seeing everyone else as competition! Things really started opening up for me when I made good contacts, and it especially helped me through the rough spots where the critics and trolls were on the attack!

- **Good content is vital, but it is also important to share it**—Though in the early days I didn't even think of self-promotion, eventually I discovered just how much more effective writing good content *and* then promoting it can be rather than relying on good writing alone. Rather than being the web's best-kept secret, by encouraging your content to spread you can help more people and reap the reputation that content can develop for you. Of course, that all depends on your content being good and useful to begin with—bad content will not spread half as well as great content!

- **Work from a position of genuine service, not just self-interest**—As mentioned earlier, I was not a natural entrepreneur, and with regards to my content, I didn't specifically go into writing it thinking I *could* make an income from it; I was just doing what my community did and was sharing solutions and the benefit of my experience. I think this was a massive element of why I succeeded in that community long-term. Turning your back on that is a mistake that, unfortunately, people often make. When your profile begins to grow, you especially need to remember that it's all about what you can do for other people rather than what they can do for you. I have seen so many people over the years get consumed by greed, believing their own hype or "faking it until [they] make it." It's not funny. Rather than think about what you can get, ask yourself why other people would want to know you, why people would want you in their network, and why someone would come to you rather than someone else.

Summary

By now you will have seen that, far from bloggers being locked into either making no money from their work or being forced down the route of selling ads or e-books, you actually have many opportunities to turn your writing into a valuable asset that can take you places far beyond blogging for its own sake!

More and more individuals and businesses are turning to blogs as a way to reach a market of people interested in what they have to say and, in turn, to offer products and services. In addition, bloggers are attracting publishing deals, speaking opportunities, and growing and strengthening their professional networks.

The reputation and connections your blog cultivates can expand your influence far beyond your blog, and I hope this chapter gives you some ideas how you can work toward attracting more of these opportunities for yourself.

Index